INVESTORS CHRONICLE

A-Z OF INVESTMENT

The Essential Guide to Tools, Terms & Techniques

Caroline Sefton

London · Hong Kong · Johannesburg · Melbourne · Singapore · Washington DC

PITMAN PUBLISHING
128 Long Acre, London WC2E 9AN
Tel: +44 (0)171 447 2000
Fax: +44 (0)171 240 5771

A Division of Pearson Professional Limited

First published in Great Britain 1996

ISBN 0 273 62521 7

British Library Cataloguing in Publication Data
A CIP catalogue record for this book can be obtained from the British Library.

10 9 8 7 6 5 4 3

Typeset by Northern Phototypesetting Co Ltd., Bolton
Printed and bound in Great Britain

The Publishers' policy is to use paper manufactured from sustainable forests.

ABOUT THE AUTHOR

Caroline Sefton has been a financial journalist for more than seven years. She writes for the UK's premier financial weekly *Investors Chronicle* and is a specialist in personal finance and companies reporting. She is also a contributor to the *Financial Times*.

Educated in Northern Ireland and England, Caroline graduated from Exeter College, Oxford in 1985 with a degree in modern history. She is married to food writer Steve Dixon and lives in south London with their young son Stanley.

ACKNOWLEDGEMENTS

I am most grateful to the many people who helped me research and write this book, particularly those generous enough to read sections of it. Any mistakes remain my own, but for the rest I would like to thank:

Phil Whiterow, Deputy Companies Editor of *Investors Chronicle*; Nick Allott of Cameron Mackintosh; Gerry Blair of the Really Useful Group; Eleanor Burton of the Association of Investment Trust Companies; Bridget Cleverly of Schroders; David Cresswell of the Investors Compensation Scheme; Ben Few Brown of GNI; Ian Francis and David Longshaw of Panmure Gordon; the Futures and Options Association; Kaly Thavarajah of Liffe; Brockbank; Jim Lodge; Chase de Vere; David Linton of Updata; Peter Fuller of Fund Research; Charlotte Morrison of the British Venture Capital Association; Brian Naylor; Matthew Orr of Killik & Co; Miranda Richards; Jo Roddan, Rufus Low and Peter Knight of Fidelity; Alan Thomas; Paul Tinslay of Lexis Pension Communications; and Peter Webster of Eiris. Particular thanks are due to Steve and Stan Dixson, Peter Smith, Philip Ryland, Ceri Jones, Chris Dillow, Jean Eaglesham, Robert Ansted, Mark Harris, Cristina Nordenstahl, Piers Leigh and all my colleagues at *Investors Chronicle*.

CONTENTS

FOREWORD

Today, more than ever, we need to make our savings and investments work hard for us. Changes to the welfare state – and the likelihood of further changes to come – mean that managing our capital properly is a key factor in financing the purchase of our home, our healthcare, our children's education and – perhaps most important – our retirement planning.

De-regulation of the financial services industry, which began in the 1980s, has led to a sometimes bewildering proliferation of financial products. The quantity and complexity of products mean investors need guidance. True, there is a world of information out there – some of it free, a lot of it cheap – but is it any good?

The *Investors Chronicle* series of investment books – like the weekly magazine – has been produced to help answer that question, with objective and authoritative advice, written from the investor's point of view.

The aim is to provide readers with a practical, jargon-free guide to all areas of personal finance and investment. Thus, whether you are a sophisticated investor, keen to learn more about the DIY approach to investing, or are new to investment, the books will arm you with the facts and understanding that you need. As such, they should be the natural complement to the high-quality, independent assessment that the magazine aims to provide every week.

MARK VAN DE WEYER, Publisher, *Investors Chronicle*,
FT Magazines

INTRODUCTION

Investment steps out of the news and into our everyday lives without waiting for an invitation. The news can be about changes in interest rates, yet another derivatives scandal or a stockmarket collapse. Yet investment belongs in our everyday lives, not just in the headlines. Galloping share prices offer everyone the chance to turn a healthy profit, as long as they make their original investment at the right time and understand that all share price stampedes have to end eventually.

WHO IS THIS A-Z FOR?

This book breaks investment into easily digested mouthfuls, classed as terms, tools and techniques. The object is to deliver the strongly practical information often missing from more theoretical investment books, beginners guides or books plugging ways to get rich. It should be particularly helpful for those wanting to invest directly in shares, whether they are experienced investors or coming to the stockmarket for the first time. But the material also bridges the knowledge gap for business students or managers who need an understanding of investment and the City, without labouring through pages of theory to explain the point.

Each chapter closes with advice on how investors can make the most of the particular term, tool or technique. For example, which stockbrokers offer a specific service for investors in new issues? How do you find the names of big shareholders in listed companies that interest you?

However, the ideas, advice and strategies described in this book are generic. If you want to put them into practice, you will need an investment adviser to adapt the strategies to your specific needs. Similarly, the fact that a firm is mentioned in this book does not imply a recommendation by *Investors Chronicle*.

MAKING THE MOST OF THIS A-Z

The A-Z structure of this book encourages a pick and mix approach. Readers should be able to use it to smooth out most of the little wrinkles that complicate investment for individuals. The same investor may want to find out the exact rules for personal equity plans, invest in new issues and understand the basics of derivatives. It is all here. The subjects covered aim to answer the questions – ranging from the basic to the highly sophisticated – asked most frequently by *Investors Chronicle* readers. They all come back to the same point – if investments are intended to earn a profit, what are the vocabulary and the mechanics of maximising that profit?

For example, the best books on derivatives are textbooks aimed at professional investors. The typical beginners' book skates over the subject because derivatives are too complicated to explain and too risky for beginners. Under D for DERIVATIVES, readers find a nutshell explanation pointing out that derivatives are more than a fancy way for bankers to lose millions of pounds. They are a legitimate investment tool used by professional and private investors to great effect. The chapter then signposts the reader to detailed explanations of each type of derivative – options, futures, warrants and convertibles. These chapters define the derivative, explain how it works, how investors can trade in it, where they can go for further information, and spell out the risks.

INVESTMENT PATHWAYS

On one level, this A-Z acts as a reference guide. However, it can also deliver a crash course in investment. Each reader can choose his or her own pathway, and may well opt for the route from A to Z without diversions. Here is an alternative contents list, taking readers from the basics to the most sophisticated end of investment.

Straight down the motorway

- Cash is the first building block of any portfolio. Investors start with it and will often run into times when cash is the best investment. Look at CASH, TESSA, ANNUITIES and YIELD.

■ Bonds can work as a half-way house between cash and shares. They are less risky than shares because they pay a fixed income, but bonds are more risky than cash because they are traded on a market so their prices move according to the levels of supply and demand. Look at BONDS, GILTS, CONVERTIBLES – bonds that can also be viewed as a type of derivative – and ZERO DIVIDEND BONDS.

■ Pooled investments offer a route into the UK and overseas stock-markets for private investors with relatively small sums to invest and without the time or interest to pick their own shares. Look at INVESTMENT TRUSTS, UNIT TRUSTS, and LIFE INSURANCE.

■ Most UK investors will put most of their money in the UK stock-market, because they know the companies and they know the currency. But there are many ways to invest directly in shares and many diversions along the way. SHARES explains the different types of share you can buy and their advantages or pitfalls. NEW ISSUES explains what happens when companies first raise money on the stock market – a particularly popular type of investment for private investors – and FUND RAISING explains what is really happening when a company looks for money from investors. Also look at TAKEOVERS.

Along the scenic route

■ Some important investment tools are easier to find, understand and use than many investors imagine. ACCOUNTS ANALYSIS explains how to assess a company using the information it publishes. PERSONAL EQUITY PLANS (*Peps*) also count as a tool because a Pep is just a tax-free wrapper that can be put on many different types of investment. Look at ACCOUNTS ANALYSIS, PEPS, HINDSIGHT, INDICES, MARGIN TRADING and SOFTWARE.

■ It is impossible to avoid some investment concepts, just as it is impossible to avoid all investment jargon. Look at RISK, JARGON and KICKBACKS.

■ Many investors take years to discover the investments that give them most pleasure and interest; this may be because people do not think of them as conventional investments. Investing in the theatre is the most obvious example. It is notoriously risky, but its investors stick with it for the enjoyment it gives them. Ethical investment is the name given to investing with a specific ethical or environmental brief, whether it is positive or negative. Ethical investors are as keen as their supposedly non-ethical peers to make a profit. Venture capital is often considered the preserve of large, institutional investors, but small investors can also put money into new businesses. Lloyd's insurance market has suffered in two ways. First it won a reputation as an investment only for the super rich or the socially ambitious. Secondly, its mismanagement almost destroyed the market. However, assuming it survives its reconstruction – due to be finished in summer 1996 – it can be an attractive investment. Look at ANGELS, ETHICAL INVESTMENT, VENTURE CAPITAL and LLOYD'S.

On the fast track

■ The best investment rule is only to put money into things you understand. The City has developed some of its most complicated strategies to make money from currencies and derivatives. As a result many private investors, often wisely, shun these areas. However, investors who can truly understand these high risk, fast-moving and often complex investments see them as an essential part of their portfolio. Look at EXCHANGE RATES, DERIVATIVES, OPTIONS, FUTURES and WARRANTS.

A

ACCOUNTS ANALYSIS

Definition: **Accounts analysis is the cornerstone of investment analysis. Investors want to know how much profit will be left to pay dividends and can the company afford to pay its bankers. It looks at what the company owns and how much money it makes to make a judgement about whether the share price reflects the value in the company by using a number of financial ratios.**

Investors rely on a company's annual report and accounts for most of the hard facts backing up their decision to buy shares. The accounts tell investors whether a company's past record supports its promises for the future and whether it has the financial strength to put the plans into action. Well, most of the time they do.

All companies must publish annual results. Listed companies must publish annual results – known as preliminary results – within six months of their financial year end. They must also publish half-year or interim results. An annual report contains a:

- Chairman's statement;
- profit and loss account, showing whether or not the company has traded profitably over the last 12 months;
- balance sheet, giving a snapshot of the company's assets and liabilities on one day;
- cashflow statement, showing how money has moved in and out of the business over the year.

Companies normally release results within two to three months of their year or half-year end. It is often a sign of trouble if companies take several months to publish their results. Good numbers are easier to add up, is a stockmarket motto. Stock Exchange rules mean companies must issue 'trading statements' if their results hold any big surprises, but sometimes the news is even worse than investors had expected.

Example: Harrington Kilbride

Harrington Kilbride, a high-profile magazines publisher and exhibitions organiser, published its results for the year to 31 December 1993 in August 1994. They revealed a £1.08m loss, compared with a 1992 profit of £1.87m. The company had stumbled into two different types of trouble. It had reported good sales, but never got paid. The situation was so bad, that the company almost went bust. New management has since rejigged the company and changed its name.

Making sense of the information can be difficult, but it is invaluable, so persevere. First, read the chairman's statement and the company's review of the business, if it gives one. Smaller companies can give particularly candid reports. The most important part of the report, even if it seems bland, is the chairman's assessment of current trading and the group's prospects for the coming year.

Only experience, or access to reports from earlier years, can tell investors whether companies are consistently over-optimistic or pessimistic. The best examples, as usual, come from small companies. For example, consider Martin International, a Marks & Spencer clothing supplier. In April 1995, the chairman said: 'The financial base is now much improved and this will undoubtedly assist development of business and release potential for growth.' In August it warned of a £1m loss in the first-half, but forecast a good second half. The full-year loss came in at £1.77m, but the chairman remained chirpy.

'Making sense of the information can be difficult, but it is invaluable, so persevere.'

By contrast, tiny Sheffield refractories maker J&J Dyson seems to enjoy disheartening its shareholders. In January 1995 it reported 70 per cent profits growth at the half-year point, but it did not want shareholders to get over-excited. It said: 'However, the underlying problem of overcapacity in the refractories industry continues, and major customers still expect to achieve price reductions when renewing contracts. In contrast, the group is experiencing renewed inflationary pressure.' Full-year profits announced in July showed 94 per cent profits growth and the interim results released in January 1996 showed further, if less dramatic, profits growth.

PE RATIOS

The PE ratio – defined in *Box A1* – is one of the most familiar measures in valuing companies. When investors say shares are cheap or expensive, they are often using the PE ratio as a benchmark.

Box A1

Accounts analysis - the phrasebook

Dividend cover is earnings per share divided by the dividend per share. You want a figure of at least one to be confident that the company will be able to maintain its dividend at the same level. If it is less than one, dividends are being paid out of reserves.

Dividend yield allows investors to compare how much income they will receive from different companies. You calculate it by dividing the dividend per share by the share price. Investors normally use the gross dividend, as investors pay different rates of tax. UK dividends are paid with 20 per cent tax deducted. You reach the gross dividend by dividing the dividend per share by 80 and multiplying by 100.

Earnings per share is the company's profit after tax, minority interests and preference dividends divided by the number of shares in issue. In profit forecasts expect differences in the earnings figures quoted for the same company, even if the profits figures are the same. Some analysts remove one-off gains or losses – such as the profit on selling a building – and others will deduct different amounts of tax.

A1 **Gearing**, or net debt, measures a company's debt as a proportion of its total assets. You calculate it by dividing the net borrowings of the company by its shareholders' funds, including minority interests and preference share capital.

Interest cover measures the interest charge paid by the company against its operating profit in the same period – divide operating profit by the interest charge. The ideal figure varies according to the type of company. Investors want to know two things – how much profit will be left to pay dividends and can the company afford to pay its bankers. Some companies, with very poor balance sheets because their business has no assets that can be valued in a set of accounts, have high gearing but also have generous interest cover. Others have low gearing but profits barely cover the interest charge.

Net asset value (NAV) is the company's shareholders' funds divided by the number of shares in issue. In theory, if the company stopped trading and shared out its assets, each share would receive this amount. NAV matters less for people-based businesses such as marketing or advertising than it does for building or engineering companies that have invested in factories and plant.

Price/earnings ratios (PE ratios) measure a company's earnings against its price and are intended to help investors decide whether a share is cheap or expensive. Divide the share price by the earnings per share to calculate the ratio. Using a ratio makes it possible to compare companies of different size and share price.

Return on capital employed (ROCE) measures how much money the company is making from the assets under its management. Divide the operating profit by the capital employed to calculate the ratio. Capital employed is total assets less current liabilities.

When you buy a share, you buy a stream of earnings. In theory, a PE ratio measures how fast the earnings will flow. One of the simplest explanations of PE is that it represents the number of years it would take for the company's earnings to match the stockmarket price. The share price alone cannot tell you whether a share is cheap or not, investors need to use ratios to help them value companies. A high PE ratio should reflect fast-growing earnings. Look out for historic and forward PE ratios. Historic PE ratios, the ones published in newspaper share price listings, are based on published accounts. Forward PE ratios are based on forecast profits.

HOW DO YOU USE A PE RATIO?

The first step in using PE ratios is to compare a share's PE ratio with the market PE ratio and with the sector PE ratio (see INDICES, page 96). Shares are cheap or dear in comparison with their peers. Here are two examples of PE ratios in practice, all based on the situation in early 1996.

Tesco, the supermarket chain, had an historic PE ratio of 13, calculated by dividing the share price of 284p by the published earnings per share of 21.6p. The market PE ratio was 17 and the PE ratio for the stores sector was 14. Tesco receives a closer look later in this chapter, but a PE below the market average and the sector average implies the shares are worth a closer look.

Bentalls, the department store group, was on an historic PE ratio of 67 at a price of 116p. The PE ratio is so far from the normal range of PE ratios that it is meaningless. However, the forecast profits for 1995–6 gave a forward PE ratio of 25. Bentalls strong balance sheet – it had net assets of 158p per share, significantly higher than its share price, and net debt of just 24 per cent – partly explained the generous rating. Hopes that it would be taken over also helped boost the rating.

Forward PE ratios, based on analysts' forecasts of future profits, are more useful than historic PE ratios, based on published accounts. Overall, the potential reward from forecasting profits correctly is worth the risk that the forecast is wrong.

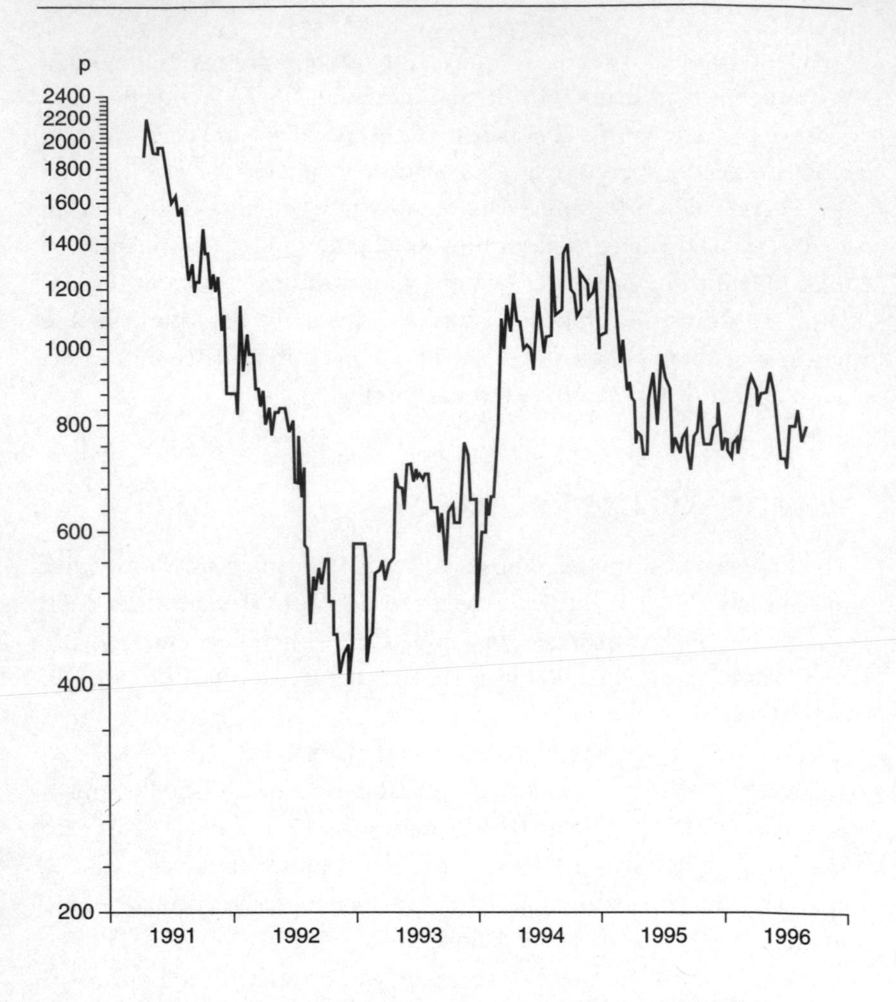

Fig A1 Tesco: share price performance 1991–96

Source: Datastream

A

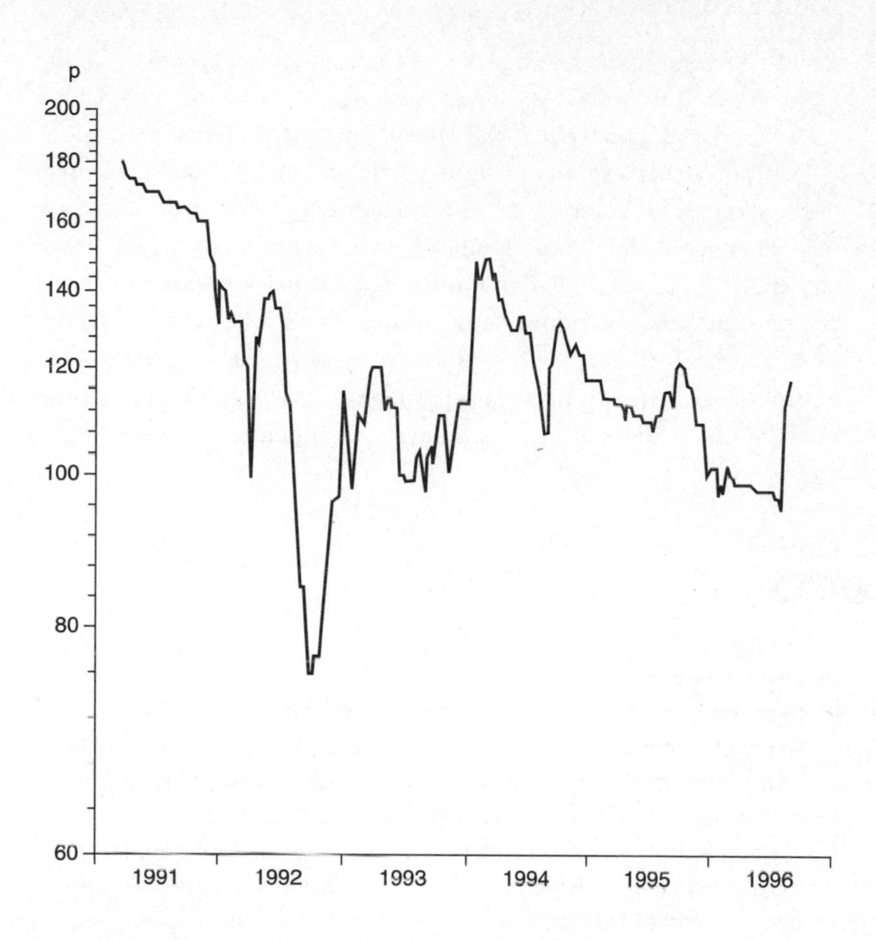

Fig A2 Bentalls: share price performance 1991–96
Source: Datastream

DIVIDEND YIELD

Yield is inversely related to price. A rising price will mean a falling yield. As with PE ratios, you need to compare the yield on any stock with the market yield. On 7 May 1996, this was 3.76 per cent.

The ratio sends a variety of signals to investors. A yield higher than the market yield is attractive, but a much higher yield implies high risk. There could be doubts about whether the company can afford to pay the current level of dividends. That means a dividend cut. At worst – and this is extreme – the company could be about to go out of business. In theory, a low dividend yield means investors can expect capital growth. However, it may mean that the company is on the skids and cannot afford to pay decent dividends.

Box A2

Track records

A single set of accounts will allow you to compare the latest results with the year before, but it is important to look at a company's long-term track record. The tables in *Investors Chronicle* show five years' worth of turnover (i.e., sales or income), pre-tax profit, earnings per share and net dividend per share. An ideal stockmarket portfolio is full of companies where all four figures rise steadily each year.

Basic statistics and investment ratios for each company are above the five-year record. A glance at the table tells you how large the company is (market capitalisation), whether its shares pay a good gross income (dividend yield), how highly the market values the shares (PE ratio) and whether it has asset backing (net asset value and net debt). *The Investors Chronicle* report on Tesco, the supermarket chain (see Figure A3), gives the basic information in the box and fleshes it out in the text. Investors want to know about what will happen next, so the story tells you what the City analysts expect Tesco to make and what should happen to dividends. Graphs of share price performance show how well the shares have fared in the past (see Figures A1 and A2).

TESCO

Food and petrol retailer

Good value

Ord price: 284p	Market value: £6.1bn
Touch: 282–286p	12 month High: 315p Low: 237p
Gross divd yield: 4.2%	PE ratio: 13
Net asset value: 166p	Net debt: 23%

Year to End Feb	Turn-over £bn	Pre-tax Profit £m	Stated Earnings per share (p)	Net Dividend per share (p)
1992	7.10	545	20.0	6.30
1993	7.58	558	20.3	7.10
1994	8.60	435	15.2	7.75
1995	10.10	551	18.9	8.60
1996	12.10	675	21.6	9.60
% Change	+20	+23	+14	+12

Market **makers: 17 Normal market size: 75,000**
Last **IC** comment: 22 September 1995, page 82 **xd**: 22 Apr

In a tough trading environment comparable sales were up 8.9 per cent, helped by the introduction of the Clubcard loyalty programme, which now has over 8m members. Add in new store openings and the integration of the Wm Low shops and group sales were up 19.8 per cent, helped by higher food price inflation running at 4.1 per cent. Tesco doesn't split out petrol sales but the petrol price war has hit profits by an estimated £30m. Overseas the focus is on France, where the Catteau supermarket chain's sales were up 13.9 per cent. The group's stores in Hungary, Poland and the Czech Republic also achieved significant sales advances. But profits in overseas activities, as a whole, fell 35 per cent to £11m.

In a push to improve customer service 4,500 staff are being recruited. This'll add to the wage bill, but management hopes they'll help the group to steal market share from competitors. Tesco plans to open 10 new superstores this year and to add to the town centre Metro store and Tesco Express concepts.

Although the dividend increase was ahead of earnings growth, future dividend growth will be kept in line with earnings. UBS forecasts profits this year of £730m giving a forward PE ratio of 12. **Good value** at a 5 per cent discount to the sector.

Fig A3 Tesco: number crunching
Source: Investors Chronicle, 19 April 1996

Example: Sims Foods – the deepest cut

In early 1996, ordinary shares in Sims Foods, a meat processor with a market value of under £15m, yielded 12 per cent. Sims had had an increasingly difficult five years, as the graph of its share price shows. It had battled against an increasingly difficult meat-processing market and falling meat consumption. The high yield reflected further worries about the effect of mad cow disease on Sims business.

Fig A4 Sims Food share price performance 1991–96
Source: Datastream

GEARING

A company with no debt cannot go bust, or that is the theory. At least if it does have to stop trading it has a better chance of returning some cash to shareholders.

However, all companies need capital to grow and some cannot grow without borrowing money – they need to buy plant, expand their workspace for example. Gearing can often be a good thing and low gearing can be a negative value for some types of company. Property investment, because their assets are so reliable, tend to have 100 per cent gearing. Here, too, there is risk – the story falls apart if the company has overvalued its property assets and finds it cannot sell them for as much as expected. It is the unexpected that turns gearing from a sensible part of the business into a looming disaster.

Eurotunnel is the great debt example of the 1990s. Its gearing at the end of 1995 was 1,787 per cent and the company had still to make a profit. *Investors Chronicle* warned readers, 'Its cashflows will never be enough to pay its interest bill.'

In general terms, companies with net debt worth more than 200 per cent of their assets have high gearing. Over 100 per cent is uncomfortable. Companies that do not borrow to make the most of opportunities may deserve criticism too. Investors need to look at how far companies' profits cover their annual interest charge, the interest cover, and whether the company has plausible reasons for borrowing so much. For example, is it borrowing to build new outlets that will transform profits in later years? Remember, too, that a company with high debt and poor cashflow is more likely to turn to shareholders for a cash injection (see FUND-RAISING, page 73).

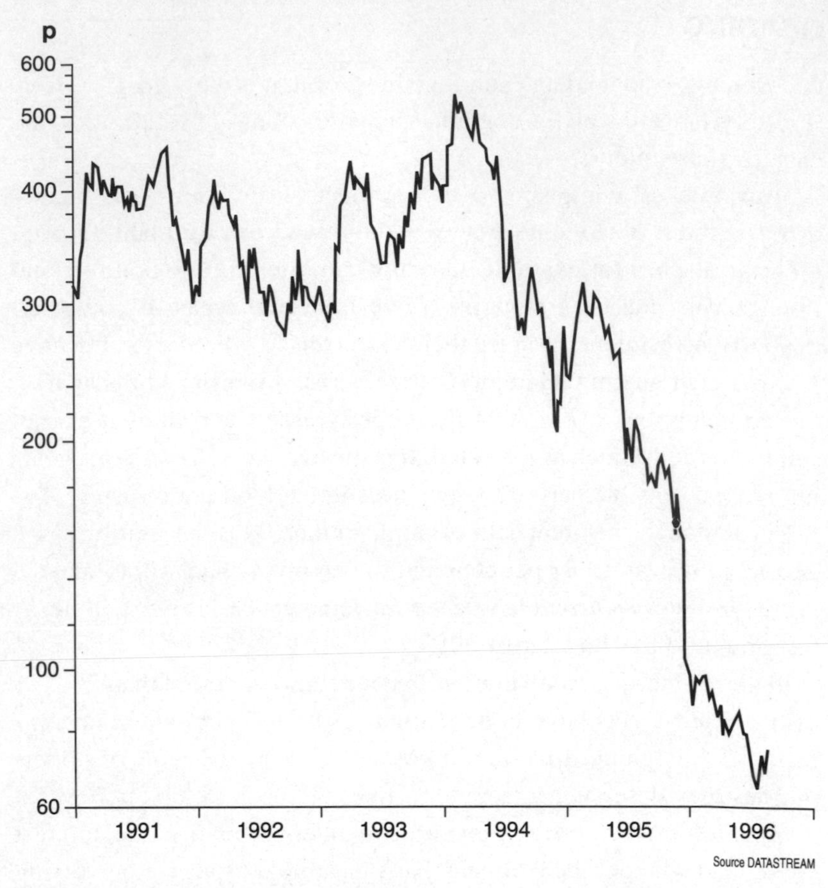

Fig A5 Eurotunnel share price per performance 1991–96

Source: Datastream

A

Box A3

Technical analysis

Technical analysis, or charting, attracts plenty of jokes, usually about train-spotting. Perhaps that is because chartists have an unfair reputation for believing they are infallible when, of course, technical analysts make mistakes too. However, growing computer power and access to PCs means charting is increasingly a valuable and practical aid to private investors. Here is a summary of the basics.

Chartists want to find the trend in share price movements, both of shares on their own and against the market. They can make money and avoid losses by following the trend and by spotting when the trend has turned. The simplest charts plot price against time with a line joining the dots. The whole point is to identify a pattern correctly. For long periods investors need to use logarithmic paper – allowing you to plot percentage changes – as a normal scale fails to show the big changes clearly enough.

Charting also shows how shares have performed against the market. Chartists call this a share's **relative strength** and calculate it by dividing the share price by the relevant index, usually the FT–SE A All-Share.

Investors can use the **moving averages** of a share price to find a trend. The chart is smoother and easier to read than a normal share price chart. Chartists tend to use 20-, 50-, 90- and 200-day moving averages. For example, a chart of the 90-day moving average plots the average price of a share in the last 90 days. At each point, you knock out the earliest figure and drop in the latest.

Resistance levels and support levels are two important charting terms. The resistance level is the point where a share price stops moving upwards because the supply of stock in the market holds it back. The support level is where a share stops falling because demand for stock has caught it up.

Volume patterns – the number of shares traded or the number of transactions – can also help investors make decisions. Charting changes in the number of bargains shows how the market's engine is running. It is business in the market that makes prices move.

Finally, here are the two of the most familiar patterns in charting. They are both made up of share price rallies and setbacks and, identified properly, signal that a price is about to change direction.

A3

- The head and shoulders formation has three stages. For the shoulder, the share price rises strongly, then slips back. It rallies again, rising further than the original rally, only to slip back again. That is the head. The right-hand shoulder comes in with another, weaker rally, peaking below the top of the head. This formation normally signals a fall, the problem is deciding whether you have correctly identified a head and shoulders.
- A double top appears when a price has rallied and slipped back, then repeats almost the same hump on the chart. Triple tops also occur.

Further reading:

Technical Analysis of Stock Trends, Robert D Edwards and John Magee (Prentice Hall)

Profitable Charting Techniques, Brian Millard (Qudos)

Charts, Profits and You, Richard Marshall (Investment Research of Cambridge)

The Stock Market Handbook, David Schwartz (Burleigh)

The Investors Chronicle Guide to Charting, Alistair Blair (Pitman Publishing)

Box A4

Taking Aim

The Alternative Investment Market (Aim) is a market for small, young and growing companies. It is a 'junior market' with fewer rules than the main market, also known as the Official List. For example, companies on Aim do not have to be a minimum size, have a three-year trading history or make sure that 25 per cent of the company is in public hands. But they must:

- appoint and retain a nominated adviser and a nominated broker (these advisers are responsible for making sure companies supply correct and appropriate information to shareholders);
- have published accounts that meet UK, US or international accounting standards;
- ensure that shares traded on Aim are freely transferable;
- adopt a code of conduct on dealing with price sensitive information, for example directors should not deal in their shares in the two months before they announce results.

For the hundreds of small companies that cannot meet the stringent rules set for having a full stockmarket listing (see **NEW ISSUES,** page 152), Aim is an important way to raise capital and make their shares easier to buy and sell.

Aim's advantages for investors are more dubious. It gives access to small, exciting companies that investors might otherwise never have the chance to follow. However, there are pitfalls for investors:

- Small exciting companies are risky by nature and Aim relies on companies' advisers and brokers to make sure the companies meet the standards expected by investors. The advisers may not always be able to keep company directors in line.
- Aim companies tend to have relatively small numbers of shares in issue or easily traded. This lack of liquidity exaggerates share price movements, making for sharp rises and falls.
- Small company markets tend to do best when stockmarkets are rising. However, Aim is likely to suffer particularly badly when share prices fall and take longer to recover than the main market. Investors who bought Aim shares for a quick speculation, rather than for the long-term, could be badly caught out.

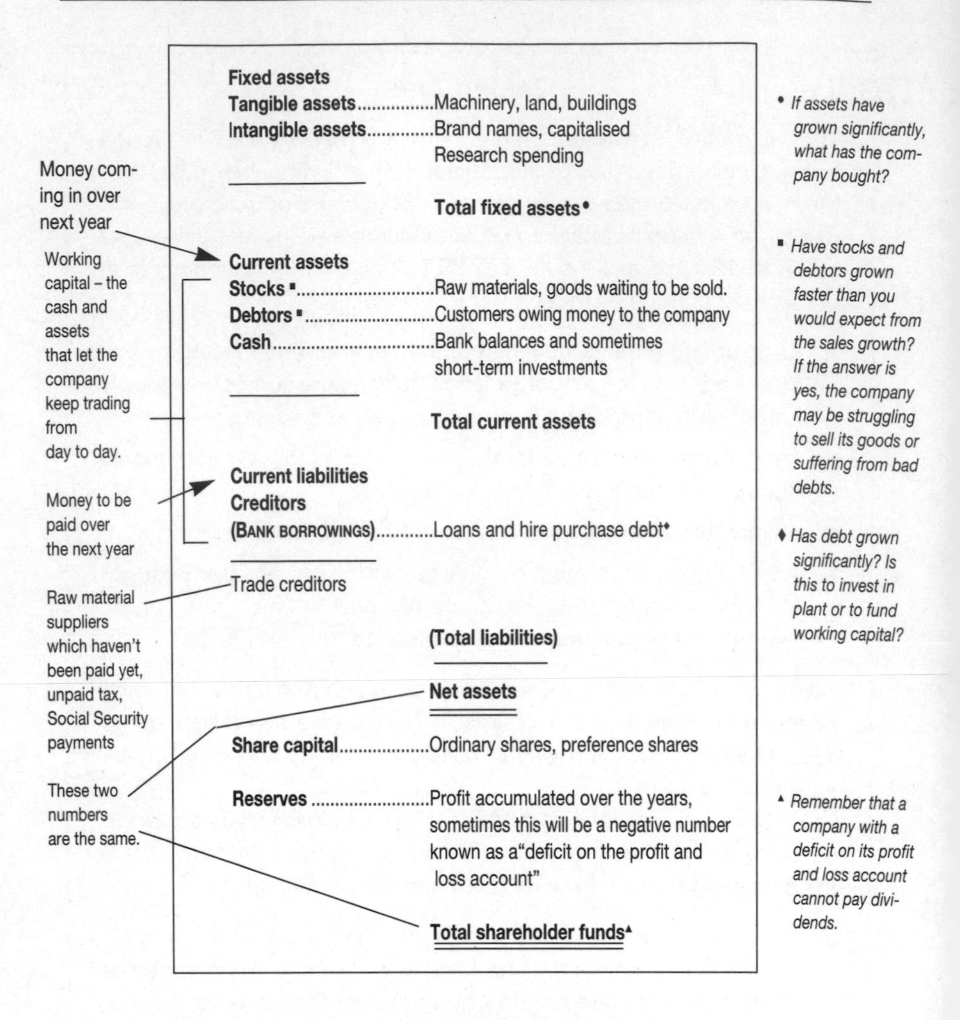

Fig A6 Balance sheets – the skeleton

Start with Sales/turnover & logically knock off following costs

Sales minus the cost of raw materials & making product.

Company's own costs or overheads.

Look out for "one-offs" or "exceptional items" in profit and loss accounts. These will be profits, losses or costs which are outside the company's normal business such as sales of assets or redundancy costs. These can make profits look unusually good or bad, distorting valuation methods such as PE ratios.

Turnover – Sales or income from trading. •

Cost of sales

Gross profit

$$\text{gross margin}^{\blacksquare} = \frac{\text{gross profit}}{\text{sales}}$$

Falling gross margins are a bad sign – either prices are falling or costs rising.

Distribution costs
Administration costs
Other operating costs/income

Operating profit

$$\text{operating margin}^{\blacksquare} = \frac{\text{operating profit}}{\text{sales}}$$

Interest receivable
Interest payable

Profit before tax

Taxation UK corporation tax is 33%, but companies can cut their tax charge in various ways so the percentage will vary widely

Profit after tax

Minorities Companies sometimes own most but not all of a subsidiary. The other shareholders in the subsidiary, the minority, receive a share of its profits.

Normally this doesn't mean a cash payment.

Preference dividends ♦

Profit attributable to ordinary shareholders

Dividends Total cash cost of dividends

Retained profit

Fig A7 Profit and loss accounts – the skeleton

- *Investors want turnover to grow each year. Beware companies where the only growth is from acquisitions.*

▪ *Margins allow you to compare how much profit companies are making. Operating margin is normally the more helpful figure. Sometimes operating margins are very low because turnover is low – fixed costs eat up the profit. A jump in turnover will improve margins dramatically. Such companies are called "operationally geared."*

♦ *Preference dividends must be met and any preference dividend arrears must be paid before a company can pay ordinary dividends.*

MAKING THE MOST OF ANNUAL ACCOUNTS

■ Look at the quality of the shareholder list of a company and its advisers.

■ Look at companies where you know the market, or use business libraries to find general information on the company's products and its competing companies.

■ Remember that some companies cannot be analysed on the basis of what has already happened – with oil and gas companies and mining companies, for example, investors are looking for forecasts of net asset value and cashflow. Investors need to use the specialist press, such as newsletters and the *Investors Chronicle* to keep up with analysts' forecasts, although some brokers offer access to stockmarket research.

■ Consider investing in reference publications such as a *Hambro Company Guide* or *Company Refs*, both from publisher Hemmington Scott (telephone: 0171-278 7769).

Further reading

Interpreting Company Reports and Accounts, Geoffrey Holmes and Alan Sugden (Woodhead-Faulkner)

Beating the Street, Peter Lynch (Simon & Schuster)

Accounting for Growth and Accounting for Growth II, Terry Smith (Century Business)

The Intelligent Investor, Benjamin Graham (Harper & Row)

The Zulu Principle, Jim Slater (Orion)

ANGELS

Definition: **Angels invest in theatre – they put up the capital to produce any type of theatrical production.** (See also *BUSINESS ANGELS*, page 233.)

Angels, more usually devoted lovers of theatre rather than hard-nosed investors, are particularly linked with London's West End. Some investments, such as the long-running musical Cats, can be spectacularly successful. However, there will always be at least one *Bernadette* – a musical version of the story of St Bernadette, the girl at the centre of the Lourdes miracle story, which closed after just 35 performances in 1990 – lurking in the wings. Everyone, including the two producers, lost their investment.

Veteran theatre investors freely admit that they invest as much for pleasure as in the hope of making money. However, they say the rising costs of staging a show have made it increasingly difficult to make a profit from being an angel. Cameron Mackintosh and the Really Useful Theatre Company, two of the most successful producers, needed £450,000 to put *Cats* on the stage in 1981. *Martin Guerre*, produced in 1996, cost £3.75m. Relatively low upfront costs meant very good returns when shows went well. Investors in *Cats* got their money back in 25–30 weeks – still the target used for Cameron Mackintosh productions. In the show's first ten years, investors enjoyed a return of 200 per cent a year. By the end of 1995, it had paid £20m in profits.

However, few producers, if any, have a record of total success. Alongside the legendary successes – *Cats*, *Les Miserables*, *Miss Saigon* – are near misses like *Follies* and *Carousel*, where investors got about 60 per cent of their investment back, and non-starters like *Moby Dick* in the early 1990s.

Also, West End theatre depends on tourism. Income from ticket sales suffers if recession in their home country, penal exchange rates or fear of terrorism deters tourists from visiting London.

'The mechanics of the investment itself are simple – investors buy units in a production.'

The Financial Services Act, the key piece of UK law in investor protection, covers theatre investment. Fund-raising by theatre producers counts as a form of collective investment scheme under the Act. As a result the producers need to be authorised and monitored by one of the investment watchdogs – probably the Investment Management Regulatory Organisation (Imro). In practice, Cameron Mackintosh and the Really Useful Group have subsidiary companies authorised by Imro and set up to raise money. Smaller producers will be authorised via one of their key advisers, such as their lawyers or accountants. Companies raising money must also quiz their investors to make sure they fully understand the risk they are about to accept. Under the terms of the Act, they cannot cold-call and they cannot advertise.

Example: Cutting the angels' cake

The mechanics of the investment itself are simple – investors buy units in a production. If the show is successful they will first receive their original capital and then share any profits according to the number of units they own. For example, a producer with a show that costs £1m decides to raise the full cost from investors, and offers 100 of units of £10,000 each. Investors should expect to put up at least £10,000, although some producers will offer part-units. In this example a part-unit might be £5,000. Profits are usually split 50:50 between the investors and the producers or 60:40 in the investors' favour. Producers may also receive a royalty and a management fee.

Angels' profit share

Producers of a show costing £1m raise the funds by selling 100 units in the show at £10,000 each. Profits will be split 50:50 between producers and investors.

In year one, the show proves a success and makes a profit after running costs of £500,000. This is split equally between the 100 investors, returning half their original capital.

In year two, the show makes a £600,000 profit. The producers use £500,000 of the profit to complete the return of capital to investors. They split the final £100,000 in half, keeping £50,000 as their own profit and dividing the last £50,000 into 100 units. Each investor receives a profit share of £500.

In year three, the show closes and there are no profits to distribute. Investors have earned a 5 per cent return on their money. That compares badly with the building society. Bear in mind also that the show in this example has been relatively successful.

It is relatively easy to become an angel, but it is almost impossible to invest in shows staged by the best-known producers. For example, Cameron Mackintosh runs three lists of investors and potential investors. The A-list includes investors who stuck by Sir Cameron in the early days of the 1970s. They have the opportunity to invest in all the company's productions. The B-list covers people who have invested in some of its productions and who really want to be on the A-list. The C-list is a waiting list. It is equally difficult to invest in productions by Sir Andrew Lloyd-Webber's Really Useful Group, or in productions by Michael Codron, who is known for producing well-known playwrights such as Alan Ayckbourn and Tom Stoppard. Michael Codron has a list of about two dozen loyal investors and it is difficult for anyone outside that list to buy a stake in his firm's productions. However, as with any producer, potential investors are welcome to ask for an opportunity to invest in future productions. As with Cameron Mackintosh, they join a waiting list.

The Really Useful Group, owned by Andrew Lloyd-Webber and producer of the musicals *Joseph* and *Sunset Boulevard*, also has a solid record. However, the main obstacle to investing in its productions may be lack of capital. The minimum investment in the German production of *Sunset Boulevard*, which opened in late 1995 in Wiesbaden, was DM225,000 (£100,000). True, the potential weekly box office of about DM1.8m (£800,000) is enticing. But £100,000 is a large sum for many private investors, given that they should invest only a small slice of their investment capital in theatre and should aim for a spread of theatre investments.

The Society of London Theatre, the body representing producers, does not organise investment or offer any investment advice, but it does act as a clearing house for information on productions. It keeps a list of people who have said they want to invest in shows and runs two systems, one for investing in the West End, and the other for investing in regional theatre.

Producers who have prepared a document on the investment potential of a show can ask the society to post the document to the names on the society's list. When potential investors write to the society, they receive information spelling out the risks, and then must write back confirming that they want to be on the mailing list.

The society keeps the names on its list confidential and makes it a condition that the producers' documents follow company and financial services law. However, it does not check that the documents meet those requirements and takes no responsibility for their content. The address of the Society of London Theatre is: Bedford Chambers, The Piazza, Covent Garden, London WC2E 8HQ and the telephone number is 0171-836 0971.

MAKING THE MOST OF BEING AN ANGEL

- Do not expect to make money. Theatre investment is highly risky. No one has done the sums, but experts believe the majority of productions fail to recoup the money invested. Only invest spare capital – you are likely to lose it.
- A minimum investment is likely to be £500–£1,000 and far more with successful producers, although some producers may allow investors to buy a part share in a show. Set aside a large enough sum to be able to invest in several shows. It is important to spread your risk in theatre, just as in the stockmarket.
- It will be difficult if not impossible, to cut any losses – or realise any gains – by selling your stake in a production to someone else.
- Remember that the minimum investment in musicals – in theory potentially the most successful form of theatre investment – will be high compared with other types of theatre investment. Even if

£100,000 for the German production of *Sunset Boulevard* was unusually high, it was £3,750 for *Martin Guerre*. Also, because musicals' upfront costs are high, they can take longer than conventional shows to make it into profit.

- Check how the producer's fund-raising is regulated, if at all. Direct regulation by Imro implies rigorous checks on the producer's financial controls. Otherwise look for well-known firms among the lawyers or accountants advising the scheme, and check that they are regulated for investment by their professional body. Regulation will not ensure a profit, but it should at least mean any losses are added up properly.
- The good news is that since early 1996, the Inland Revenue has made it official that UK investors in theatre productions can set losses against gains in theatre investment for tax purposes under Schedule D case VI. Only profits count as gains, not the return of capital.

ANNUITIES

Definition: **An annuity is an insurance contract that pays an income which must be regular in payment and be sufficiently secure for that payment to be guaranteed for life, in exchange for a lump sum.**

If you reckon annuities offer an enticing degree of security – income for life, no worries about stockmarket ups and downs – think again. Annuities tend to be a poor investment for the young or middle-aged. They work best for men aged over 70 or women aged over 75 and even here, in their natural habitat, annuities can be a tricky investment.

Anyone can buy an annuity. However, given that the annuity payable is largely based on your life expectancy, it is just that the rates for young or middle-aged people are remarkably poor value. If you have not reached your seventies, but want to invest a lump sum to earn a regular income do consider an alternative form of investment (see YIELD, page 250). However, investors with very little capital may find that an annuity is the only way to get a reliable investment income.

Most annuities are sold to people converting their pension fund into an annual income. Until recently pension scheme rules insisted that you buy an annuity to unlock your fund. For example personal pension schemes only allowed investors to withdraw up to 25 per cent of their pension fund as a lump sum, with the remaining 75 per cent used to purchase the annuity.

The UK government's rationale for insisting that investors bought annuities was that it is important to stop people frittering away their money or putting it in poorly performing investments. Otherwise they will end up depending on the State. Recently the Department of Social Security, which looks after pension matters, has relaxed the rules slightly, but annuities continue to dominate pension planning.

Box A5

Annuities – the basics

- Life insurance companies sell annuities and the older you are, the better the return they offer. The insurance company gambles that it will have to pay out less to someone who starts his annuity at 80 than it would to someone starting an annuity at 70. It cuts the risk on the gamble by using its actuarial tables of mortality and life expectancy patterns. In a sense, annuities are life insurance in reverse.
- You cannot change your mind about the annuity and be repaid your lump sum. (A temporary annuity, also known as a purchased life annuity and running for a set term only, can be surrendered, however.)
- Your annuity payment is partly interest on your money and partly a return of your original lump sum – your capital. The Inland Revenue taxes the interest element of the annuity payment, but not the return of capital. Usually the insurance company deducts basic-rate tax and the investor pays any higher rate tax separately. However, payments can be tax-free if you are a non-taxpayer. In other words, non-taxpayers do not have to fill in a fresh layer of paperwork to reclaim the tax.
- Women receive lower annuity rates than men, because women are expected to live longer.
- You can, in effect, pay more to get a better quality of annuity. The trade-off is between accepting a lower income in the early years of the annuity and having some protection against inflation or unexpected death. The basic choices boil down to single or joint-life annuities, flat-rate annuities, annuities with a guaranteed period, index-linked annuities, escalating annuities and unit-linked annuities.

Box A6

Pensions – the basics

Money-purchase pension schemes require investors or their pension fund trustees to buy an annuity. A money-purchase scheme means the size of your pension depends on the amount you save in the scheme and the investment performance of your fund. The other main type of pension scheme in the UK is the final-salary pension scheme. In this your pension is related to your salary and length of service when you retire, not the amount you have invested. You still need an annuity to unlock your pension, but it is all arranged by the pension scheme. As a rule self-employed people, people in executive pension schemes, investors in personal pensions and pension scheme trustees have to worrry about annuities. Most people in occupational pension schemes – pensions run by your employer – do not have to worry about the details of annuities. Their pension scheme trustees sort it out for them whether the scheme is money-purchase or final-salary.

THE HIGHEST INCOME MAY BE THE WORST DEAL

Annuity investors face tremendous pressure to opt for the annuity paying the largest income. After all, that seems the best value for money. In fact the single life annuity taken out on the life of a man, which normally gives the biggest annual payment compared to other annuities, is often the worst one to choose. The income stops as soon as the man dies. Say, for example, that on retirement a 65-year-old man immediately buys an annuity intended to provide a pension for him and his 60-year-old wife. In early 1996, a single-life annuity brought them an annual income of £1,124 per £10,000 invested.

A joint-life annuity bought on the same terms would have brought an annual income of just £987 a year, or 12 per cent less than the single-life annuity. In other words you get 12 per cent less for your £10,000. The difference is that the joint-life annuity will continue to be paid to the spouse even if the husband dies. The misery is that so many people make the wrong decision at this point and leave one partner financially dependent on relatives or the State.

Annuities can be guaranteed. This means the annuity continues for a stated number of years after the commencement date of the annuity. However, the guarantee costs more. In early 1996 a guaranteed single-life annuity for our 65-year-old man bought £1,100 for £10,000. The guarantee, in this case for five years, added barely 2 per cent to the cost of the annuity. It is a small price for some degree of security.

In all the examples so far the income from the annuity has been fixed. If the annuity pays £1,124 in 1996 and the pensioner lives 20 years, the annuity will still be paying £1,124 a year in 2016, whatever happens to inflation. Escalating and index-linked annuities are the two ways to build in a safeguard for your income against rising prices. Escalating annuities rise in steps each year, say 5 per cent. In early 1996, a 5 per cent escalating annuity, bought on a single-life basis for £10,000, paid £802 in the first year. Index-linked annuities rise in line with the retail price index, and until the early 1990s they were hugely expensive even compared with escalating annuities. However, as the belief has grown that high inflation may be a thing of the past, index-linked annuities have come down in price. In early 1996, £10,000 invested in an index-linked annuity policy bought £761 of income in year 1, in comparison with the £802 paid by the 5 per cent escalating annuity above.

'Escalating and index-linked annuities are the two ways to build in a safeguard for your income against rising prices.'

Two further types of annuity, also intended in part as protection against the effects of inflation, are with-profits and unit-linked annuities. Both are rare. They allow investors to link their annuities to the stockmarket, which may seem a contradiction in terms when annuities are supposed to be all about securing an income beyond the vagaries of the stockmarket. A with-profits annuity pays annual income linked to the bonuses on the life insurer's with-profits fund (see LIFE INSURANCE, page 140). With-profits funds are a relatively low-risk form of stockmarket investment, but they can still deliver nasty surprises, i.e., bonuses can fall. Unit-linked annuities mean the annuity fund is split into units in a stockmarket fund of funds. Each unit earns dividends and capital growth – in the good years – and the annuity investor receives a fixed number of units each year. However, if the fund goes through a bad patch, the risk is that the unit prices fall in value and the investor ends up with a much lower income than expected.

The Stalwart insurance company has introduced a smokers' annuity which pays particularly attractive annuity rates to smokers, because of their shorter life expectancy. In early 1996, Stalwart's single-life annuity for a 65-year-old man paid 5 per cent more than the next highest annuity.

THE COST OF MONEY

Annuity providers for the most part will use your pension fund to invest in UK gilts, as gilts will give the annuity provider the security for the life-time commitment they have made to you. Falling interest rates in the early 1990s – bank base rates fell from a peak of 15 per cent in 1989-90 to 6 per cent in 1993 – therefore hit annuity rates with the interest on the gilts also reducing (see GILTS, page 85). Falling interest rates meant that gilts grew more expensive. In turn people cashing in their pensions found annuities growing more expensive month by month. In 1991 £10,000 bought a basic annuity income of £1,390. By 1993 it bought just £1,180 a year and investors had little scope to improve the income from their pension fund.

True, you can convert the pension fund to an annuity at any time between 50 and 75 and faced with relatively low annuity rates, investors' first option is simply to postpone buying an annuity in the hope that rates will improve. The risk is that rates keep on falling and the continued investment does not compensate.

However, two further options opened up to pension investors as the government recognised the level of pension income depended too much on annuity rates on the day an investor converts his fund. The options are known as income withdrawal – orginally known as having a flexible annuity – and phased retirement. Both routes work best for people with large pension funds – say £100,000 – and ideally with other forms of income as a further buffer against loss.

Income withdrawal only won the green light from the government in 1994. It had been highly suspicious of insurance companies' attempts to introduce more flexibility into annuities. Income withdrawal means investors in personal pensions can postpone buying their annuity until they are 75, but can withdraw some income in the meantime directly from the fund. Inland Revenue rules fix the ceiling as equivalent to the income from a single life annuity if the pension fund were cashed in as normal. The minimum is 35 per cent of that ceiling. Unlike phased retirement (see below) you can take all your tax-free cash upfront.

The rules also say that the pension company must review the position every three years to make sure the fund has enough money left in it to buy an appropriate annuity at 75. However, investment advisers remain nervous about income withdrawal. Keeping your pension fund invested for longer should allow it to keep growing, but that depends on investment returns being good. It is also possible that the fund will shrink, particularly as investors have to pay charges for being able to withdraw income from their fund. The safeguards imposed by law may be too little to protect investors' cash in some cases.

Phased retirement works on the same principle as freezing food in ice cube trays. You can just defrost as many ice cubes or segments as you need instead of having to defrost your whole supply at once. You transfer your pension fund into a number of separate pension policies – as many as 1,000. You encash each policy as you need it, receiving tax-free cash and income from an annuity. At 75, you must convert all the remaining segments into tax-free cash and annuity income.

Box A7

Case study: Retirement options

Mr Smith is a farmer, owning the farm, the farm house and about 18 acres of land. He has three pension policies with a combined fund value of about £100,000 and has no mortgage or other liabilities. He and his wife are due to inherit about £300,000 from relatives. In retirement Mr Smith will lease the farm and the lease will provide about two-thirds of his retirement income. However, the income from the lease depends on having a tenant and Mr Smith would like the income from his pension funds to be as flexible as possible.

Mr Smith does not need to withdraw his tax-free cash, but if he changes his mind the three pension funds would give him total tax-free cash of just over £29,000. His attitude to risk scores two on a range of one to five, where one is the lowest risk and five is the highest risk.

The three main options open to Mr Smith are:

- Buying an annuity, either from his existing pension providers or using the open market option to shop around.
- Phased retirement.
- Income drawdown.

Annuity

The three pension funds could buy an annual income of £9,452 with a single-life annuity, guaranteed for five years. However, using the open market option would bump his annual income up to £10,413 – a 9 per cent improvement. If Mr Smith chose to take his £29,000 of tax-free cash, the annuity income would be £6,741, or £7,795 with the open market option.

Phased retirement

This option allows a tax-efficient income, flexibility on timing and the option to vary the level of income. But it limits access to the tax-free cash and it may not be economically viable. Investors need to set a target income and work out the annual investment return needed to achieve this income. If Mr Smith aims for £10,412, the amount an annuity would bring him, his underlying investments would need to grow at 10.3 per cent a year. That is an ambitious growth rate.

A7 **Income drawdown**

Here investors have instant access to the tax-free cash, avoid buying a conventional annuity and get a variable income, within certain limits. But two factors work against income drawdown. First, conventional annuities offer a mortality premium – in effect investors who die early subsidise the income of the investors who live beyond the average life expectancy. Investors who take the income drawdown route sacrifice the mortality premium in favour of flexibility. This means that the investments backing their income must work harder to achieve the same return.

Access to the tax-free cash means that the appropriate target income is £7,795 – i.e., matching the equivalent annuity income. However, the income drawdown rules mean a fund of his size could only pay £7,618. Moreover, the underlying investments would have to achieve an annual return of 12.2 per cent to back up the income payments.

The best route for Mr Smith is phased retirement. He needs flexibility, but not the tax-free cash and the required investment return is steep but more realistic than that needed for income drawdown.

Source: Lexis Pension Consultants Ltd April 1996

BUYING AN ANNUITY? SHOP AROUND

The range of annuity choices means buying an annuity is a complex investment decision. It is vital to shop around. The annuity rates paid by the life insurance companies vary enormously. There can even be a large difference within the top layers of annuity rates. *Pensions Management*, a sister magazine of *Investors Chronicle*, publishes a snapshot of the top six annuity rates each month. In early 1996 there was up to a 5 per cent difference between the highest and lowest rates for some annuities just within the top six. Across the whole market the difference can be as much as 20 per cent.

The companies maintain that investors will go elsewhere to buy their annuities if they offer poor rates. However, a surprisingly large number of people fail to shop around for an annuity. They buy their annuity from the company which has run their pension fund out of inertia, a mistaken belief that a company that runs pension funds successfully will also pay good value annuities. They are wrong. Investors have a legal right to shop around under the open-market option. Life insurers that do not want to attract annuity business – they prefer to focus on other forms of investment – will pay lousy rates.

Annuities check list

- Find out the value of your pension fund.
- Aks your own pension provider, normally an insurance company, for a quote on the annuity value your pension fund will buy.
- Buy a specialist pensions magazine to check the annuity rates in the market. How does your original company compare?
- Is your pension fund value greater than £100,000? Consider phased retirement or income drawdown if you want more flexibility than a basic annuity can offer.
- Take specialist annuities advice before you commit any funds.

Given that decisions about your pension income will affect as much as 30 years of your life, it is worth taking the time to visit a fee-based annuity adviser and to buy a specialist pensions magazine.

Box A8

Annuities phrasebook

A **single-life annuity** lasts only as long as the person who buys it – the annuitant. A **joint-life annuity** lasts until the second person named in the annuity policy dies. A **guaranteed-period annuity** will ensure that the annuity will run for a given number of years from the annuity commencement date even if the annuitant dies during this period.

Escalating annuities look expensive, but allow your income to grow in annual steps of say 5 per cent from a relatively low base. **Index-linked annuities** allow income to grow with inflation.

A **with-profits annuity** is linked to stockmarket growth through a life insurer's with profits fund – annuity income will depend on the with-profits bonuses. A **unit-linked annuity** has an even more direct link to the stockmarket than its with-profits peer and is therefore more risky because it depends on the performance of the fund selected for investment. Backed up by a life insurer's fund, the annuity income depends on stockmarket performance.

Phased retirement means you unlock your pension in stages, allowing greater flexibility on when and how you receive your income until you reach 75. **Income drawdown** means you can keep your pension invested until you are 75, but can draw income from it in the meantime. Both options carry more risk than a conventional annuity and are expensive.

MAKING THE MOST OF ANNUITIES

- Take advice on buying your annuity and use a fee-based specialist adviser – few generalist advisers fully understand the annuities market. The three best-known annuity specialists are the Annuity Bureau (telephone: 0171-620 4090), Annuity Direct (telephone: 0171-375 1175) and Lexis Pension Consultants (telephone: 0171-283 2828).
- Avoid purchased life annuities (PLAs), annuities sold to people

who want a guaranteed income, but are not cashing in their pension. They may seem attractive compared to other forms of guaranteed income, but remember you cannot cash in your investment if you change your mind. However, PLAs are only partly taxed and for basic-rate taxpayers, only at 20 per cent. Therefore unlike a pension annuity, a PLA can provide a tax efficient income.

- Be careful about phased retirement and income drawdown. Their flexibility comes at higher cost and higher investment risk. They are most useful for people with at least £100,000 to invest.

Further reading

These books cover all forms of pensions planning, including annuities.

The Which? Guide to Pensions (Which? Books)

Pension Power, Debbie Harrison (Wiley)

BONDS

Definition: **Bonds are a form of traded IOU issued by governments, local authorities or companies. They carry a fixed rate of interest and, normally, a date at which they will be repaid. The bond universe includes gilts, preference shares, convertibles and many other types of fixed interest investment. The coupon is the nominal rate of interest paid by the bond when it is issued.**

Buying a bond means lending money to someone. The advantages are that you receive a pre-determined level of income and you know when and how much you will receive when the borrower repays you. That sounds like, and is, a comfortably low risk, assuming you trust your borrower to pay up. Being able to buy and sell bonds is supposed to make lending the money that much more attractive in the first place.

Moreover, bonds are useful and attractive to investors because they offer a halfway house between the very low risk of savings accounts with banks and building societies and the high risk of stockmarket investment. The certainty of a pre-determined rate of interest and a known repayment, or redemption, date means bonds work equally well for insurance companies expecting to pay pensions or individuals expecting to pay school fees.

If bonds are so pre-determinedly wonderful and straightforward, why do relatively few UK investors hold them? The answer is that investing in bonds has one big disadvantage. If prices in the shops start rising quickly, the fixed income will be unable to keep up. Given the UK's history of high inflation, it is no surprise that UK investors have avoided bonds for fear of eroding their income and capital.

Also, investing in bond markets can seem as much like a roller-coaster as investing in shares. That is because you only know exactly how much your bond is worth to you if you plan to hold it to redemp-

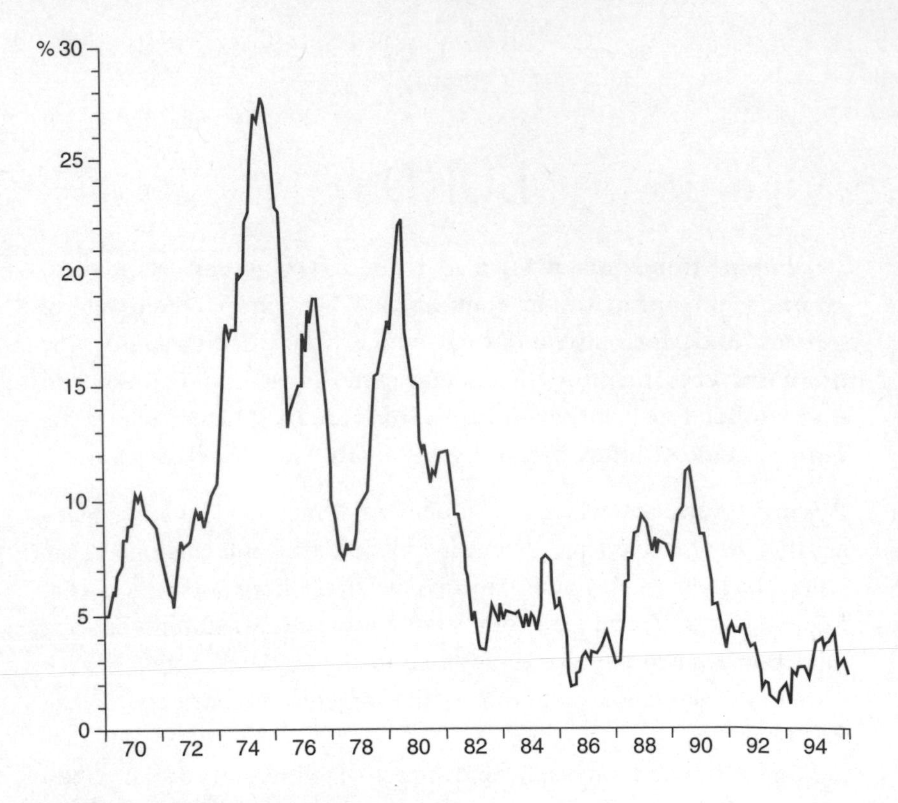

Fig B1 UK inflation since 1970
Source: Datastream

tion. The price of a bond can move very sharply between the time it is issued and the time it is repaid. It need not be a roller-coaster ride for private investors, but here are the reasons why bond markets make headline news.

Three main factors affect bond markets – interest rates, inflation and movements in overseas bond markets. All three factors tend to interlock.

- Interest rates matter because higher bank base rates will attract investors from bonds into cash. The coupon is fixed, and the capital value of the bond must change to reflect the level of other interest rates. Bond prices will fall and yields rise when interest rates go up. The reverse will happen when interest rates go down.

- Inflation matters because the market will adjust to allow for its effect on income. Fear of rising inflation means bond prices will fall and yields rise, and the reverse will happen when inflation looks set to fall or stay low.
- Overseas bond markets matter because international investors will switch from one market to another to find the best return. The German and US bond markets have a strong influence on the UK market.

The flowchart of the elements affecting bond markets shows that further factors can lie behind the three listed above. Changes in the value of the currency, in government and and the economy are all important to bond markets.

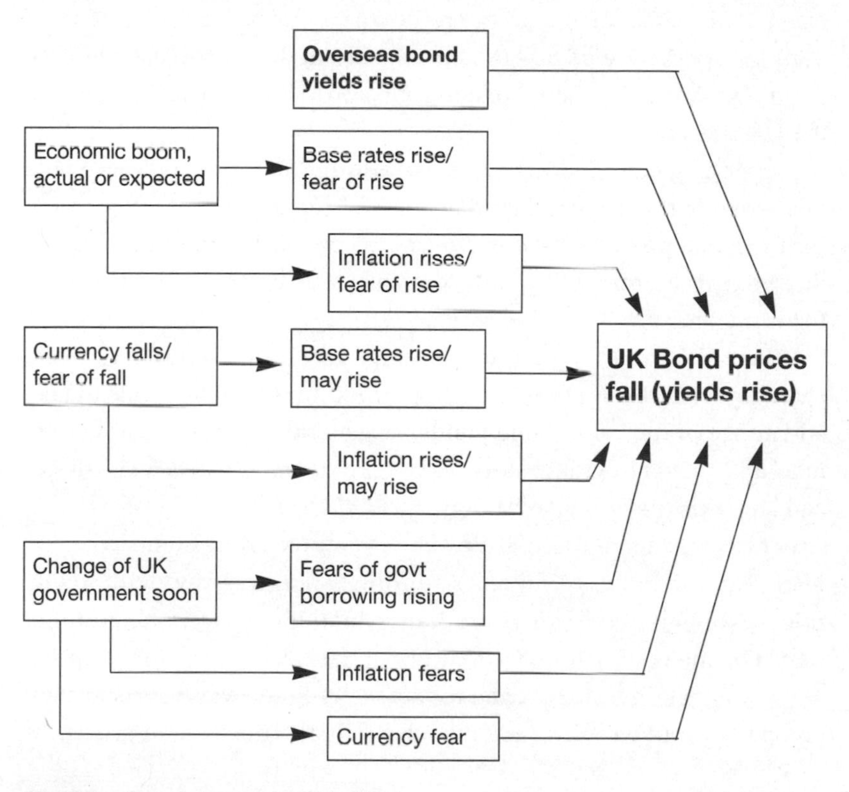

Fig B2 Bonds: cause and effect

Source: Investors Chronicle, 15 March 1996

> ***'Changes in the value of the currency, in government and the economy are all important to bond markets.'***

Every so often these factors swing into action so dramatically, that the result jumps out of newspapers' financial sections on to the front pages. Bond markets reacted sharply to some good economic news early in 1996. The number of jobs in the US jumped by 624,000 in February and 140,000 in March. Bond prices fell. Yields on long-dated US bonds, barely 6 per cent at the beginning of 1996, had nosed up to almost 7 per cent by early April. US bond investors decided that the US government, which had been cutting interest rates to encourage economic growth, would now stop the rate cuts because of the good employment news. The same line of thinking sparked fears that inflation would make a comeback as economic growth picked up. Higher yields on US bonds spilled over to the UK market.

A sneezing bond market can mean equities catch a cold too. Share markets move when bond markets move because they are competing for the same money. But they will not necessarily move in the same direction. Investors will jump from shares to bonds if bonds offer a better income.

When US bond markets fell in early 1996 and yields improved, share prices fell sharply in response – investors bought bonds to take advantage of the better bond yields. In general, when bond prices are high and yields low, investors will accept a lower yield from shares and share prices will also be high.

However, shares normally react differently from bonds to news affecting inflation. Companies' profits should grow with rising prices, so their share prices are less vulnerable to news about inflation. The interesting little wrinkle about the US bonds panic in spring 1996 was that investors began to factor in higher wage costs to their company profit forecasts and that also helped knock share prices.

B

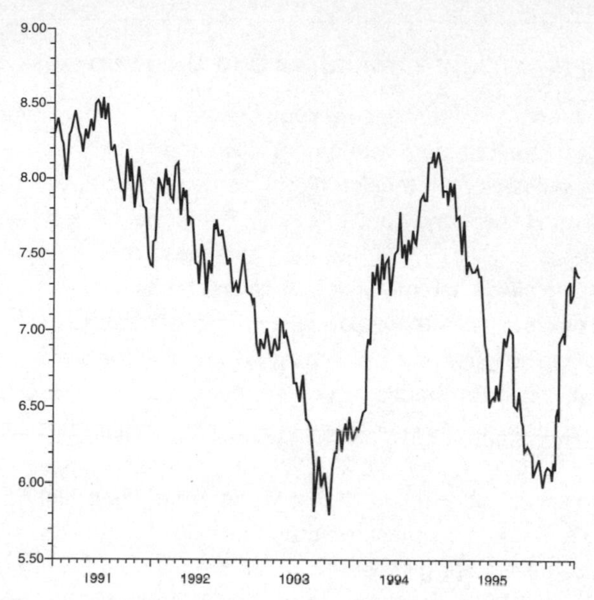

Fig B3 US treasury 30-year benchmark bonds: redemption yields

Source: Datastream

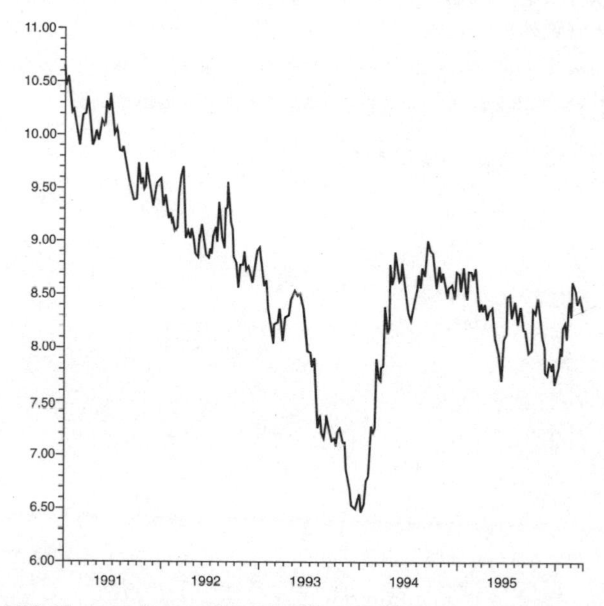

Fig B4 UK 15-year (long-dated) gilts: redemption yields

Source: Datastream

Box B1

Yield - the curve and the ratio

Yield tells you how much income you are getting from an investment, which you then compare with others. Changes in the yield earned on different investments can also alert investors to particular trends in interest rates share and bond prices. Two important investment measures based on yields are the yield curve and the gilt/equity ratio. Plotting the yields and maturities of different gilts on a graph creates a **yield curve**. Investors would expect the yield curve to be on a positive slope. The longer the life of the gilt, the higher the yield. It is called a normal curve. In practice the yield curve can look very far from normal, if for example interest rates are high and people believe that in the long term inflation will be high too. Figure B5 shows the yield curve in early 1996 – it shows that yields are better on longer-dated stocks, and is more or less normal. The **gilt/equity ratio**, shown in Figure B6 measures gilt yields against the yield on shares. Historically, the gilt/equity ratio has been as high as three, i.e., gilts have yielded as much as three times more than shares, and the low has been 1.5. The rule of thumb for interpreting the ratio is that equities are set to rise if the ratio falls below 2 and set to fall if it rises above 2.5 to three. The reverse applies for gilts prices. The gilt market is set to fall if the ratio is below 2 and rise if it goes above 2.5.

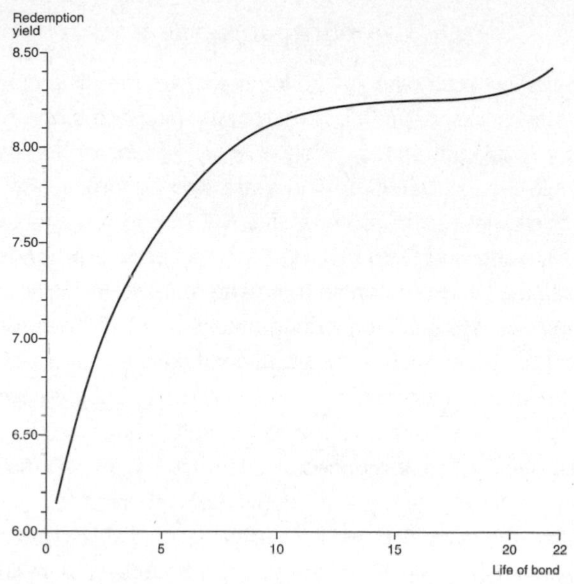

Fig B5 UK gilts: yield curve April 1996

Source: Datastream

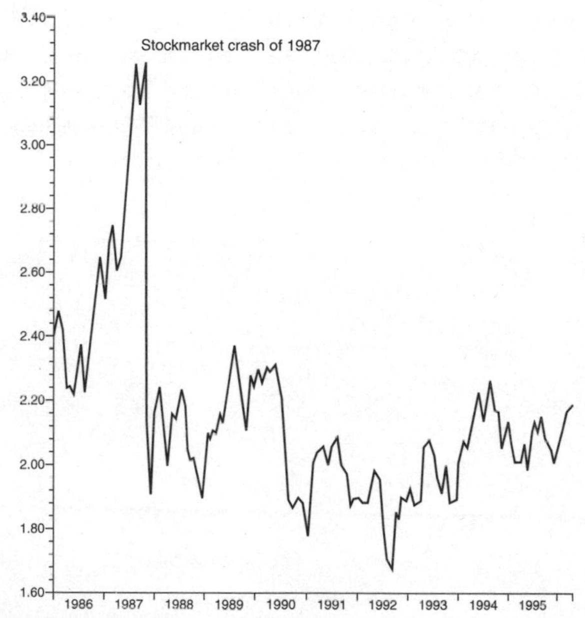

Fig B6 UK gilt/equity ratio

Source: Datastream

Box B2

The bond universe

Gilts, bonds issued by the UK government, are the main category of UK bond (see GILTS, page 85). Investors will also come across bonds issued by local authorities, such as City of Bristol 11½ per cent redeemable, and universities. There are also hundreds of corporate bonds, bonds issued by companies. UK bonds fall into two main camps – sterling and Eurosterling. Sterling bonds are bonds traded and held in the UK. Eurosterling bonds are bonds, normally issued by UK companies, available for trading outside the UK. They tend to be bearer bonds, which means the bond certificate is your proof of ownership. Private investors are most likely to encounter preference shares (see SHARES, page 198) and convertibles (see CONVERTIBLES, page 52). Debentures and unsecured loan stock, also forms of debt, are safer than preference and convertible shares. However, it is unusual for the typical private investor to hold this type of bond. Credit rating agencies give ratings to bond issuers – Figure B7 shows the ratings used by the main credit rating agencies. The rating does what it says – gives an opinion on whether the borrower is good for the money. But the ratings agencies are not all-knowing. The perpetual bonds issued by Barings, the well-respected and long-established bank that collapsed in 1995 and was bought by Dutch bank group ING, had a good credit rating. In early 1996, the holders of the £100m worth of bonds were still pursuing repayment of their investment.

B

RISKY BUSINESS

S&P	Moody's	IBCA	
AAA	Aaa	AAA	The highest rating awarded. The ability to service debt is extremely strong
AA	Aa	AA	A very strong capacity indeed to service debt. High-quality bonds
A	A	A	A strong capacity to service debt although more vulnerable to changes in circumstances
BBB	Baa	BBB	Adequate capacity to service debt and adequate protection but more susceptible to circumstances that affect these measures
Each of the above ratings bands, except AAA, also has above and below average ratings, marked by +/– for Standard & Poor's and IBCA and the numbers 1 and 3 for Moody's. Ratings continued down through BB/Ba via B to CCC/Caa.			

Fig B7 Credit ratings – the main names

Sources: BZW and Investors Chronicle

MAKING THE MOST OF BONDS

- Bonds offer higher income and less risk than shares, but investors still need to be careful in buying bonds. You are only sure of your return if you hold the bond to redemption, so it is important to look for bonds which offer a profit on redemption. In times of low interest rates, this may be relatively difficult. See CONVERTIBLES and GILTS for an explanation of the language of bonds and some ideas on choosing your investment (pages 52 and 85).
- It is important to have a spread of bonds to reduce your risk, otherwise one disaster could wipe out a large part of your portfolio. But avoid bond funds as far as possible unless they offer a specialist edge – such as convertible bond funds – or have an outstanding long-term record. It is difficult for a bond fund to achieve good enough performance to justify its charges.
- Check where your bonds stand in the pecking order for repayment if the issuer goes under. Some bonds pay a generous yield only because they are relatively risky.

CASH

Definition: **Widely used and readily accepted medium of exchange for goods.**

Stockbrokers, when they know the stock they are pushing could be a bottomless pit of disaster, like to end the sales pitch by saying: 'Of course, only invest money you can afford to lose.' In practice the same rule applies to all stockmarket investment, even when it is low-risk, and two factors make it a good rule to follow.

First, stockmarket investment is a long-term commitment. Secondly, moving into cash can be the best of all investments. It may well be possible to make money overnight on the stockmarket if you take big risks, but most stockmarket speculators work at it full-time and even they keep a disaster fund. The typical part-time investor is looking at a five-year view, or longer.

All investors need ready cash, but no one wants to be a forced seller. The cash could be for unexpected disasters or big treats. But it is important to keep some money in cash. Selling shares at the wrong time can lose a large slice of any gains and make a mess of your tax-planning. Worse, cashing in a packaged investment such as a unit trust, investment trust or an insurance-linked fund, normally means that the investor does not even get back his original lump sum. The charges will have been deducted, but the fund has had no chance to grow.

Professional fund managers can move large proportions of their portfolio into cash when they decide that stockmarkets have reached a peak. The truly successful investors are those who sell up at the right time. Sir James Goldsmith is as famous for moving some of his fortune out of the stockmarket before the 1987 crash as for his views on European union. Nick Leslau and Nigel Wray made a fortune in property in the 1980s and sold up before the collapse in property prices of 1989. Their reputation by 1996 was good enough to win backing for highly speculative projects such as developing the Trocadero shopping and entertainment complex in London's West End. The private investor – working on a more personal level than the wheeler-dealers, but with the same capacity for good luck – can aim to make equally astute decisions. It is also worth remembering that high interest rates attract money away from the stockmarket. After all, why should investors risk their money in the stockmarket when they can earn a good return on their money at relatively little risk? But investors need to consider the real interest rate earned by their money – the rate of interest less the rate of inflation. If the real rate of interest is low, then they have a better chance of protecting their capital through stockmarket investment than through a building society.

'The truly successful investors are those who sell up at the right time.'

KNOWING THE CASH CHOICES

The options for people wanting to keep money in cash are enormously varied. Even savers who restrict their choice to the largest banks and building societies – normally the top 20 building societies and the top four banks – face too many choices.

Here are the basic options.

- Instant access savings accounts run through high street branches by banks and building societies offer poor rates of interest, even for large sums, i.e., over £1,000.
- Notice accounts, normally ranging from seven-day to three-month, can pay slightly better rates, particularly for large sums. If you fail to give notice, you lose interest built up in the notice period instead.
- Term accounts, where savers commit large sums – normally at least £2,000 – for one year or more. Interest rates on such accounts

C

will often be fixed for the term, or will rise in pre-determined steps.

- Money market accounts pay rates of interest directly linked to rates in the money market, for fixed periods. The minimum investment is about £10,000, although some banks and building societies accept small deposits.
- Postal accounts, generally the preserve of the building societies, offer premium rates of interest on the grounds that they do not incur the cost associated with running a high street branch and investors accept that they must wait for their money.
- Cash unit trusts are run by the unit trust companies alongside their stockmarket funds, mainly to give investors an in-house cash haven when they choose to switch out of stockmarket investments. These pay competitive rates of interest – the gross yields, net of costs, are published in newspapers' normal unit trust listings – and offer near instant access.
- Offshore accounts, usually operated by offshoots of the familiar high street names based in the Channel Islands or the Isle of Man, can pay slightly better rates of interest than the UK-based equivalents. However, these are aimed at ex-patriates or at seriously wealthy individuals who have sheltered large chunks of their capital overseas. The main benefit for the typical investor, who lives in the UK and is taxed wholly as a UK resident, is that interest is paid gross of tax. On conventional UK-based savings accounts tax – at 20 per cent – is deducted at source by the bank or building society.
- Tax exempt special savings accounts (Tessas) are one of the most attractive options for savers and are covered at length later in the book (see TESSAS, page 219).
- National Savings – see *Box C1*.

Box C1

National Savings

National Savings is the UK government's version of the building society account. It is another way for the government to borrow from its citizens and, like gilts, National Savings products are one of the safest investments on offer. The risk that the government will go out of business is considered to be zero. National Savings products tend to offer highly competitive rates, despite their low risk. However, as with any savings product, it is important to shop around. The tax-free products are particularly attractive to higher-rate taxpayers. For a higher-rate taxpayer, 5.35 per cent tax-free is equivalent to a gross rate of 8.9 per cent. But the trade-off is that savers have to leave their money with the government for several years to earn the best returns. Cashing in National Savings certificates early means you will receive far less than the headline rate – the rates are *guaranteed over five years*, not fixed. National Savings products are sold through post offices, newspaper advertising or the Sales Information Unit, National Savings, Freepost BJ2092, Blackpool FY 9XR.

The main products, with their April 1996 rates of interest, are:

- Guaranteed rates
- National Savings Certificates: 5.35 per cent tax-free over five years
- Index-Linked National Savings Certificates: 2.5 per cent plus index-linking tax-free over five years
- Pensioners Guaranteed Income Bonds: 7 per cent gross over five years (taxable)
- Capital Bonds: 6.65 per cent gross over five years (taxable)
- Children's Bonus Bonds: 6.75 per cent tax-free over five years
- FIRST Option Bonds: 6.25 per cent gross over 12 months (taxable)

Guaranteed rates offered by National Savings are equivalent to fixed rates. The variable rate options are the Ordinary and Investment accounts and the Income Bonds. National Savings also runs the Premium Bonds prize fund.

So far this chapter has dealt with the merits of keeping a back-up fund in cash, and cash as an investment in its own right. However, sometimes investors have a choice between building up capital and paying off debt. It is a more difficult choice than it seems. After all, companies borrow to expand their business and the same thinking can apply to personal finance. The best rule of thumb in choosing which route to follow is to think about real interest rates (see page 46). When inflation is high, real interest rates can be very low even if nominal interest rates are in double figures. Our table of interest rates and inflation shown in Figure C1 shows how real interest rates can tell a very different story from the mortgage rate.

	Mortgage rate %	Inflation %	Real interest rate %
1975	11.00	6.4	4.6
1980	15.00	18.0	–3.0
1985	12.00	6.1	5.9
1990	15.40	9.5	5.9
1995	6.99	3.4	3.6

Fig C1 Tables of interest rates and inflation 1975–95

In the 1970s, real interest rates were low, inflation seemed unlikely ever to disappear, and it made sense to run a mortgage. The real cost of borrowing was low, the debt was shrinking in real terms, and the value of property was rising. However, by 1995, the rules of the game had changed. Now the cost of borrowing is relatively high and inflation is no longer working in homeowners' favour. When that is the case, mortgage holders with spare cash on top of their disaster fund should consider paying off some of their mortgage debt.

However, it is important to make it clear to your mortgage lender that you are paying in extra capital to reduce your debt. Some lenders will set extra payments against the mortgage only once a year, and spare cash sits in limbo for the rest of the year when it could be earning interest.

MAKING THE MOST OF CASH

- Narrow your field of choice by deciding exactly how much you have to save and for how long.
- Look at building society accounts rather than banks. Building societies still pay better interest rates on savings accounts than banks. Moreover, although the main rush of conversions from building society to bank is over, saving with a building society that has held on to its mutual status opens up the chance of a bonus should your society convert or be acquired.
- Consider a postal account. Savers who invest large sums for long periods earn the highest rates of interest. At its most extreme that means locking up cash for years, in which case you could simply invest on the stockmarket. However, building societies pay premium rates on accounts run by post, because savers are implicitly accepting a wait of a few days to withdraw their cash. Even agreeing to a notice period of one week or a fortnight can make a significant difference to the rate of interest you earn.
- Scan the financial press and weekend finance pages for tables of the highest savings rates once you have found your savings account, as well as when you are looking for the right one. Rates can slip far behind the competition as time passes and you may find that your account is paying a very poor rate compared to a more recent version of the account run by the same bank or building society.
- Avoid small banks and, if possible, very small building societies. These tend to top the savings rate league tables because they are paying you a risk premium. The Bank of England and the building society compensation schemes will repay you most of the money you lose (see *Box K2* on page 137) up to a given ceiling if the bank or society goes out of business. However, you will lose some of your capital and you can wait a long time to receive your compensation.
- Consider using spare cash to reduce debt if real interest rates are low.

- If you are an active investor – as opposed to someone who wants to let their capital build up in a unit trust over 20 years – be alert to the advantages of cashing in investments which have earned a spectacular return.

CONVERTIBLES

***Definition:* Convertibles are loan stock or preference shares that can be exchanged for ordinary shares at predetermined dates. They pay a fixed rate of interest and normally have a fixed maturity date.**

Convertibles lead a double life. They pay a fixed level of interest, so they look like a bond. But investors can also convert them into the ordinary shares of the issuing company. The attraction for private investors is that convertibles deliver income, with the prospect of capital growth.

'... even if investors are interested only in income, they should buy convertible shares only if they like the company.'

In times of low interest rates, such as the early 1990s, income is the main attraction of convertibles. For most investors it is the prospect of earning a better income from the convertible than from the ordinary shares, or equity, of a company that makes them buy a convertible stock. However, few investors would buy convertibles in a company with no chance of growing its profits, or at least reversing its losses. Convertibles will rise or fall in value along with the ordinary shares according to how well the company trades. That is why, even if investors are interested only in income, they should buy convertible shares only if they like the company.

But what about the option to convert – isn't this an unnecessarily complicated way of investing? In practice, it is unusual for investors, institutional or private, to hold the convertible for long enough to get involved in the conversion process.

THE CONVERSION PREMIUM

The conversion premium is the main investment yardstick associated with convertibles – it tells you how much extra you are paying for the reliable income stream from the convertible shares compared with the price of the ordinary shares. That is fine. But convertibles experts will always remind investors that a convertible with a premium of 100 per cent can be cheap, and one with a 5 per cent premium can be expensive, depending on the amount of extra income received on the convertible. In other words, investors need to apply common sense to conversion premiums. As with PE ratios and return on capital employed (see ACCOUNTS ANALYSIS, page 1) it is easy to get into a pickle with conversion premiums.

The conditions for conversion are normally given in the company's annual report – available directly from the company or through one of the annual reports services run by, for example, the *Investors Chronicle* or the *Financial Times*. It is worth reading the terms carefully. However, it is also worth checking with your broker in case the annual report omits an important little wrinkle in the terms.

Knowing the conversion terms means you can work out the premium – it is a simple sum as you can see from the example of Lookers (*Box C2*). A high premium tells you that using the convertible as a way to buy the equity would be much more expensive than just buying the equity. For example, the premium on Frederick Cooper, which makes bakeware and architectural hardware, was over 170 per cent in early 1996. A convertible with such a big distance between itself and the underlying equity should behave like a fairly low risk fixed-interest stock. Its price will move less dramatically than the price of the equity, so investors would avoid the worst of any serious dips in the price, but would also miss the highs. A premium of over 50 per cent can be considered 'high'.

A very low premium – say below 20 per cent – tells you that using the convertible to buy the equity might be good value. It also tells you that the convertible will move much more closely in line with the underlying equity, allowing convertibles investors to enjoy any peaks and troughs. However, premiums can be misleading. British Aerospace slashed its dividend in 1993 – dividend payments fell from 24p a share for 1991 to barely 7p for 1992 – and briefly deferred payments on its convertibles. The convertible hit a premium of 400 per cent, in theory, a sign that the convertibles were expensive. But Figure C2 shows how well British Aerospace convertibles have done since 1993.

Box C2

Conversion premiums – the arithmetic

In March 1996, Lookers 8 per cent convertible cumulative redeemable preference shares were 98p in the market, and Lookers ordinary shares were 129p.

The convertibles can be exchanged at a rate of 20 ordinary shares for 44 convertibles on 31 March in each and any of the years 1993 to 2000 inclusive. The company has the option to redeem – 'to call' – the shares at their par value of £1 between 2000 and 2004.

The price at which you can reasonably exchange the convertibles for shares, i.e., the conversion price, is:

$$\frac{\text{Convertible price x number of convertibles}}{\text{Number of ordinary shares}} = \frac{\text{98p x 44}}{20} = 215.6\text{p}$$

That is much higher than the price of the ordinary shares, but a figure in pence is hard to compare with other stocks on the market. Working out the conversion premium gives you a benchmark for comparing Lookers convertibles with other convertibles. If the conversion price is 215.6p and the ordinary shares are trading at 129p, the conversion premium is:

$$\frac{\text{Conversion price}}{\text{Ordinary price}} - 1 = \left(\frac{215.6}{129}\right) - 1 = 1.67 - 1 = 67\%$$

In March 1996, Lookers had suffered because of the general problem afflicting motor dealers, but the dividend on the convertible was still covered by profits. The 11 per cent yield made the convertibles an attractive income buy. The ordinary shares yielded 8 per cent. The relatively high conversion premium implied that the convertibles would behave more like a fixed-interest bond than an ordinary share, i.e., the price movements should be less dramatic. In textbook terms, the premium also told you that it would be expensive to use the convertibles to switch into the ordinary shares.

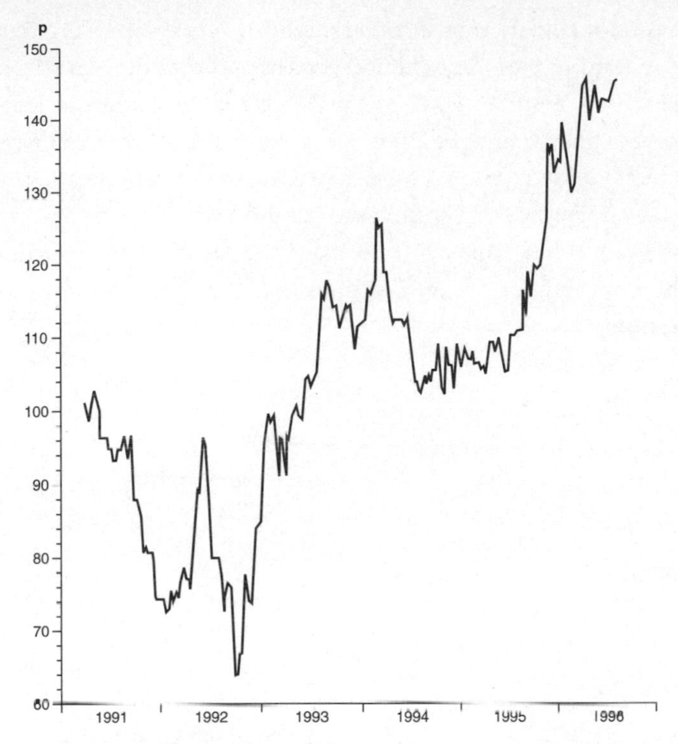

Fig C2 'Oh ye of little faith': British Aerospace 7.75 per cent convertibles

Source: Datastream

By contrast, Cable & Wireless's convertible loan stock tends to trade at a very low premium or at par. In theory, that is a signal to convert. But converting on 31 August – the only conversion date in the year – means you receive no income for 11 months. You miss the September convertible dividend and the next equity dividend.

The most frequently quoted rule of thumb for judging conversion premiums is to think about converting if the premium falls below 0 per cent i.e. disappears. In fact, you need to look at the dividend yield as well as the premium if you want to decide whether holding the equity makes more sense than holding the convertible. If the yield on the ordinary shares is better than the yield on the convertible, think about switching. But take advice as to whether you are better to convert than to sell in the market. Converting may not be the best option when you look at alternative investments. For example, Dixons 5 per cent convertible preference shares traded at a premium of 61 per cent in early 1995, but had sunk to an 8 per cent premium a year later. Someone who had bought Dixons convertibles at 78p in March 1995 when they yielded 8 per cent gross had an 80 per cent profit by March 1996 (see Figure C3). The investor could switch – sell the convertible and buy the ordinary – if he liked the Dixons story, or he could sell the convertible, pocket the gain and buy another high-yielding convertible.

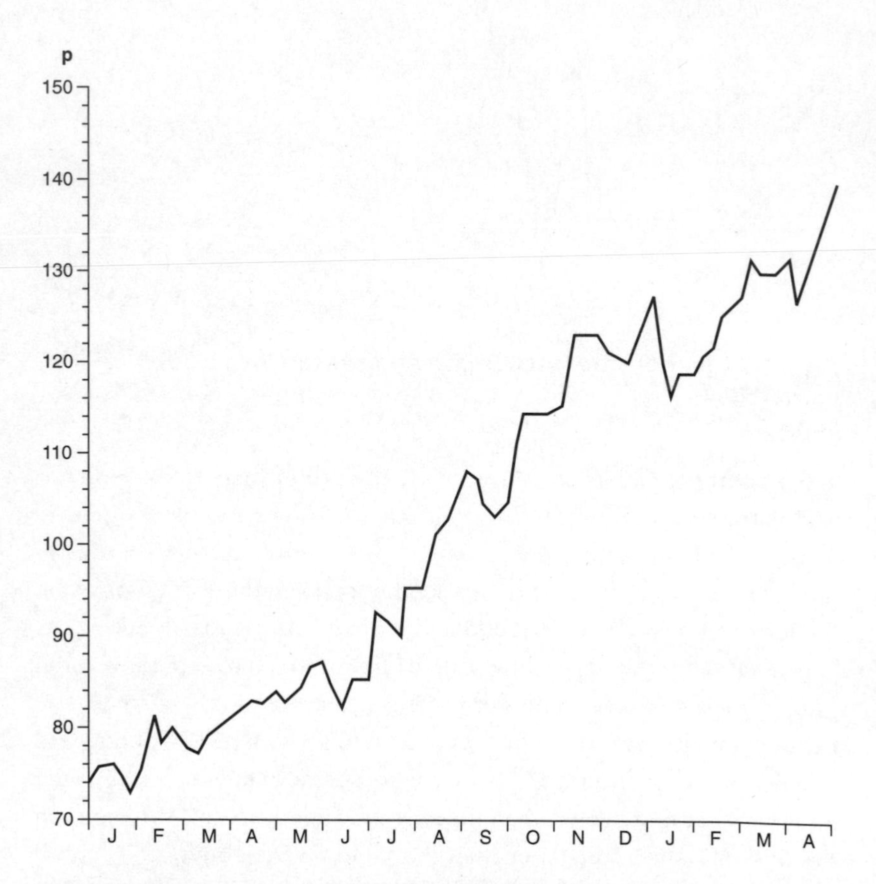

Fig C3 'Days of glory': Dixons 5 per cent convertibles

Source: Datastream

CONVERTIBLES FOR INCOME

The yield makes convertibles a less risky investment than the ordinary shares – in theory, the convertible price will fall more slowly than the price of the ordinary shares because the yield becomes increasingly attractive as the price falls. At least that is what the textbooks tell you, but practised investors point out that convertibles can fall almost as fast as ordinary shares, despite the so-called yield protection. For example, Reckitt & Colman convertibles have fared badly since early 1994, and slipped again in early 1996 (see Figure C4). Investors decided they were reluctant to hold the household goods company in any form, good yield or not.

C

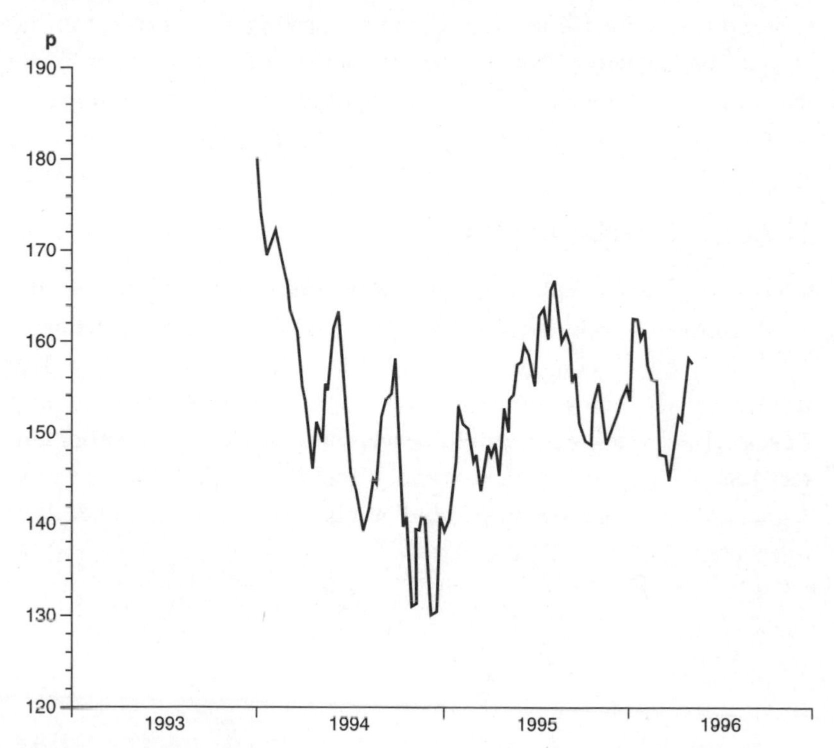

Fig C4 'No-one likes us, we don't care': Reckitt & Colman 9.5 per cent 2005 convertibles

Source: Datastream

It is worth repeating that convertibles are an attractive investment only if the underlying shares are worth buying. A very high yield on a convertible implies that the market has doubts about the company's trading or its financial strength. For example, in early 1996 Ticketing Group, now known as First Call, had a yield of 28 per cent. That reflected Ticketing's enormous debt problems. Only a drastic refinancing stopped the ticket sales company from going out of business. A high yield is worthless if the company is unable to pay its convertible dividends. The trick is to spot companies on a high yield where the fears are overdone.

CONVERTIBLES FOR GROWTH

Convertibles will rise in price if the underlying shares rise, but the bigger the premium, the slower the price rise. That is because investors realise the convertibles are an expensive way of buying into the company, and the rising price also makes the yield less attractive.

TRACKING THEM DOWN

Convertibles are listed with the company's ordinary shares in the *Financial Times* share price listings. Here is a list of some of the more commonly traded convertibles in March 1996 (see Figure C5). The difference between domestic and Eurosterling convertibles is that Eurosterling bonds are traded in bearer form for Euroclear settlement (see SHARES, page 198). Now some of these bonds are also traded in registered form, but they are traded in lots with a minimum of £1,000 or £5,000.

Domestic Convertible	Coupon %	Eurosterling Convertible	Coupon %
BBA	6.75	Allied Domecq	6.75
BICC	10.75	BAA	5.75
BAA	5.75	BPB Industries	7.25
British Land	8.625	British Land	6.00
British Airways	9.75	Cookson	7.00
Cable & Wireless	7.00	Inchcape	6.25
Caradon	7.25	Land Securities	9.375
Carlton Commun'ns	5.50	Legal & General	6.75
Carlton Commun'ns	6.50	National Power	6.25
Carlton Commun'ns	7.50	NFC	7.75
Cookson	7.00	Royal Insurance	7.25
Dixons	5.00	J. Sainsbury	8.50
Granada	7.50	Tarmac	9.50
Greenalls	7.00	Thames Water	9.50
Hambros	7.50		
Hunting	8.25		
Rank Organisation	8.25		
Reckitt & Colman	9.50		
Rexam	7.75		
Slough Estates	8.25		
Tate & Lyle	7.25		
Williams Holdings	8.00		

Fig C5 Convertibles: some of the big names

Source: Panmure Gordon

The 1995 arrival of corporate bond Peps (see PERSONAL EQUITY PLANS, page 181) has given convertibles a higher profile than ever before and the *Investors Chronicle* frequently publishes a list of bonds that can be used in a corporate bond Pep. It also runs regular features spotlighting high-yielding convertibles.

Greater demand for convertibles has also pushed up prices and depressed yields compared with earlier times. Factors such as a strong gilt market or improving company profits will further strengthen prices. However, there will always be some convertibles worth considering, thanks to the wide range on the market – there are about 200 convertible stocks.

Box C3

Convertibles – knowing what you want

Just what should investors look for in a convertible? Here is a note on the merits of the convertible stock issued by Cookson, an industrial materials manufacturer, by the convertibles analyst at Panmure Gordon, the City stockbrokers. Remember that the market has moved on since the note was written in early 1996, so the reasons for buying the stock may no longer apply. However, the note is an excellent summary of the points any investor in convertibles should consider.

Cookson 7% CB 2004[1]

The last interim figures were well up to expectations, and as a result our analyst upgraded future forecasts. This company is very sensitive to the US markets. This allied to our view on the £/$ exchange rate (mildly bullish of sterling) makes for an interesting call[2] on the equity.

The attractions of the convertible listed below are particularly strong arguments for holding the company via the convertible.

- The premium of the convertible is very close to the bottom of its range at 9.9 per cent on a range of 9.9 per cent up to 35.7 per cent during the last 12 months[3].
- The discounted dividend growth rate[4] of the convertible at 15 per cent per annum until the call[5] in November 1999 is equal to or above most dividend forecasts for the next two years; this closely allied to the low premium already mentioned should guarantee that the convertible will perform in line with the equity in any bull run in the market.
- The flat yield at 5.7 per cent is just under 2 times the yield on the underlying equity (3.14 per cent). This large yield pick up should protect the convertible against any major downward movement in the equity[6].
- This is an unfranked convertible[7] and as such is treated like a gilt for accounting purposes in unit and investment trusts, and is especially attractive for those which pay income quarterly. The other advantage of unfranked income stocks is that, if there were to be any change in ACT, then 'gross' paying stocks will outperform.

  We therefore advocate either a buy of the convertible or switching from the ordinary shares into the convertible.

Source: Panmure Gordon

C3 ***Notes***

1. The name of the company, the interest rate, the bond type (capital bond) and the year the convertible is due to be repaid.
2. A reminder that a convertible is a form of option – a call gives the right to buy the equity.
3. The relatively low premium tells investors the convertible should follow the equity closely.
4. Discounting matters because investors are always trying to measure the future in today's terms. Working out future income flows at today's values helps choose which investment to buy.
5. In this case, call refers to the company's option to force conversion.
6. The income gives 'yield protection' in case investors turn against the underlying shares.
7. Dividend income on unfranked stocks is paid gross of tax. Franked income is taxed at source. Choosing unfranked stocks means investors are safely on the sidelines if the goverment changes its rules on this form of taxation.

MAKING THE MOST OF CONVERTIBLES

- Convertibles are suitable for any investors needing to boost income, but it is essential to take advice on buying them. There are plenty of little wrinkles which only people dealing in the convertibles market from day-to-day will follow. For example, some convertibles do not switch into the ordinary shares of the issuing company, but into another company altogether. Newspaper group the Daily Mail & General Trust has a convertible which is exchangeable into Reuters shares.
- Know the small print of the conversion terms and of the dividend payment dates. It is all too easy to convert at just the wrong time. Bear in mind the 11-month income gap for investors who switch out of the Cable & Wireless convertible to the equity.

DERIVATIVES

Definition: **Derivatives are securities whose value relates to the value of another investment. The main forms of derivative are futures, options, forward contracts and swaps. Warrants and convertibles are also forms of derivative. Derivatives have many attractions – such as flexibility, potential for large profits on a small stake – but they also carry enormous risks.**

Private investors are particularly vulnerable to derivatives losses, as relatively few have the capital, experience or access to market information needed for successful dealing. However, warrants (see WARRANTS, page 235), convertibles (see CONVERTIBLES, page 52) and traded options (see OPTIONS page 161) can all be good investments for private investors who have a good broker, or devote time and resources to following the market. Some investors will also deal successfully in futures (see FUTURES, page 78), but successful futures investment is particularly risky. It is important to take professional advice on dealing in all these areas.

Barings, brought to its knees in 1995 by runaway derivatives trading, is one of the latest examples of what can go wrong for investors. By the end of February, Nick Leeson, a Singapore-based trader with Barings, had run up losses of £625m on derivatives trading. Barings had capital of only £541m. The Bank of England's attempt to rescue the bank failed, because the losses on the futures were still rising. Mr Leeson, in prison in Singapore since 1996, had been trading futures and options on the Nikkei 225, the

'... warrants, convertibles and traded options can all be good investments for private investors who have a good broker, or devote time and resources to following the market.'

main index for the Japanese stockmarket, expecting the market to rise. But it kept falling. He had hidden his rising losses in an error account. Although in 1994 Barings internal auditors had flagged the fact that Mr Leeson was more or less his own boss, no-one had curbed his freedom. Dutch banking group ING bought most of Barings, so the banking group survived. But private investors cannot expect anyone to step in to rescue them if their deals go wrong.

In 1996 well-respected Japanese investment house Sumitomo suffered serious losses as a result of rogue trading in copper futures by one of its senior dealers. The copper market was forced into crisis. This further illustrates the dangers for private investors of exposure to the fast-moving derivatives markets, futures in particular. The copper crisis was serious for institutions with large capital backing, but potentially disastrous for private investors.

However, the chapters on futures and options show how even the most notorious forms of derivative can be a worthwhile investment when used properly. Private investors should not be frightened away from derivatives by scandals in the institutional markets. The scandals are just a good reminder never to get too cocky.

Further reading

Big Bets Gone Bad – Derivatives and Bankruptcy in Orange County, Philippe Jorion (Academic Press)

The Collapse of Barings, Stephen Fay (Richard Cohen Books)

Rogue Trader, Nick Leeson with Edward Whitley (Little Brown & Co)

See also the reading lists for FUTURES (page 84), OPTIONS (page 180) and WARRANTS (page 243).

ETHICAL INVESTMENT

Definition: **Ethical investment is shorthand for ethically and environmentally sensitive stockpicking. It means avoiding companies which break a given ethical or environmental code. It also implies deliberately looking for companies which represent good practice or have a strategy for improving their ethical and environmental conduct.**

Almost two-thirds of people interested in investing would rather put their money in an ethical fund than any other type of unit trust. Well over half of potential investors believe ethical and environmental issues are important or very important in investment decisions. And all of the investors questioned agreed that sin is a thoroughly bad thing.

The research done for the ethical fund industry – the figures quoted here come from opinion polls carried out for fund managers Friends Provident and NPI – is all too vulnerable to parody. But how many individual shareholders in Shell would admit to being proud of owning a share in the oil company's profits from Nigeria after the allegations about its conduct of business in the country? The research has also revealed that barely a fifth of investors realise there is an ethical investment choice. It is likely that even fewer people understand that ethical investment, and in practice, 'ethical' tends to cover environmental concerns as well, is accessible and good value.

It is true that only a handful of FT-SE 100 companies qualify as ethically acceptable investments. Perhaps 40 per cent of the companies listed in the FT-SE Actuaries/All-Share index would meet the demands of the typical ethical and green investor. Yet despite the apparent drawback of having a smaller choice of investments, some ethical funds, particularly the pension funds, have a highly respectable pedigree.

Ethical funds	Launched	Size £m
Abbey Life Ethical Trust	1987	30.2
Abtrust Ethical Fund	1992	2.2
Acorn Ethical Unit Trust	1989	4.2
Allchurches Amity Fund	1988	24.5
Barchester Best of Green Life Fund	1991	7.4
Barchester Best of Green Pension Fund	1991	0.7
CIS Environmental Trust	1990	47.5
Clerical Medical Evergreen Trusts	1990	17.6
Co-operative Bank Ethical Unit Trust	1993	11.4
Credit Suisse Fellowship Trust	1986	17.8
Commercial Union Environmental Trust	1992	17.7
Eagle Star Environment Opportunities Trust	1989	16.2
Ethical Investment Fund	1986	1.1
Equitable Ethical Trust	1994	15.8
Framlington Health Fund	1987	24.1
Friends Provident Ethical Investment Trust	1993	30.4
Friends Provident Stewardship Income Trust	1987	64.0
Friends Provident Stewardship Pension Fund	1984	240.4
Friends Provident Stewardship Unit Trust	1984	258.9
Homeowners Green Chip Fund	1989	15.0
Henderson Touche Remnant Ethical Fund	1995	13.6
Jupiter Ecology Fund	1988	22.1
Jupiter International Green Investment Trust	1989	28.9
NPI Global Care Income Unit Trust	1995	2.5
NPI Global Care Unit Trust	1991	21.4
NPI Pension Global Care	1994	1.1
Scottish Equitable Ethical Unit Trust (including pension fund)	1989	44.6
Sovereign Ethical Fund	1989	12.0
Sun Life Global Portfolio Ecological Fund	1992	8.4
TSB Environmental Investor Fund	1989	14.4

Fig E1 Ethical funds

Source: Eiris, April 1996

Money & Ethics, published by Eiris (telephone: 0171-735 1351) in 1996, gives full details of all the funds listed here and ethical broker funds.

AH Ball
Powerscreen International
Protean
Senior Engineering
United States Filter
Low & Bonar
David S Smith
Treatt
Court Cavendish
Crestacare
Goldborough Healthcare
Huntleigh Technology
Takare
Columbia/HCA Healthcare
Abacus Polar
Abbott Mead Vickers
Blenheim
Cassell
Dorling Kindersley
Shandwick
Tinsley Robor
Argyll
Corporate Services
CRT
Sherwood Computers
Microsoft
Clean Diesel Technology
Fuel Technology
Go-Ahead
Tobu Railway
Visual Action
Waste Recycling
London Electricity
Northern Ireland Electricity
Enron Oil & Gas
California Energy
British Telecom
Telecom Italia
Telmex
MCI
Telecommunications A
Nippon Telegraph & Telephone
Abbey National
London & Manchester
Federal National Mortgage
Thermo Electronic
Engelhard
Imco Recycling
Legrand
NRJ
Union Assurances Fédérales
Praktiker Bau & Heim

Fig E2 NPI Pension Global Care fund – a portfolio snapshot as at 4 April 1996

Source: NPI

Investors can choose from almost 30 ethical and environmental unit trusts, life insurance funds and pension funds (see Figure E1). In early 1996 they managed about £1bn. Where do they put it? Figure E2 gives a snapshot of part of the NPI Pension Global Care fund in April 1996. Some of the holdings are classic ethical investments – David S Smith makes cardboard boxes and some years ago decided to invest heavily in recycling plant. The paper shortage in 1995 meant the investment finally paid off. Smith's share price galloped ahead, rising 90 per cent in two years compared with a 14 per cent rise in the FT-SE Actuaries All-Share Index over the same period (see Figure E3).

'... despite the apparent drawback of having a smaller choice of investments, some ethical funds, particularly the pension funds, have a highly respectable pedigree.'

However, at least one of the holdings represents the other extreme of green investment stereotypes – tiny companies in stockmarket backwaters. AH Ball is a small firm of construction contractors specialising in pipelaying. Based in the south-east of England, the company found its profits falling sharply in the early 1990s (see Figure E4). The housebuilding slump meant there were fewer drainage systems to install, and work dwindled further when the water companies' infrastructure spending dried up. The shares enjoyed a renaissance in 1996, doubling in value after AH Ball directors bought shares in the company.

NPI's green and ethical investment strategy is, in practice, based on the same basic idea as most conventional funds' strategy. The fund managers want to spot the companies that are going to be the Marks & Spencer and Sainsbury's of the next 20 years. It believes: 'Many of the winners will be companies solving problems facing society and the environment.' That means recycling, telecommunications, computer networking, nursing home and healthcare, water management, alternative energy, energy efficiency and pollu-

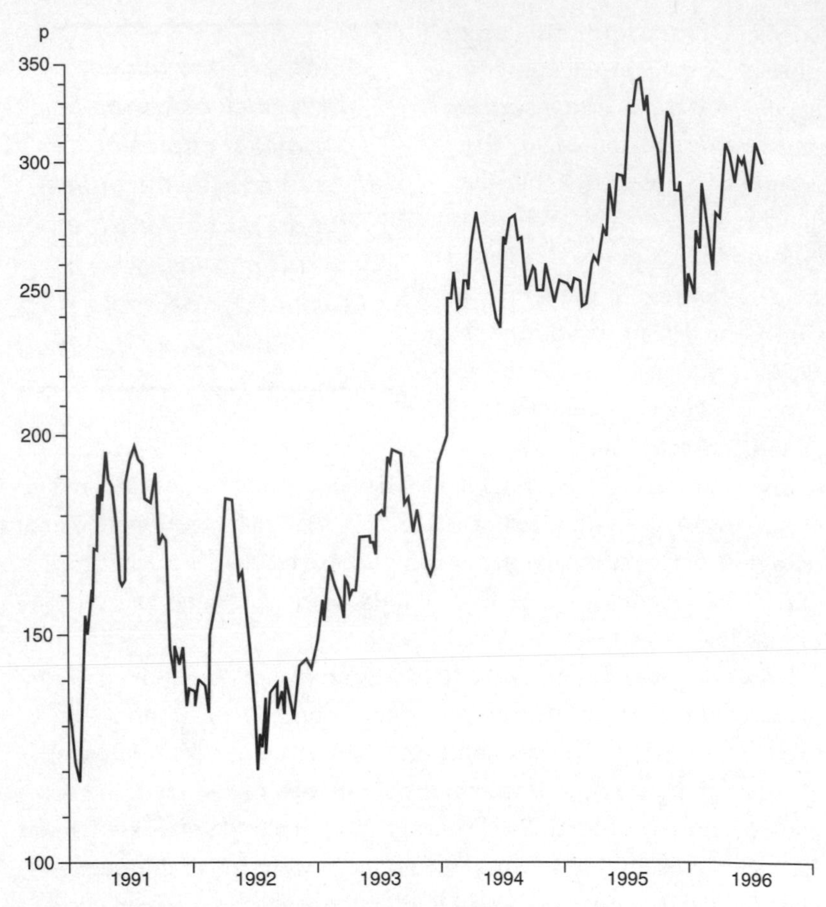

Fig E3 David S Smith: share price performance 1991–96
Source: Datastream

tion control. Some of the holdings must be flattered to find itself in such company.

Ethical and environmental funds tend to be lumped together and are to some extent interchangeable. As a rule, environmental funds have more self-imposed restrictions than ethical funds, and it is worth looking at the different ethical and environmental approaches, even if you like the first fund management group you consider.

For example NPI's green investment team avoids mining shares,

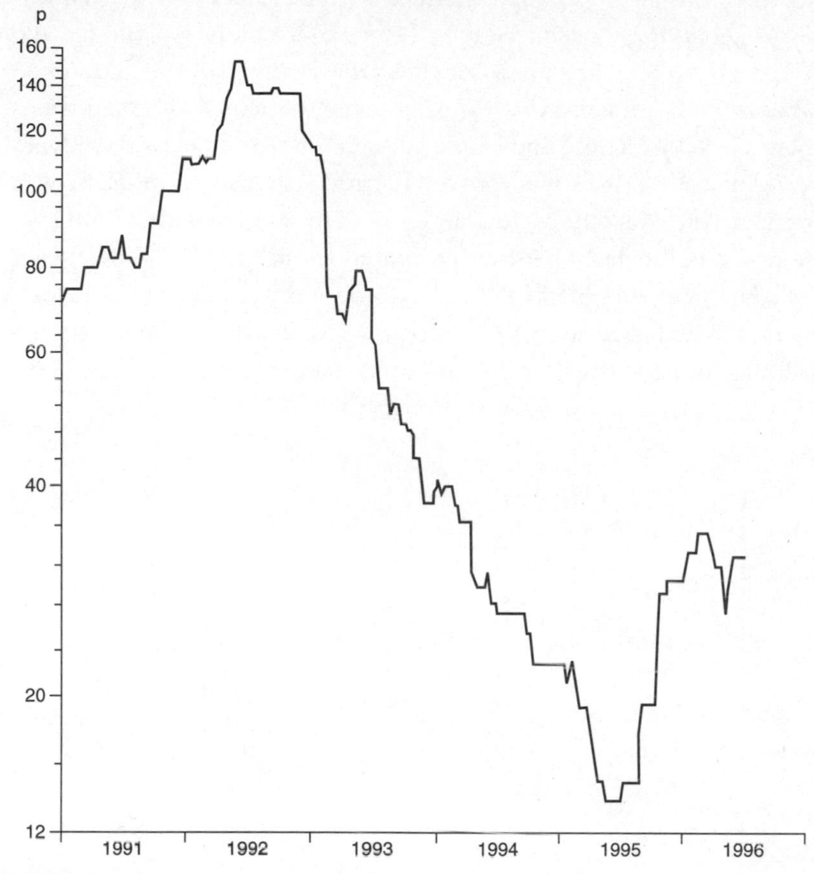

Fig E4 AH Ball: share price performance 1991–96
Source: Datastream

but funds following ethical rather than environmental criteria might have no problem with responsible mining investments. The Friends Provident Stewardship funds, the longest-established ethical and green funds in the UK, include some mining companies in their portfolios, and have done very well from one in particular. RJB Mining, which bought most of the English coal mines when British Coal was privatised, was a Stewardship holding. The company attracted almost universal criticism. Commentators asked whether, in general, private operators would pay enough attention to mine safety and raised questions about RJB itself, largely because a company run by the founder's brother had gone out of business. The City also doubted whether RJB's finances were strong enough to cope with the investment it had taken on. Fund manager John Singleton decided the fears were overdone and was proved correct. Investing in RJB was arguably an ethically correct action – RJB was providing employment for particularly hard-hit communities in the UK. Either way, RJB is a fine example of the tricky little wrinkles of ethical investment. Floated at 250p in 1993, RJB rose to 550p by December 1995 (see Figure E5). The Stewardship funds had sold the shares by early 1996.

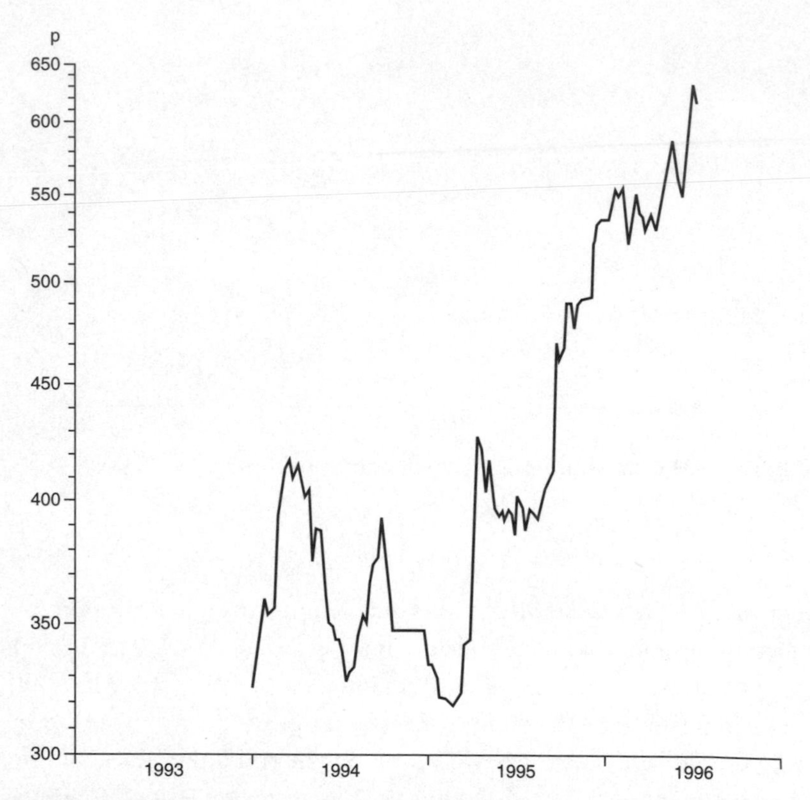

Fig E5 'A hole in the ground that came good for Friends Provident Stewardship': RJB Mining: share price performance 1994–96
Source: Datastream

UK private investors can devise their own ethical investment strategy and, depending on their enthusiasm, can lobby companies for change. Eiris, the Ethical Investment Research Service, has a questionnaire intended to help investors define their own ethical investment guidelines. It will screen portfolios, although this quickly becomes expensive. The screening service starts at £50 for a portfolio of 15 to 20 shares, but goes up to several hundred pounds for large portfolios.

Shareholders are also in a good position to lobby companies on ethical and environmental issues. Individuals may have too few shares to swing votes at annual general meetings, but shareholders' letters are taken seriously. The shareholders own the company. The *Shareholder Action Handbook* (see *Further reading*, page 72) gives advice on letter-writing and behaviour at AGMs.

MAKING THE MOST OF ETHICAL INVESTMENT

- Define your ethical criteria – positive and negative – before you start looking at potential investments.
- Check whether funds have independent ethical committees which monitor the funds' holdings and investment criteria. Eiris's book *Money and Ethics* is probably the most useful guide for ethical investors in personal equity plans, pensions, endowments and funds.
- Find out whether funds are pro-active – the NPI team pioneered the idea that fund managers could influence a company's attitude to the environment. Other funds stick to investing in companies which already meet their ethical criteria.
- Read funds' annual reports before you invest. They list the funds' main holdings and the major sales and purchases within a year. They are good snapshots of funds' investment styles.
- So far ethical unit trusts have largely failed to cut their upfront charges. A financial adviser will probably be able to cut the upfront fee by offering you a discount on his commission.

- If you use a financial adviser, make sure he takes your ethical and environmental investment preferences into account.
- Ethical investment is not an excuse for below-average investment results over the medium- to long-term. An ethical fund manager can lose money just as quickly as a conventional fund manager. Do not be sentimental if your ethical fund is performing badly. Switch funds. There are plenty of good ethical funds.
- As well as your ethical screening, use the same rules for choosing an ethical fund as you would in choosing a conventional unit trust (see UNIT TRUSTS, page 222).

Further reading:

The Shareholder Action Handbook, Craig Mackenzie (New Consumer)

The Ethical Investor, quarterly (Eiris, 504 Bondway Business Centre, 71 Bondway, London SW8 1SQ)

Money and Ethics (Eiris, address as above)

FUND-RAISING

Definition: **Companies, once they are listed on the stockmarket, can raise money from shareholders through rights issues, placings and open offers. Companies can also raise money when they first come to the market (see NEW ISSUES, page 152).**

The ability to raise money from a wide shareholder base is one of the great advantages of having a stockmarket listing. A private company can turn to its shareholders for cash, but it also normally depends on its bankers. A bank, which has normally secured its lending on the assets of the business, will be less generous than shareholders in shoring up a company's finances. After all, the shareholders face losing their money if the company goes under. But a bank calling in the receiver knows it will still get its hands on the assets securing the loan, even if the business disappears.

So, companies wanting to expand, fed up with paying interest on their debt, or in financial trouble have an incentive to turn to shareholders for cash rather than their bankers. The main ways of raising further money are rights issues – the most common method – and placings.

A rights issue gives existing shareholders in a company the right to buy new shares in the company in proportion to their existing holdings and at a discount to the current share price in the market. The new shares will normally be ordinary shares, but sometimes companies issue other types of share (see SHARES, page 198). A rights issue will usually be underwritten by an institution such as a merchant bank. Underwriting the issue means the bank will make up the difference if shareholders fail to take up their rights. The underwriter earns a commission of 2 per cent of the total sum being raised.

Shareholders who choose to ignore a rights issue may still receive some money for the rights they have given up. Normally the company will arrange to sell the rights in the market on behalf of shareholders – that is the nil paid rights price you will see quoted in the *Investors Chronicle*'s rights issue tables and in the Press. It depends on the market price of the shares when you choose to sell your rights.

Example: The arithmetic of rights issues

The best way to work through the arithmetic of rights issues is to look at an actual fund-raising.

In 1996 Persimmon, a Yorkshire-based housebuilder, announced it needed £91m to help buy the Ideal Homes housebuilding business from Trafalgar House for £170m. Buying Ideal almost doubled the size of Persimmon and made it the fourth largest housebuilder in the UK. The *Investors Chronicle* advised readers to take up the offer. 'Persimmon will have snatched a cheap deal if, as it appears, it has bought at the bottom of the market,' it said.

The terms of the Persimmon rights issue were one-for-two at 155p, i.e., shareholders were offered the right to buy one share at 155p, for every two they already owned.

If the market price was 185p, the rights issue price of 155p gave investors a 19 per cent discount. Using these two figures and the terms of the rights issue, investors could work out roughly where the share price would settle once the rights issue went through.

- A shareholder with 1,000 shares in Persimmon could apply for 500 new shares (1,000/2 x 1).
- The 1,000 shares already owned by the shareholder are worth £1,850 at the market price and buying the rights issue shares will cost £775 (500 x 155p). The total holding would be worth £2,625.
- The ex-rights price, i.e., the price of the shares after the rights issue, will be £2,625/1,500 = 175p.

The difference between the ex-rights price and the market price is 185p –175p = 10p, and investors who chose to sell their rights in the market could expect to receive roughly this sum per share, less brokers' commission. Of course, this example assumes that the markets behave according to the rules in the textbooks and in practice they do not.

Footwear retailer Owen & Robinson also set out to raise money in 1996, but for different reasons. The company went into administration – a form of receivership – late in 1995. In the new year, it announced that it wanted £5.5m to cut its debt, pay its administration costs and beef up its working capital. The terms of the issue were a warning in themselves – investors would receive five shares for every four they owned at an issue price of 10p. The shares were suspended, i.e. temporarily stopped from being bought or sold, at 16p. This is a classic example of a rescue rights issue, where shareholders' main reason for putting in more money is to protect their original investment.

The cynics argue that private investors are best to ignore all rights issues on the grounds that if the company was any good it would not need to raise any more money. It would have generated enough cash for growth from its existing activities. What is more, continue the cynics, private investors normally own too few shares in a company for it to be worth their worrying about diluting their holding.

However, it is reasonable to consider taking up rights if an investor likes the company's record and likes the reason for the fund-raising. A rights issue offering one new share for every 10 already held counts as small, since relatively few new shares are being issued. However, a rights issue with one share issued for every three held, or worse as in the Owen & Robinson fund-raising described above, is heavy and would need a big discount to the market price. The typical discount tends to be around 20 per cent.

PLACINGS AND OPEN OFFERS

In a placing, a company raises money from selected investors, normally only institutions, not private individuals. A placing will sometimes be accompanied by an open offer. The name is misleading, as the offer is open only to existing shareholders. The open offer means shareholders have the right to clawback the shares they would have been entitled to in a rights issue, so cutting back the number of shares taken up by institutions. Increasingly, companies are offering new

'Be doubly cautious if the company is buying a business outside its traditional markets – consider the water companies' expensive efforts to diversify – or has a record of several rights issues or placings within a relatively short time.'

shares at a range of prices instead of one fixed price. For example, SkyePharma, a drugs company, wanted to raise £135m in a placing and open offer. The terms were 105–125 shares for 100 already held, at a price of 84p to 100p. Companies and their advisers have decided that by effectively inviting bids for the shares, they tend to get a better price, and can save money on underwriting. The practice is already well-established outside the UK. By the time private investors have a chance to take part, the terms are fixed.

Be doubly cautious if the company is buying a business outside its traditional markets – consider the water companies' expensive efforts to diversify – or has a record of several rights issues or placings within a relatively short time. With hindsight, investors can see that companies have expanded too fast for their own good, but few spot the trend before it is too late.

MAKING THE MOST OF A CASH CALL

- Be absolutely sure why the company needs more money. It will normally be one of two main reasons: to fund growth, which could mean buying other businesses or expanding their existing facilities, and to get themselves out of trouble with their bankers. Putting in fresh cash is usually more risky if the company says it needs to cut debt or improve its working capital.
- Check who is underwriting the rights issue. Companies in serious trouble may have to fall back on second-rank institutions to underwrite the fund-raising, and will probably have to pay more for the privilege. These costs come out of the money raised –

investors' money. Sometimes the company directors or a large private shareholder will underwrite the issue. For most investors, this is a sure warning to steer clear, despite the argument that at least the directors are putting their own money in the business.

- Consider the discount to the current market value. Even if you are lukewarm about the reasons for the fund-raising, a large discount may make it worth while taking up your rights. Companies anxious to make their rights issue a success and avoid underwriting costs sometimes offer deep discount rights issues. That can mean offering shares at as little as half their market value.
- If you are in two minds about the deal, compromise. In a rights issue, particularly one with a large discount, it may be possible to sell some of your rights in the market and use the proceeds to take up at least some shares in the fund-raising.
- Remember the capital gains tax implications of selling your rights in the market. As long as the rights are worth 5 per cent or less of the market value of an investor's holding in a company, there is no capital gains tax liability and no problem. However, there may be a liability with a deep discount rights issue.

FUTURES

Definition: **Futures are contracts to buy or sell a fixed quantity of an asset – goods or securities – at a fixed price and a fixed date, regardless of any intervening change in price or circumstances. Futures fall into two main camps – financial and commodities – and cover foreign currencies and interest rates as well as stock indices, potatoes or orange juice.**

Futures, like options, allow investors to take big risks for a small upfront payment. Unlike options, the potential losses are unlimited. As a result private investors will normally be shepherded away from futures towards less risky investments. The problem is that investing successfully in futures is a full-time job. Private investors can easily understand the mechanics of futures, but they are unlikely to have access to enough information to make money from them.

Box F1

Futures – the phrasebook

Arbitrageurs Mainly traders who exploit anomalies in the futures market, such as unusual differences between the futures price and the cash price, are arbitrageurs. As a rule, only professional investors can command enough information to arbitrage successfully.

Backwardation The opposite of 'contango'. When an asset is in short supply, forward prices will be lower than current prices. Consumers need the item and will pay a premium to have it. They will not pay a premium to have it in three months' time.

Basis The basis is the relationship between the actual price of an asset, and the price of the futures contract. There is normally a difference to allow for the fact that assets can pay income, but a futures contract does not pay income. For example, a futures contract for copper may cost $3,030, compared with $3,000 for a cash copper contract. But by the time the investor closes the contract there is no difference between the futures and the copper price. The gap is called the basis risk.

F1

Contango Also known as 'forwardation'. A situation where futures prices of assets are higher than current prices. The further a contract is from delivery, the higher the futures price will be. The difference reflects storage costs and the lost interest – someone is paying for an asset they do not have, when the money could be earning interest elsewhere. Contango applies when supplies of an asset are plentiful.

Gearing Being able to put down just £1,000 on a contract to buy £10,000 worth of cocoa means the investor can benefit from gearing. If the price of cocoa rises 10 per cent during the contract, the investor can sell the cocoa for £11,000 and nets a £1,000 profit, doubling his money. However, the investor has to fill the gap if the price falls. In this case he loses his £1,000 if the price falls 10 per cent, but it can be more. It is important to keep gearing sensible, after all, you would not buy shares in a company with net debt running at 500 per cent of net assets.

Margin Money put up by investors when they buy or sell a futures contract. It is normally only a small proportion of the total cost of the deal, but it will vary according to the type of contract from perhaps a few hundred pounds to several thousand. The relevant futures exchange will set the minimum margin, and brokers will normally ask clients for slightly more than the minimum. Investors pay initial margin when they open a contract – also called a 'lot' – and the broker works out variation margin. If prices have moved the right way, an investor's margin account will receive payments if they have moved against an investor, he must put up more cash.

THE MECHANICS OF FUTURES

The best way to explain the mechanics of buying futures is to use a commodity as an example. Say an investor wants to speculate on the future cost of robusta coffee without actually buying any coffee. He expects the price to rise, and in July buys a contract for 10 tonnes of coffee at $1,500 a tonne to be delivered in December. The total cost of the contract is $15,000. He pays a fraction of the actual cost of the contract, perhaps 10 per cent or $1,500, and the price of coffee rises to $1,700 a tonne. The investor sells his contract before delivery and makes $2,000. His return is 133 per cent, although the coffee price has risen just 13 per cent. However, if prices had moved as much the other way, the investor would have faced a $2,000 loss.

In broad terms there are three main players in futures markets – investors, traders and arbitrageurs. The investors are using futures to gain exposure to shares. Futures have all sorts of attractions for institutional investors. For example, futures can be more liquid – easier to deal in – than the underlying securities. Investors who need to change their exposure to an investment – gilts, equities, currencies – can do it quickly and cheaply by buying a futures contract. That is why stockmarket reports will often refer to activity in the futures market – the changes in futures prices of investments can be a better short-term guide to a market than changes in the market itself.

'Private investors can easily understand the mechanics of futures, but they are unlikely to have access to enough information to make money from them.'

Traders are the people taking a view on how prices in a particular market are going to move. Futures are particularly attractive to traders because they need to put up relatively little cash, as described above. The arbitrageurs make their money by exploiting the pricing differences between the future contracts and the underlying asset – times when the market has got it wrong and failed to adjust the price to fit changed conditions.

Box F2

Good advice – the search continues

Finding a private client stockbroker experienced in futures dealing may prove difficult. The London commodities exchanges – the London Commodity Exchange, London Metal Exchange and the International Petroleum Exchange – can provide lists of their members, but these are mainly large institutions or specialist firms dealing on behalf of corporate clients. Specialist firms may tend to be reluctant to accept private clients, but some of the best-known names include GNI (telephone: 0171-337 3500) – a subsidiary of stockmarket-listed discount house Gerrard & National, Berkeley Futures (telephone: 0171-629 1133) and BZW Futures (telephone: 0171-696 3080). Further information may be obtained from the Exchanges listed below or the Futures and Options Association (telephone: 0171-488 4610), the trade body for participants in the derivatives industry in the United Kingdom.

The law obliges brokers to make sure their clients are 'suitable'. A reputable broker will make sure that private investors planning to deal in futures or options have enough capital to set aside a portion as pure risk capital. A rule of thumb is up to 10 per cent of your investment assets – excluding your house. Be prepared to put money upfront – some firms ask for £20,000. Your broker should also want to know your stop-losses (see **RISK**, page 195) – an essential guard against disaster. Broad rules of thumb are to:

- assume a potential loss to be greater than any potential profit;
- risk no more than 10 per cent of your trading capital on a single position and to cap the total of all positions at 30 per cent of trading capital;
- measure your potential profit against the amount you will pay in charges – profit should be about 10 times the charges.

F

Box F3

Funds – trimming the futures risk

Futures funds are probably the best option for all but the wealthiest private investors interested in futures or specifically in commodities. But do not make the mistake of thinking they are the easy option. The commodities unit trusts based in the UK – the two main ones are run by Save & Prosper and M&G – are heavily biased towards mining and invest in companies rather than directly in commodities. For example, the Save & Prosper fund limits its exposure to agricultural commodities – in this case palm oil – to a small holding in the REA plantation company. There are some UK-based futures and options funds run by specialist managers such as John Govett, but most pure futures funds are based offshore. Offshore funds fall outside most UK financial regulation, although they are subject to laws in their home territory, and some funds are 'recognised' by the UK watchdogs and allowed to carry out some marketing in the UK. However, the futures funds are not allowed to volunteer information about themselves to private investors. Investors must go through an authorised adviser. International fund managers include John Henry, Tudor Investment Partners, Trout Trading and Chesapeake. Their funds under management run to billions of dollars, and their investors are institutions and very rich individuals. UK futures fund managers include Sabre, Rudolf Wolff, BZW Asset Risk Management and GNI. The funds are registered offshore, but the fund managers are in London. Some of these funds offer guarantees on your capital, which sounds good, until you remember that if you want guarantees, you should hardly be investing in futures. The cost of a guarantee will eat into your fund performance.

It would be wrong to say that private investors should never get involved in the futures markets. In some ways they are easier to understand than traded options (see OPTIONS, page 161). But futures can mean bottomless losses for the unwary, and are for investors with a thorough knowledge of the underlying market.

Box F4

Futures for hedging

Futures can be highly risky, but in the main are used to manage financial or commodities risk rather than for speculation. They can do this, because there are traders and arbitrageurs who effectively take on the risk. For example, a company has agreed to deliver an order of copper piping in six months' time. The price is agreed, but reasons beyond its control mean the company has still to buy the copper to make the pipes. It can protect itself against a rise in the price of copper by buying a futures contract. The company still may not make a profit on the deal, but buying the futures contract means it can put a ceiling on how much it will lose. It is buying certainty. This is hedging against a price rise. Here is an example prepared by GNI, a London-based futures specialist.

A stockholder is nervous that the stockmarket will fall if poor figures on the economy are released later in the week. As a large holder of equities, he wishes to cover some of his exposure to this capital risk without acutally selling his stock (as this is costly in commission terms, and he wishes to hold this stock for the long term).

On Monday, the stockholder checks the FT-SE futures price, which stands at 2843, and decides to make a selling hedge trade.

He wishes to cover £1.5m of stock so he sells 21 lots of FT-SE to cover his risk as nearly as possible:

Index 2843 x £25 (value of one point) x 21 = £1,492,575 of value

Monday: Sells 21 lots of FT-SE at 2843

Thursday: Poor economic figures are released and FT-SE falls

Friday: Buys back his short futures position at 2791 to re-open the underlying exposure.

By hedging, the stockholder has made a profit on his hedge (and therefore has cut possible losses on his portfolio).

Hedging profit = 52 index points x £25 x 21 lots = £27,300

Source: GNI

F

MAKING THE MOST OF FUTURES

- Treat your futures investment as risk capital – limit it to a small part of your total portfolio.
- Keep track of news affecting the assets underlying your futures – call your broker regularly and leave clear fail-safe instructions to cover times when your broker may not be able to contact you.
- Avoid futures where the markets are thinly traded.
- Consider futures funds which guarantee the return of your original capital (see Box F4), but remember that the charges you will pay for the guarantee will cut your profits.

Further reading

An Introduction to Commodity Futures and Options, Nick Battley (Probus)

Options, Futures and Other Derivative Securities, John C Hull (Prentice Hall)

Strategic Futures Trading, Jake Bernstein (Dearborn)

Where are the Customers' Yachts? Fred Schwed Jr (Wiley)

Money Management, a sister magazine of the *Investors Chronicle*, offers some coverage of futures and options funds. Specialist futures magazines include the US-based *Futures*, published by Oster Communications Inc, 219 Parkade, PO Box 6, Cedar Falls, Iowa 50613 USA; *Futures & Options World* and *Derivatives in Fund Management*, both published by the Metal Bulletin publishing company in London. They publish performance statistics on the futures funds, and any serious investor should take the time to read at least one of these before looking for an adviser and selecting a fund.

Useful telephone numbers

Exchanges avoid promoting futures to private investors but may give some background information.

London International Financial Futures & Options Exchange (telephone: 0171-623 0444)

London Metal Exchange (telephone: 0171-264 5555)

London Commodity Exchange (telephone: 0171-481 2080)

International Petroleum Exchange (telephone: 0171-481 0643)

G

GILTS

Definition: **Gilts are bonds issued by the UK government (see BONDS, page 35).**

Gilts, if held to redemption, are a solid, low-risk investment. The problem is choosing the right one at the right price. Stockbrokers can advise investors on which gilts to buy, and the advice normally justifies the commission on the deal. In fact buying and selling gilts costs much less than dealing in shares, but it is still too much for investors who know what they want. Use an execution-only or dealing-only stockbroker – one that charges less because you do not receive advice – if you need to deal as soon as possible at a given price, or deal through National Savings, if you are prepared to deal by post.

Figure G1 shows the gap in costs between the different ways of buying gilts.

	£1,000 worth of gilts £	**£5,000 worth of gilts** £
Unit trusts*	50.00	250
Advisory stockbroker	33.00	70
Dealing-only stockbroker	22.00	25
National Savings	12.50	35

* plus 0.5 per cent annual management charge

Fig G1 Typical costs of buying gilts
Source: Investors Chronicle

Gilt unit trusts are the most expensive route, not just because of their high charges, but because they are almost always a poor investment. Over the 10 years to February 1996, the average gilt and fixed-interest unit trust has turned £1,000 into £2,200. Over the two years to February 1996, £1,000 has turned into £987, according to Micropal statistics. By contrast, the average unit trust has managed £3,048 and £1,036 respectively.

Box G1

How do you choose a gilt?

The current yield tells you how much you will earn from a gilt on a day-to-day basis. It is much less than the 15½ per cent nominal rate or coupon, reflecting the change in the price since the bond was issued. But the redemption yield reflects the capital loss. If the redemption yield is less than the current yield, you will lose money on the gilt if you hold it to maturity.

In a nutshell, investors planning to sell in the market face a capital loss if interest rates or inflation look set to pick up, and investors planning to hold the gilts to maturity face a capital loss when they redeem their investment.

Changes in the prices of futures contracts tell investors whether the market expects interest rates to move up or down. Look at the three-month sterling futures prices in the Financial Times. Subtract the settlement price – given in the column headed 'Sett' and you have an idea of the expected interest rate in three months' time.

You can gauge market expectations of inflation by looking at the gap between the gross redemption yield on conventional gilts and the gross redemption yield on index-linked gilts. The difference is normally close to the average rate of inflation expected by City economists. Investors need to look out for signs that the gap is narrowing or widening. However, one rule of thumb when gilt prices are high is to find a gilt that still offers a gain on maturity, and be prepared to hold it until its maturity date.

Some unit trust companies charge a full 6 per cent upfront charge, despite the lower costs of running gilts funds. Even when the upfront charge is low – it can be 3 per cent or sometimes zero – annual charges of 0.5 per cent or more can soak up a large part of your capital and income. Investors who really want professional help in buying a portfolio of gilts should pay for a stockbroker's advice rather than use a unit trust.

INDEX-LINKED GILTS

Inflation is an important factor in the direction of gilts markets, because gilts investors, having bought a fixed rate of interest, are particularly vulnerable to inflation. The income from a conventional gilt is fixed, whatever happens to the cost of living. Investors in consols, the undated gilts with their origins in the 18th century and now paying either 4 per cent or 2½ per cent, can bear testimony to the damage inflation can do. Investors who paid £100 for stock in the late 19th century had an investment worth £30 in 1996, before making any allowance for the effect of inflation. In 1974, the UK's inflationary peak, the price was just £14.

Index-linked gilts were launched in 1981 as an antidote to the inflation problem, and, in the year to March 1996, made up 15 per cent of new gilt issues.

Index-linked gilts pay a lower coupon or rate of interest – than conventional gilts. It is typically 2 or 2½ per cent when issued. But the interest and the capital sum due on maturity will grow in line with inflation. There is an eight-month time lag in indexing the gilts, however, because the indexing sums are based on the retail prices index (RPI) eight months before the gilt's issue date, and eight months before any interest payment.

'Inflation is an important factor in the direction of gilts markets, because gilts investors, having bought a fixed rate of interest, are particularly vulnerable to inflation.'

Investors in indexed-linked gilts need to check whether they are paying more or less than the indexed value of the gilt. If you pay less than the indexed value, you should make a capital gain ahead of

Current or running yield

Gross redemption yields

Assumes inflation at 5%

Assumes inflation at 10%

UK GILTS PRICES

Notes	Yield Int	Yield Red	Price £	+ or –	52 week High	52 week Low
Shorts" (Lives up to Five Years)						
Treas 15 1/4pc 1996‡‡....	15.05	6.36	101 5/16	...	108 5/8	101 5/16
Exch 13 1/4pc 1996‡‡.....	13.09	6.10	101 7/32	...	106 9/16	101 7/32
Conversion 10pc 1996.	9.75	6.03	102 9/16	...	104 15/32	102 9/16
Treas 13 1/4pc 1997‡‡....	12.52	6.09	105 17/32	...	109 25/32	105 17/32
Exch 10 1/2pc 1997.........	10.11	6.12	103 7/8	...	105 25/32	103 7/8
Treas Cnv7pc 1997‡‡..	6.94	6.33	100 27/32	...	101 15/32	98 3/32
Treas 8 3/4pc 1997‡‡......	8.48	6.36	103 3/16	...	104 7/32	101 17/32
Exch 15pc 1997............	13.29	6.49	112 27/32	...	117 3/16	112 23/32
Exch 9 3/4pc 1998...........	9.26	6.61	105 5/16	...	107 5/16	103 5/8
Treas 7 1/4pc 1998‡‡......	7.18	6.70	101	...	102 5/16	97 5/16
Treas 6 3/4pc 1995-98‡‡....	6.76	6.80	99 7/8	...	100 9/32	95 29/32
Treas 15 1/2pc '98‡‡.......	12.95	6.90	119 23/32	+1/16	124 1/8	119 9/32
Exch 12pc 1998............	10.71	6.97	112 3/32	+1/16	114 5/8	110 7/32
Treas 9 1/2pc 1999‡‡......	8.94	6.99	106 1/4	+1/8	108 9/16	103 13/32
Treas Fltg Rate 1999....	–	–	99 15/16	...	100 31/32	99 15/16
Exch 12 1/4pc 1999.........	10.77	7.09	113 25/32	+1/8	116 21/32	112 1/2
Treas 10 1/2pc 1999........	9.60	7.14	109 3/8	+3/32	112 3/16	106 15/16
Treas 6pc 1999‡‡.........	6.21	7.14	96 9/16	+5/32	98 23/32	91 5/16
Conversion 10 1/4pc 1999	9.37	7.28	109 13/32	+5/32	112 17/32	106 3/8
Conv 9pc 2000‡‡.........	8.53	7.33	105 9/16	+3/32	108 27/32	101 15/16
Treas 13pc 2000...........	10.82	7.45	120 3/16	+3/32	124 15/32	118 5/16
Treas 14pc 1998-1........	12.24	6.82	114 11/32	+1/16	117 3/4	113 31/32
Treas 8pc 2000‡‡.........	7.82	7.39	102 1/4	+1/16	105 7/8	98
Five to Fifteen Years						
Treas 10pc 2001...........	9.10	7.54	109 15/16	+3/32	114	106 5/16
Treas 7pc 2001‡‡.........	7.20	7.58	97 9/32	+3/32	101 3/32	92 3/16
Treas 9 3/4pc 2002..........	8.87	7.76	109 29/32	+1/8	114 5/8	105 23/32
Treas 8pc 2003‡‡.........	7.93	7.82	100 7/8	+7/32	105 23/32	96 5/16
Treas 10pc 2003...........	8.95	7.88	111 23/32	+7/32	117 5/32	107 5/8
Treas 11 1/2pc 2001-4	9.95	7.69	115 9/16xd	+5/32	119 15/16	112 15/32
Funding 3 1/2pc 1999-4...	4.39	6.79	79 13/16	+1/2	83 31/32	70 1/2
Conversion 9 1/2pc 2004.	8.72	8.02	108 15/16	+1/4	114 9/16	105 7/32
Treas 6 3/4pc 2004‡‡......	7.33	8.00	92 1/8	+3/16	96 15/16	88 1/16
Conv 9 1/2pc 2005...........	8.71	8.05	109 1/16	+3/16	114 23/32	105 9/16
Treas 12 1/2pc 2003-5.....	9.97	7.99	125 13/32	+1/4	131 3/8	121 5/8
Treas 8 1/2pc 2005‡‡......	8.26	8.04	102 7/8	+7/32	108 21/32	99 1/2
Treas 7 1/2pc 2006‡‡......	7.83	8.08	95 25/32	+7/32	101 23/32	94 25/32
Treas 7 3/4pc 2006‡‡......	7.97	8.12	97 1/4	+3/16	103 1/4	93 15/16
Treas 8pc 2002‡‡.........	8.10	8.18	98 13/16	+3/32	104 11/32	95 13/32
Treas 11 3/4pc 2003-7.....	9.81	7.95	119 23/32	+7/32	125 3/32	115 7/8
Treas 8 1/2pc 2007‡‡......	8.31	8.17	102 5/16	+5/16	108 27/32	99 15/32
Treas 13 1/2pc 2004-8.....	10.22	7.99	132 3/32	+5/32	138 13/32	128 7/32
Treas 9pc 2008‡‡.........	8.48	8.20	106 1/8	+5/16	112 13/16	103 15/32
Treas 8pc 2009............	8.17	8.24	97 29/32xd	+1/8	104 1/2	95 1/4
Treas 6 1/4pc 2010..........	7.56	8.30	82 21/32	+1/4	88 5/16	80 7/16
Over Fifteen Years						
Conv 9pc Ln 2011‡‡.....	8.51	8.31	105 3/4	+11/32	112 13/16	103 25/32
Treas 9pc 2012‡‡.........	8.50	8.32	105 7/8	+11/32	113 3/16	104 1/32
Treas 5 1/2pc 2008‡‡......	7.15	8.04	76 7/8	+7/32	82 3/4	73
Treas 8pc 2013‡‡.........	8.26	8.33	96 7/8	+5/16	103 13/16	94 15/16
Treas 7 3/4pc 2012-15‡‡.	8.21	8.33	94 3/8	+3/16	101 13/32	92 5/8
Treas 8pc 2015............	8.26	8.31	96 7/8	+1/4	104 5/32	95 1/4
Treas 8 3/4pc 2017‡‡......	8.43	8.36	103 25/32	+3/8	111 5/8	102 7/32
Exch 12pc 2013-17.......	9.08	8.46	132 1/8	+11/32	141 19/32	130 5/16
Treas 8pc 2021............	8.25	8.28	96 15/16	+9/32	99 7/8	95 7/8
Undated						
Consols 4pc..................	8.51	–	47	...	50 13/16	46 1/8
War Loan 3 1/2pc‡‡.........	8.35	–	41 15/16	...	45 9/16	40 15/16
Conv 3 1/2pc '61 Aft.	5.92	–	59 3/32	...	62 1/4	57 9/16
Treas 3pc '66 Aft...........	8.47	–	35 13/32	...	38 1/16	34 11/16
Consols 2 1/2pc..............	8.35	–	29 15/16	–1/8	32 27/32	29 1/8
Treas 2 1/2pc..................	8.33	–	30	...	32 3/16	28 7/16

	Notes	Yield (1)	Yield (2)	Price £	+ or –	52 week High	52 week Low
Index-Linked	**(b)**						
2pc '96.............	(67.9)	–	0.86	216 13/32xd	...	216 7/16	205 11/32
4 5/8pc '98‡‡......	(135.6)	1.84	3.05	111 3/8	+3/8	113 5/16	107 29/32
2 1/2pc '01..........	(78.3)	3.15	3.62	176 17/32xd	+1/8	180 1/32	168
2 1/2pc '03..........	(78.8)	3.32	3.69	172 5/32	+5/32	176 1/32	164
4 3/8pc '04‡‡......	(135.6)	3.38	3.72	113 1/8	...	116 13/16	109 1/4
2pc '06.............	(69.5)	3.46	3.72	179 7/8	+3/32	185 17/32	170 5/8
2 1/2pc '09..........	(78.8)	3.55	3.76	161 5/8	+7/32	167 3/4	154 7/32
2 1/2pc '11..........	(74.6)	3.57	3.77	167 7/32	+7/16	173 9/16	159 11/32
2 1/2pc '13..........	(89.2)	3.63	3.81	137 1/32	+3/16	143	131 7/32
2 1/2pc '16..........	(81.6)	3.66	3.82	145 27/32	+13/32	152 1/4	139 11/16
2 1/2pc '20..........	(83.0)	3.69	3.83	139 11/16	+13/32	146 7/32	133 23/32
2 1/2pc '24‡‡......	(97.7)	3.68	3.81	115 15/16	+3/8	122 3/8	110 27/32
4 1/8pc '30‡‡......	(135.1)	3.69	3.82	114 13/32	+3/8	120 15/16	109 27/32

(b) Figures in parentheses show RPI base for indexing, (ie 8 months prior to issue) and have been adjusted to reflect rebasing of RPI to 100 in February 1987. Conversion factor 3.945. RPI for June 1995: 149.8 and for January 1996: 150.2.

Other Fixed Interest

Notes	Yield Int	Yield Red	Price £	+ or –	52 week High	52 week Low
Asian Dev 10 1/4pc 2009....	9.09	8.59	112 13/16	...	120	110 11/16
B'ham 11 1/2pc 2012..........	9.52	9.07	120 3/4	...	128	119
Ireland Cap 8 1/2pc '10.......	8.04	–	105 3/4	...	106	98 1/4
9pc Cap 1996	8.65	–	104	...	104 3/4	101
13pc Cap '97-2..............	11.72	–	110 7/8	...	111 7/8	107 7/8
Hydro Quebec 15pc 2011	10.46	9.52	143 13/32	...	154 15/32	141 7/16
Leeds 13 1/2pc 2006..........	10.38	–	130	...	136 1/2	128
Liverpool 3 1/2pc Irred........	9.09	–	38 1/2	...	41	33
LCC 3pc '20 Aft...............	9.09	–	33 13/16	...	35	27 3/4
Manchester 11 1/2pc 2007.	9.73	8.92	118 1/4	...	124 1/2	115 1/4
Met. Wtr. 3pc 'B'............	4.08	7.93	73 1/2	...	76	70
N'wide Anglia 3 7/8pc 2021	–	4.61	136	...	143 1/2	132 1/2
4 1/4pc IL 2024.................	–	4.57	130 1/2	...	140 5/8	127 1/2
Utd Mex States 16 1/2pc 2008	13.36	–	123 1/2	...	136 1/2	113 1/2

● 'Tap' stock. ‡‡ Tax-free to non-residents on application. E Auction basis. xd Ex dividend. Closing mid-prices are shown in pounds per £100 nominal of stock. Prospective real Index-Linked redemption yields are calcualted by HSBC Greenwell from Bank of England closing prices.

Other bodies apart from HM Government such as building societies and local authorities, also use fixed interest bonds to raise money. However, these are aimed at institutional investors.

Fig G2 Table of UK gilts prices

Source: Financial Times, 15 March 1996

inflation. But your capital will slip behind inflation if you pay more than the indexed value. Again, the *Financial Times* UK gilts prices table (see Figure G2) can tell you whether the current price is below the indexed value – look at the real redemption yields for the gilt. If these are higher than the coupon of the gilt, then the gilt price is below its indexed value.

The problem with index-linked gilts is that, if inflation fails to rise, they can deliver a worse return than some of their fixed-interest peers. Good stockbrokers are normally able to offer a break-even inflation rate where it makes sense to buy index-linked gilts rather than conventional gilts. The break-even rate varies according to your tax rate.

MAKING THE MOST OF GILTS

- Decide why you want to invest in gilts. They can be particularly useful in meeting predictable cash needs, such as school fees. Individuals pay no capital gains tax on gains from gilts held to redemption, so higher-rate income tax payers may want to lock into a tax-free gain.
- Avoid high charges by using the National Savings Stock Register or a low-cost execution-only broker – you will find their charges listed in the annual *Investors Chronicle Stockbrokers Survey*. The National Savings booklet *Government Stocks* tells you which gilts are on offer through the National Savings Stock Register, as well as the maturity date of the gilt, the nominal rate of interest and the dates when the interest is paid. The booklet, complete with application form, is available through post offices. But you need a newspaper to find out the price and the true interest rate you will receive.
- Find the table of UK gilts prices (see Figure G2) in the second section of the *Financial Times*. It splits gilts into short, 0–5 years left to maturity; medium, 5–15 years left; and long, over 15 years left. Undated gilts have no fixed redemption date.
- Choose a gilt according to when you want your cash back and whether you want high income, which will be taxed, or a tax-free

capital gain. A spread of gilts could give you both. Choosing gilts you can hold to maturity will also save you selling costs.

- Remember that gilt prices move according to the market's feeling about future interest rates and future inflation rates. The prospect of low interest rates and low inflation make gilts more attractive. Investors can track sentiment by reading the financial press, or use the statistics in the *Financial Times* to check market expectations for themselves.

HINDSIGHT

Definition: **All investors know that past performance is no guide to the future, but statistics about the past record of a company or fund are the only concrete evidence available to investors.**

H

Hindsight makes everyone wise. The problem is to relate past performance to your opinion of how an investment will do in future. Investment performance collators such as Micropal and HSW publish monthly tables showing how each unit trust has performed. *Money Management*, a monthly magazine aimed at financial advisers and also part of the the *Financial Times* group, is the most accessible source for these statistics.

'Apart from the fact that investors are gambling that their chosen unit trust can continue its good record, the numbers can be intrinsically misleading.'

Past performance tables split the hundreds of trusts into 24 sectors ranging from UK Growth to Far East funds and from North American to Futures and Options funds. The meat of the tables is in the cumulative performance figures – six columns going from one month to 10 years. The tables also tell you whether you can invest in a trust through a regular savings plan, whether the trust offers an in-house personal equity plan, the age of the fund, its size, the dividend yield, its compound annual return over five years and its volatility. All of this information is invaluable to private investor, whether or not they use a financial adviser.

All investment advertisements warn, correctly, that past performance is no guide to the future, yet investors have little alternative but to use near-derelict performance figures in choosing a fund. The point is to use the information intelligently. Apart from the fact that investors are gambling that their chosen unit trust can continue its good record, the numbers can be intrinsically misleading. They measure cumulative growth between two points in time. The single figure leaves the investors ignorant of the ups and downs in between the two dates, or whether there was anything unusual about investment conditions at the start date.

Using hindsight

- Decide the type of investment you want – UK or overseas? Developed or developing economies?
- Find past performance statistics for the unit trusts and investment trusts covering your chosen sector.
- Look for above average performance in comparison with other funds in the sector.
- Look for funds that have beaten or at least matched the relevant market index.
- Does the good performance show up over several years?
- Contact the fund management company for a copy of the fund's annual report – it gives more detail on past performance over several years.
- Is the fund covered by Fund Research?

For example, the cumulative figures from Micropal show that £1,000 invested in one of the best-performing UK unit trusts in January 1986 was worth £5,400 ten years later. This performance beat the average return on the stockmarket in the same period.

In between the UK stockmarket boomed in 1986–7, crashed in October 1987, groaned in despair at the Gulf War in 1990, limped through most of 1992, jumped for joy at the devaluation of sterling and the UK's exit from the European exchange rate mechanism in October 1992, chugged through 1994 and climbed to record highs during 1995–96. Only the 10-year graphs (see Figures H1 and H2) hint at the ups and downs suffered by the original £1,000 and show where the fund made most of its money. The graph of the worst

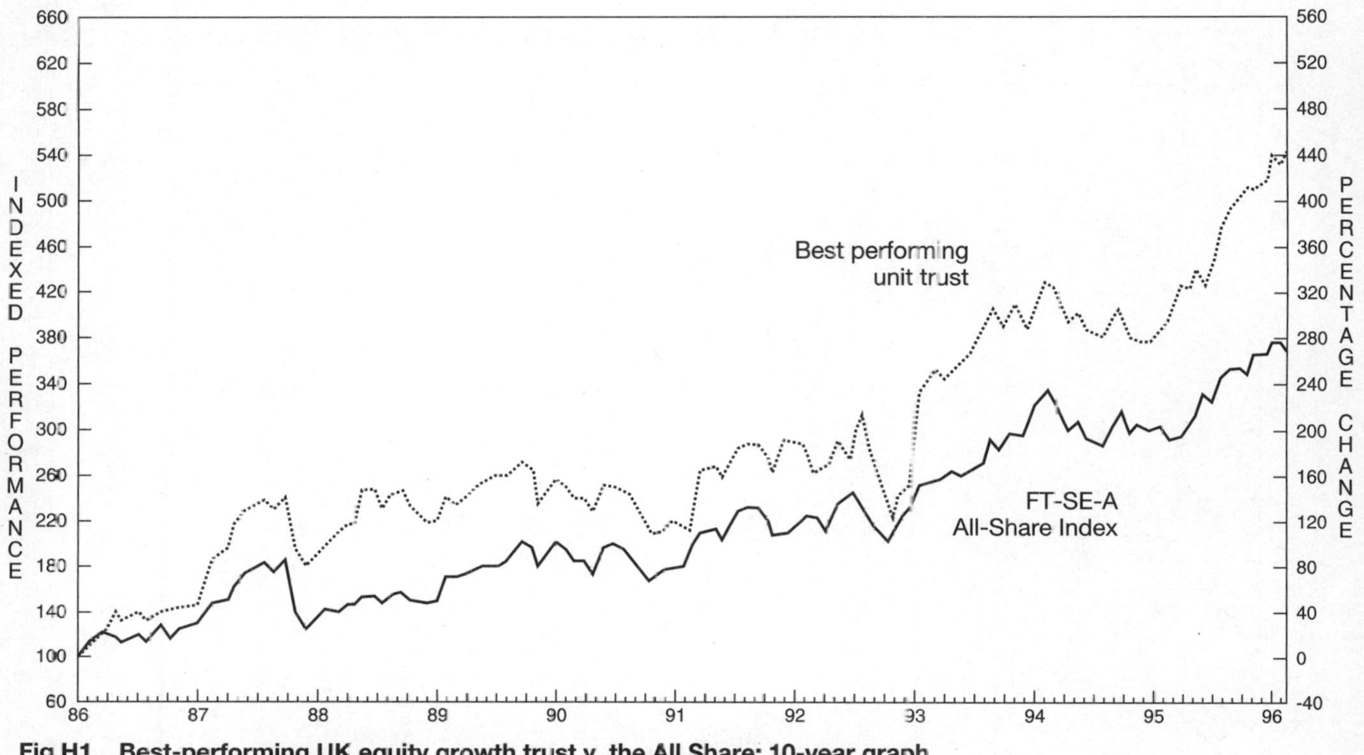

Fig H1 Best-performing UK equity growth trust v. the All Share: 10-year graph

Source: Micropal

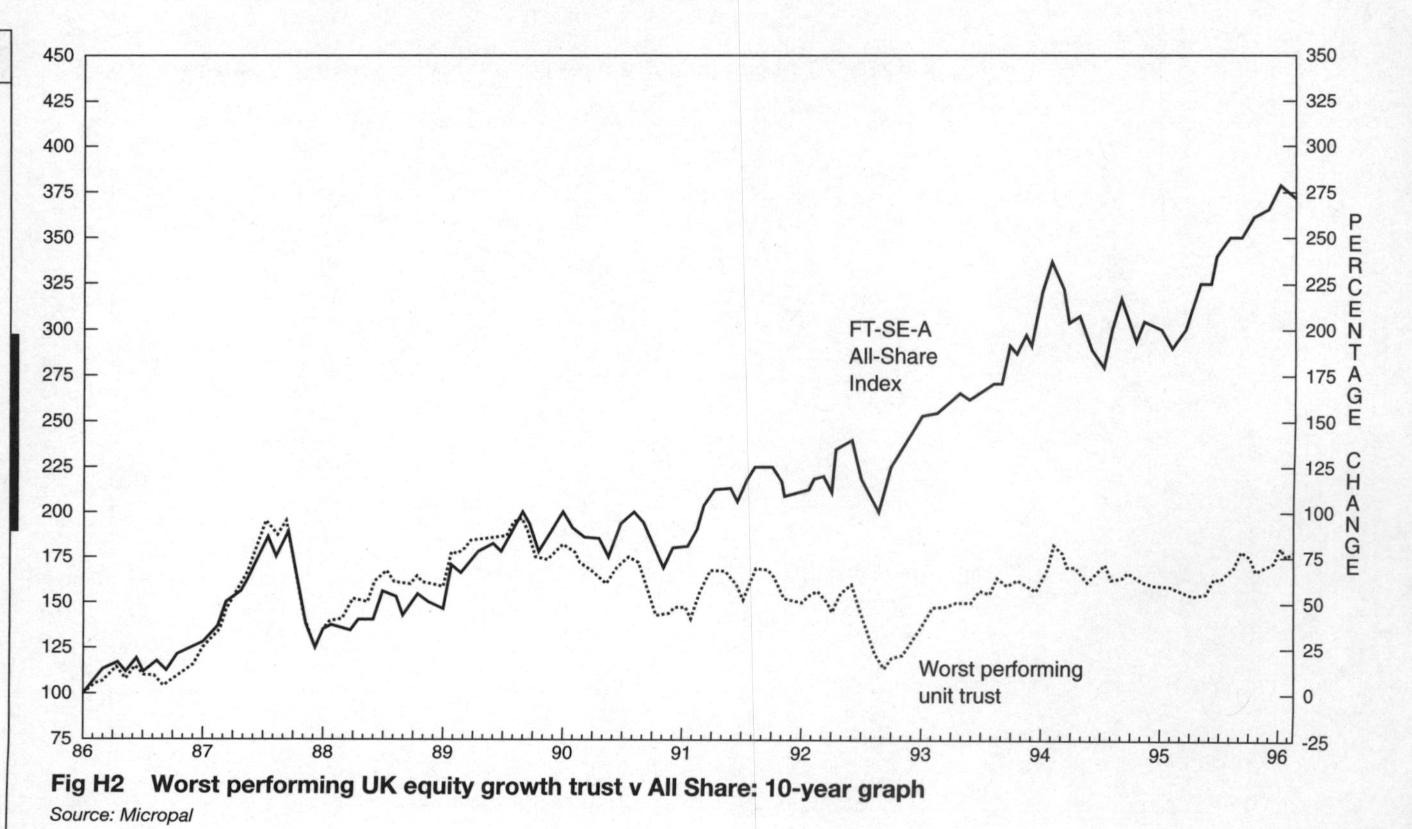

Fig H2 Worst performing UK equity growth trust v All Share: 10-year graph

Source: Micropal

performing trust in the same period shows how badly the fund slipped behind the average stockmarket performance. Money in this fund had not even doubled in value. An investor who ignored the performance tables might think this was good result, however.

However, new investors would normally only win easy and inexpensive access to such information through a financial adviser. Most large firms of advisers have either their own research department or access to one. The leading name in unit trust research is Fund Research. As a dedicated research company, it analyses performance and interviews the fund managers in order to rate funds worldwide. Its highest rating is AAA, but it only considers funds with a three-year record and more than £10m under management. Its research is well-respected and any Fund Research rating is a good sign.

MAKING THE MOST OF HINDSIGHT

- Always compare an individual trust's cumulative performance with the benchmarks. These will normally be an index of shares from the market covered by the trust in the same period.
- Ask your financial adviser to provide graphs of funds' performance over five years.
- Look for independent ratings such at the Fund Research scores.
- Use hindsight to trigger questions rather than answer them.
- Beware. The best-performing unit trust out of all 1,600 funds may only be perched at the top of the league tables because of a quirk.

INDICES

Definition: **An index is a numerical scale that allows investors to compare share prices with some base number.**

A share can rise in value, and still do badly compared with the rest of the stockmarket. Stockmarket indices not only tell investors whether the market has moved up or down, but how their own investments are shaping up. They are investment benchmarks.

It is possible to create your own index (see Box I1), but there is a wealth of index information already available in the financial Press, particularly the *Financial Times*.

Box I1

Make your own index

Step 1

Calculate the capitalisation of your constituent companies at your chosen starting date. The starting date in this example is 5 March 1996.

Company	Share price p	Shares in issue m	Market value £m
Glaxo Wellcome	920	3,509	32,283
British Petroleum	543	5,589	30,348
British Telecom	377	6,290	23,713
Total market value			**86,344**

Step 2

Set starting value of your index (say 100).

I1

Step 3

Calculate an index divisor on the starting date – the divisor is an arbitrary number chosen to fix the starting value. It can be adjusted when the share capital of the index constituents change and that allows the index value to remain comparable over time.

$$\text{Index divisor} = \frac{\text{Total market value}}{\text{Index value}} = \frac{86{,}344}{100} = 863.4$$

Step 4

Calculate the capitalisation of the constituent companies on the end-date (21 March 1996).

Company	**Share price p**	**Shares in issue m**	**Market value £m**
Glaxo Wellcome	819	3,509	28,739
British Petroleum	561	5,589	31,354
British Telecom	340	6,290	21,386
Total market value			**81,479**

Step 5

Calculate index value at the end date.

$$\text{Index value} = \frac{\text{Total market value}}{\text{Index divisor}} = \frac{81{,}479}{863.4} = 94.4$$

Index starting value: 100.0 **Index end value:** 94.4

Source: FT-SE International

FT 30-SHARE INDEX

The oldest surviving stockmarket index is the FT 30-Share Index, or FT Ordinary. Set up in 1935, it goes back to 1930 and, as its name implies, measures the performance of shares in 30 of the market's largest companies. The formula is based on the US Dow Jones Average index, and it sets out to show changes in the market's mood. Its historical value is clear – the index tells investors how the stockmarket has moved over the last 60 years (see Figure (I1). However, it has been dominated by huge industrial companies, with no representation from, for example, property companies. Companies stay in the index until circumstances force them out – they have to be taken over or go out of business – while constituents of the more modern indices are subject to rigorous review. So the FT 30's practical usefulness to private investors in the 1990s can seem limited. However, made up of 30 heavily traded stocks – not just the 30 companies with the largest market capitalisation – the FT 30 is still considered a very effective short-term measure of how the market is moving (see Figure I2).

'The search for useful investment measures means the number of indices can seem ridiculous.'

The search for useful investment measures means the number of indices can seem ridiculous. Fund managers are expected to 'beat the index' and, understandably, some believe that even if they have slipped behind one index, there will always be another index that suits their purpose. Beware of fund management companies that like to compare their performance to the retail prices index, for example. However, there is a hard core of indices which should give private investors the full picture and which are used by all UK fund managers.

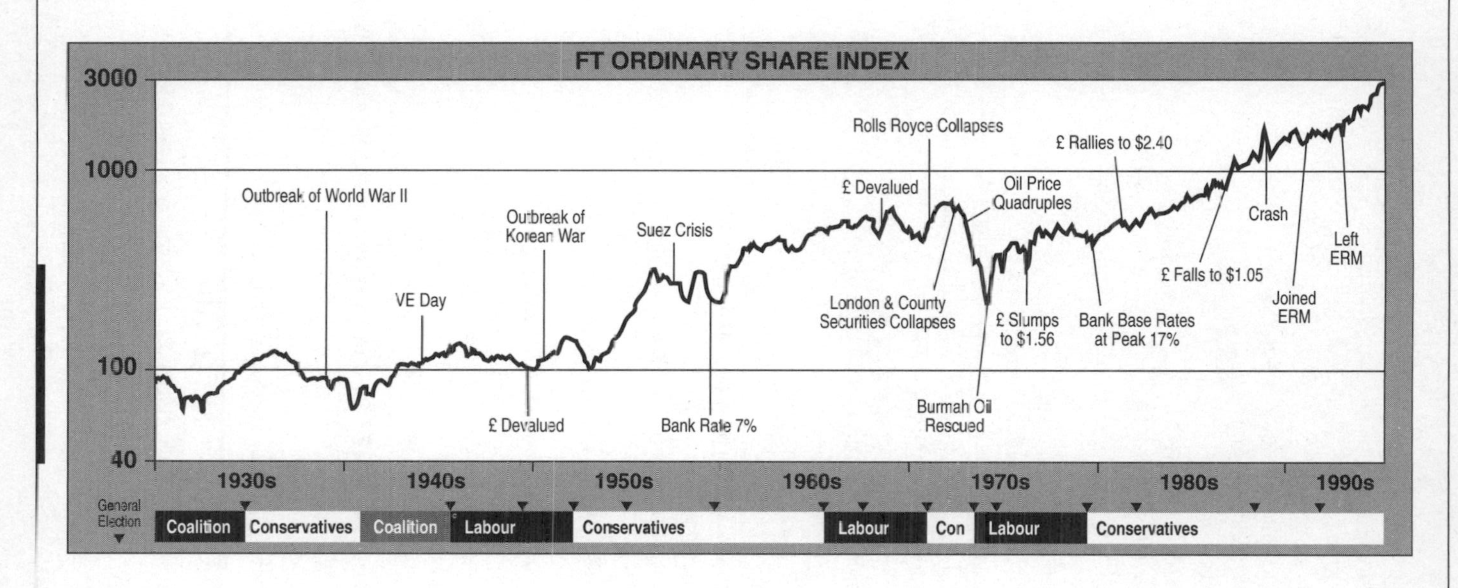

Fig I1 FT Ordinary Index

Source: Investors Chronicle

Allied Domecq (Alcoholic beverages)
Asda (Food retailers)
BP (Oil, integrated)
BICC (Electronic & electrical equipment)
Blue Circle (Building materials)
BOC (Chemicals)
Boots (General retailers)
British Airways (Transport)
British Gas (Gas distribution)
British Telecom (Telecoms)
BTR (Diversified industrials)
Cadbury-Schweppes (Food producers)
Courtaulds (Chemicals)
General Electric (Electronic & electrical equipment)
GKN (Engineering, vehicles)
Glaxo Wellcome (Pharmaceuticals)
Grand Metropolitan (Alcoholic beverages)
Guinness (Alcoholic beverages)
Hanson (Diversified industrials)
ICI (Chemicals)
Lucas Industries (Engineering, vehicles)
Marks & Spencer (General retailers)
National Westminster Bank (Retail banks)
P&O (Transport)
Reuters (Media)
Royal Insurance (Insurance)
Smith Kline Beecham (Pharmaceuticals)
Tate & Lyle (Food producers)
Thorn-EMI (Media)
Vodafone (Telecoms)

Fig I2 Constituents of the FT 30 and their sectors at 22 March 1996

FT-SE ACTUARIES ALL-SHARE INDEX

The FT-SE Actuaries (FT-SE-A) All-Share Index remains the mother of all indices simply because it gives the most accurate picture of the whole stockmarket. Set up in 1962 by the *Financial Times* and the Faculty and Institute of Actuaries, the All-Share includes some 900 shares of companies, representing 98 per cent of the market by value. About 2,000 companies are listed on the market in total. The All-Share is an arithmetic, market-capitalisation-weighted index. That means it weights each company by its size so that a 15 per cent rise in the price of British Telecom, which has a market capitalisation of over £20bn, will have a bigger effect on the index than a 15 per cent rise in the price of Alexandra Workwear, a clothing manufacturer with a market capitalisation of just £50m. Each issue of the *Financial Times* carries the All-Share cross-section of the market by sector, and the Saturday newspaper carries extra information. The two pages of share price information in the *Financial Times* can seem like a nightmare of meaningless names and numbers. But the table summarising the FT-SE-A All-Share Index, normally on the back page of the paper's second section, compresses that maze of information into something more digestible – a single figure for how the whole market has fared, and figures for each of the 40 or so sectors (see Figure I3).

Each company has a home in its own sector, even if some end up in 'rattlebag' sectors such as support services or diversified industrials. The smallest sector is tobacco – its only company is BAT Industries. The biggest sectors, ignoring the investment trusts, are engineering, support services, media and general retailers. The sectors make it easier to find the information you want, to compare like with like, and to help work out why a given share has done well or badly.

An industry can be out of favour with the City, even if the rest of the market is storming ahead. For example, food retailers, which includes the big supermarkets such as J Sainsbury, Asda and Tesco, as well as chocolate shop group Thorntons, suffered in 1995–96, as the major supermarkets dived into a fresh price war. The media sector, including takeover targets such as Yorkshire Television and HTV, soared as changes to the media ownership rules fuelled takeover speculation. But within the sector, some individual shares, such as publishers, still did badly. They 'underperformed' the sector and the market.

Value of the index as at close of trading on 14 March.

Measure of how much investors will pay in relation to a company's earnings.

FT-SE Actuaries Share Indices — The UK Series

	Mar 14	Div. yield%	Net cover	P/E ratio	Total Return
FT-SE 100	3681.8	4.03	2.11	14.74	1482.40
FT-SE Mid 250	4232.9	3.49	1.72	20.84	1682.67
FT-SE Mid 250 ex Inv Trusts	4264.6	3.60	1.77	19.64	1697.68
FT-SE-A 350	1847.9	3.91	2.03	15.75	1522.57
FT-SE-A 350 Higher Yield	1814.1	4.90	1.89	13.51	1240.31
FT-SE-A 350 Lower Yield	1888.7	2.89	2.28	18.97	1299.41
FT-SE SmallCap	2064.05	3.07	1.80	22.64	1675.14
FT-SE SmallCap ex Inv Trusts	2051.49	3.27	1.88	20.32	1673.71
FT-SE-A ALL-SHARE	1826.73	3.84	2.02	16.13	1528.88

■ FT-SE Actuaries All-Share

	Mar 14	Div. yield%	Net cover	P/E ratio	Total Return
10 **MINERAL EXTRACTION(24)**	3296.60	3.93	1.51	21.08	1396.88
12 Extractive Industries(6)	4165.05	3.82	2.39	13.68	1218.81
15 Oil, Integrated(3)	3331.37	4.14	1.35	22.28	1444.20
16 Oil Exploration & Prod(15)	2338.84	2.10	1.41	42.32	1388.25
20 **GEN INDUSTRIALS(275)**	2081.53	4.03	1.87	16.55	1122.05
21 Building & Construction(34)	1132.69	3.53	2.03	17.48	934.59
22 Building Matls & Merchs(29)	1883.73	3.97	2.00	15.76	935.18
23 Chemicals(23)	2563.02	3.91	1.99	16.06	1204.93
24 Diversified Industrials(21)	1806.17	5.60	1.50	14.89	994.73
25 Electronic & Elect Equip(38)	2350.06	3.07	1.82	22.40	1207.12
26 Engineering(70)	2352.04	3.23	2.40	16.11	1412.62
27 Engineering, Vehicles(13)	2759.48	3.83	1.66	19.72	1407.08
28 Paper, Pckg & Printing(28)	2696.61	3.73	2.03	16.47	1106.32
29 Textiles & Apparel(19)	1476.26	4.75	1.64	16.01	889.82
30 **CONSUMER GOODS(81)**	3506.13	3.99	1.86	16.83	1276.50
32 Alcoholic Beverages(9)	2788.70	4.36	1.67	17.18	996.71
33 Food Producers(23)	2548.39	4.21	1.75	17.01	1132.35
34 Household Goods(15)	2520.25	3.92	2.08	15.35	947.60
36 Health Care(20)	1926.69	2.71	1.82	25.43	1159.81
37 Pharmaceuticals(13)	4936.08	3.41	1.94	18.94	1652.73
38 Tobacco(1)	4358.27	5.83	2.03	10.53	1054.40
40 **SERVICES(253)**	2361.18	2.96	2.10	20.14	1217.69
41 Distributors(32)	2602.48	3.77	1.84	18.00	949.86
42 Leisure & Hotels(23)	2965.53	2.81	2.16	20.63	1579.25
43 Media(46)	3920.61	2.20	2.09	27.21	1409.08
44 Retailers, Food(15)	1899.07	3.85	2.40	13.51	1190.93
45 Retailers, General(43)	1952.87	3.04	2.21	18.60	1104.17
47 Breweries, Pubs & Rest.(24)	2959.05	3.34	2.08	17.98	1411.07
48 Support Services(49)	2096.54	2.32	2.52	21.35	1321.67
49 Transport(21)	2398.16	3.61	1.41	24.57	987.75
60 **UTILITIES(33)**	2446.41	5.07	2.06	11.95	1038.13
62 Electricity(12)	2684.46	5.18	2.60	9.30	1314.47
64 Gas Distribution(2)	1553.05	7.72	1.37	11.84	779.19
66 Telecommunications(7)	2024.42	4.17	1.76	17.07	916.38
68 Water(12)	2163.82	5.64	2.59	8.55	1173.42
69 **NON-FINANCIALS(666)**	1950.98	3.83	1.91	17.03	1464.39
70 **FINANCIALS(108)**	2779.23	4.23	2.57	11.52	1188.67
71 Banks, Retail(8)	3844.65	4.03	2.83	10.97	1253.42
72 Banks, Merchant(6)	3366.45	2.91	2.33	18.46	1056.71
73 Insurance(24)	1367.58	5.71	3.07	7.13	1017.75
74 Life Assurance(6)	3536.71	4.128	2.06	14.50	1440.86
77 Other Financial(23)	2491.23	3.71	1.88	17.90	1407.65
79 Property(41)	1420.08	4.40	1.30	21.87	863.64
80 **INVESTMENT TRUSTS(126)**	3059.88	2.21	1.07	52.79	1062.76
89 **FT-SE-A ALL-SHARE(900)**	1826.73	3.84	2.02	16.13	1528.88
FT-SE-A Fledgling	1152.95	2.96	2.18	19.38	1196.08
FT-SE-A Fledgling ex Inv Trusts	1157.93	3.22	2.35	16.51	1200.56

Gross dividend yield based on last 12 months' dividends.

Measures ability of a company to pay its dividends out of its current earnings.

Measures total return on the underlying index, combining capital performance and reinvested income. Started in 1993.

Fig I3 FT-SE Actuaries All-Share Index

Source: Financial Times, 15 March 1996

FT-SE 100 INDEX

The FT-SE 100 Index, also known as the Footsie, covers the shares of the 100 largest companies listed on the UK stock market. Each has a market capitalisation of at least £1bn, and together they account for 70 per cent of the UK stockmarket. Started at 1,000 in 1984, the FT-SE has become the main UK index, mainly because it stays right up-to-date throughout the day – it is calculated by computer every minute. It was created to meet demand for options trading (see OPTIONS, page 161).

The FT-SE committee, made up of about 15 people working with indices, reviews the constituents of the index every three months. It is normal for one or two companies to drop out of or come into the index, and the market will drive up the price of companies expected to join the FT-SE.

Many UK fund managers, particularly those running so-called tracker funds, have to invest in FT-SE companies to keep their fund running in line with the market. The whole point of tracker funds, which own as much as 15 per cent of the market, is that they buy the constituents of the index in order to track it as exactly as possible.

Failing to match the market – known as underperforming – is considered professional failure by many fund managers, whether or not they admit it. When National Grid joined the FT-SE, its share price picked up. Partly, the share price rises reflect the market's good opinion of companies, but the scramble to own shares in a new FT-SE member also pushes up the price. The graph in Figure I4 shows the price of National Grid climbing in December, only to slip back badly.

Box I2

Tracking the index

Tracker funds, assisted by computers, track the market by investing in the exact constituents of a particular index. This technique makes for foolproof (well, almost foolproof, see QUANTITATIVE FUND MANAGEMENT, page 191) and relatively cheap investment because the fund manager wants to match the market, not beat it. Few fund managers consistently achieve a better result than the market, as measured by the index of your choice. The unit trust fund managers presently offering tracker funds include: Schroders, Norwich Union, Morgan Grenfell, Legal & General, Govett, Fidelity, Midland, Gartmore, Marks & Spencer, Virgin and HSBC.

Look for a fund with low charges and a record of accurate tracking. Tracking accuracy varies between funds for a number of reasons: for example do they buy every single stock in the index, or a sample of stocks? Experts say that a fund needs to have at least £15m under management in order to track the All-Share accurately. Remember that funds that capture most of the rise in a stockmarket will also capture most of the fall.

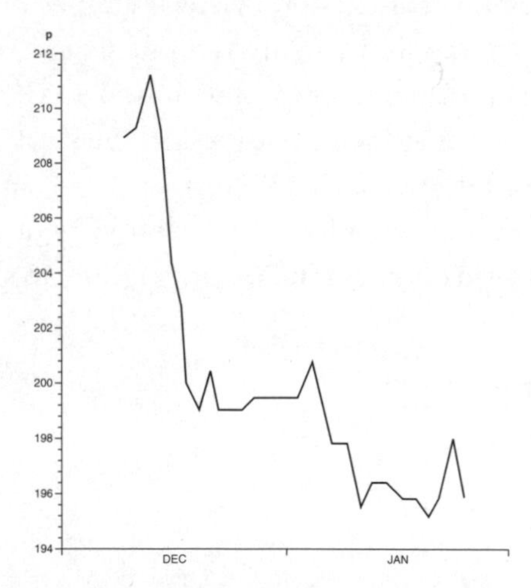

Fig I4 'The excitement was just too much' National Grid share price performance December 1995 to January 1996

Source: Datastream

FT-SE MID 250 INDEX

The FT-SE Mid 250 Index captures the performance of the next 250 companies by size after the FT-SE 100 companies. It represents about a quarter of the UK stockmarket, making it bigger than the Hong Kong stockmarket. The index reflects the performance of UK public limited companies more directly than the multinationals making up the FT-SE 100 can measure it. FT-SE 250 companies react strongly to UK economics, such as changes in interest rates, while the FT-SE 100 companies follow global trends.

FT-SE-A 350 INDEX

The FT-SE-A 350 Index combines the FT-SE 100 and the FT-SE 250. Both the 350 and the 250 are calculated on a continuous basis and, although they only started in 1992, they have been backdated to 1985.

FT-SE SMALLCAP INDEX

The FT-SE SmallCap Index covers the rest of the companies in the All-Share not included in the FT-SE-A 350: essentially smaller companies worth more than £40m. As of 1996, it is calculated every minute.

FT-SE A FLEDGLING INDEX

The FT-SE A Fledgling Index covers the companies too small to qualify for the All-Share – all companies with market capitalisations below £40m. This index is calculated just once a day.

FT-SE AIM INDEX

The FT-SE Aim Index started in January 1996. It covers the widely diverse companies – which just about fit under the umbrella term of 'growth companies' – quoted on the Alternative Investment Market, launched in 1995 (see page 15).

OTHER INDICES

Investors will also find more specialist indices, such as the FT Government Securities Index, which covers a cross-section of gilts. The Fixed Interest Index covers fixed interest bonds issued by the UK government, local authorities and UK companies; other indices follow specific types of gilts. The gilts indices are due for a thorough review in 1996–7. The Gold Mining Index is based on South African, Australian and North American mining shares traded in London. All these indices, and more, can be useful in making investment decisions as well as assessing the performance of your own portfolio.

UK investors should also keep an eye on international stockmarkets. The main indices are: Dow Jones Industrials and the Standard & Poor's 500 for the US, the Nikkei 225 for Japan, the Dax for Germany, the CAC 40 for France and the Hang Seng for Hong Kong. You will find them, and others, in the *Financial Times*. Each week the *Investors Chronicle* gives a snapshot of the main indices and of investment trends.

MAKING THE MOST OF INDICES

A unit trust or investment will normally tell investors which index it uses as a benchmark. You will find details of the indices and comparable funds in specialist magazines such as *Money Management* – also part of the *Financial Times* group – or *Planned Savings*. It is worth checking how your fund's performance measures up against its chosen benchmark, and the competition in between the half-yearly and yearly reports from your fund manager. The graph in Figure I5 shows how an average UK growth fund has performed against the All-Share.

- Investors running their own portfolios need to choose their own index. The FT-SE-A All-Share will normally be the best choice for a broadly based UK portfolio, but a portfolio of very small companies should be measured against the FT-SE A Fledgling.
- Be sure whether an index is a measure of capital return on its own

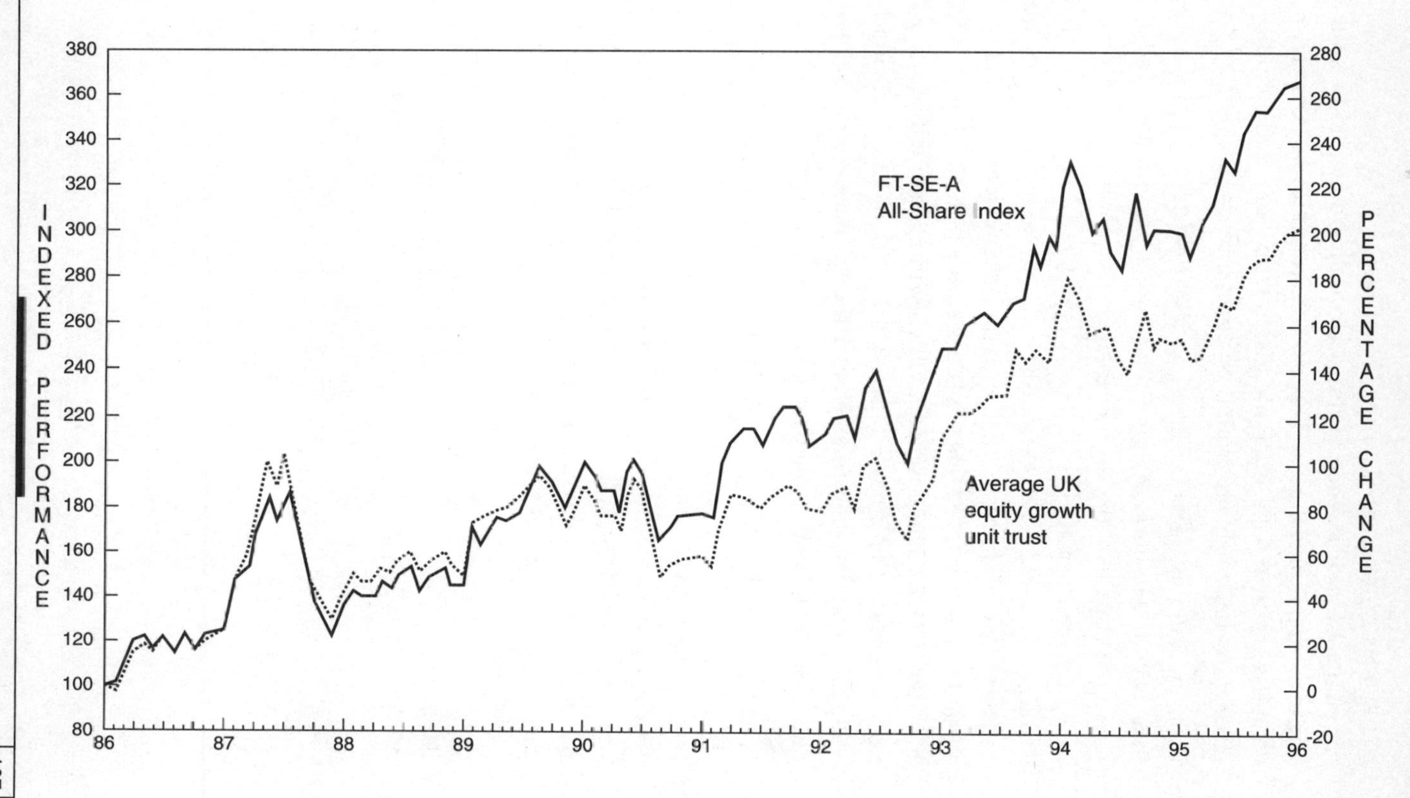
FT-SE-A
All-Share Index
Average UK
equity growth
unit trust
INDEXED PERFORMANCE
PERCENTAGE CHANGE
380
360
340
320
300
280
260
240
220
200
180
160
140
120
100
80
280
260
240
220
200
180
160
140
120
100
80
60
40
20
0
-20
86
87
88
89
90
91
92
93
94
95
96

or includes re-invested income. The effect of re-invested income can make a big difference to the performance based only on the original capital investment. The FT-SE Actuaries indices can be calculated with or without dividends, but most of the main indices throughout the world are capital performance only.

- Portfolio fund managers, who look after investors' portfolios on their behalf, will normally give their clients performance updates measured against the fund manager's chosen benchmark. Investors can turn to stockbroker Capel-Cure Myers or to fund manager Cantrade for specialist indices tailored to private investors. FT-SE International, the company which owns and runs the indices, was due to launch indices aimed directly at the private investor in 1996. These indices, which will appear in the newspapers alongside the other FT-SE figures, should be particularly valuable to private investors because they will give separate measures for capital and income performance.
- Consider an index tracker fund as part of your investment portfolio.
- Avoid index fever – fund managers can be excused for slavishly following indices, because, rightly or wrongly, their professional reputation stands or falls by their ability to beat or at least match the market. However, with investment, as with so much else, it is the pound in the hand that counts.

INVESTMENT TRUSTS

Definition: **Investment trusts are set up to invest mainly in other companies' shares. Developed in the 19th century, they have become increasingly popular among small investors wanting to plug into stockmarket growth. With both unit trusts (see** **UNIT TRUSTS, page 222****) and investment trusts, the small investor subcontracts his investment decisions to a professional fund manager. Putting his money in a pool with other investors' cash is cheaper and less risky than investing the same sum in individual shares.**

When you buy shares in an investment trust, you join a club that hopes to share growing returns from the trust's assets. You buy and sell your investment trust shares through a stockbroker, as with other quoted companies. And like other quoted companies, the trust's size depends on its share capital. Its stockmarket value will vary according to the changing prices of the shares in its portfolio. Its share price often does not reflect its underlying asset value.That is a big difference between an investment trust and a unit trust. The size of a unit trust depends on how many people want to buy and sell units, and the value of its units directly reflects the value of its underlying assets.

Shareholders in an investment trust have effectively bought a double-layered investment – the shares in the investment trust and the assets underlying these shares. As a result, there is normally a gap between an investment trust's share price and its net asset value. The net asset value means the chunk of the trust's assets belonging to each share. A premium means the share price is higher than the net asset value per share. A discount means it is lower. Historically, investment trusts' net asset values have outpaced their share prices, and the shares have traded at a discount. In the 1970s, the discount reached 40 per cent, and even in the early 1980s it was about 25 per cent. Now it is about 10 per cent. Discounts on most trusts have narrowed as investment trusts worked harder at marketing and made their shares more fashionable.

Investment trusts also have a good investment record. On share price alone, the 10-year average return on £1,000 invested in investment trusts in February 1996 was £3,693, compared with £2,897 in unit trusts – allowing for costs – and £2,111 in a building society (source: Association of Investment Trust Companies MIS March 1996). To be fair, investment trust returns do not reflect broking costs, while unit trust returns include the trusts' upfront charges. But investment trusts still come out better. The management costs passed on to investors can be lower for investment trusts than for unit trusts. Investment trusts can normally set costs against their corporation tax charge, instead of taking them out of the income after tax. And like 'authorised' unit trusts, investment trusts can be 'approved' by the Inland Revenue to be exempted from capital gains tax on share trading within the trust. Investors will still pay tax on their personal gains. However, investment trusts' costs have caught up with unit trusts in some areas, particularly their marketing costs in launching new funds. The result is that more of investors' money is working for the fund management company and less for the investors.

The company structure of investment trusts gives managers two other main advantages. The fixed share capital structure means that managers know exactly how much they can invest, giving them a strategic advantage over unit trust managers. A unit trust is constantly changing in size because new investors are bringing money to go into the market, or investors are cashing in their units.

Secondly, being a company means that an investment trust can borrow money if it wants to invest more than its share capital size permits. A trust's borrowing or gearing should allow it to earn more money for shareholders. Part of the fund manager's skill is assessing the risks and rewards of gearing up the fund correctly. A highly geared fund, i.e., one with large borrowings in proportion to its share capital, also stands to lose more if markets turn against the fund manager's expectations. Two most dramatic examples of this are Govett Strategic and the Invesco English & International investment trusts. Figures I6 and I7 show how the fund managers had miscalculated and geared up at the wrong time. Each has had a long struggle to get back on track. It is worth noting that some fund managers, such as Foreign & Colonial, have a record of using gearing to great advantage, however.

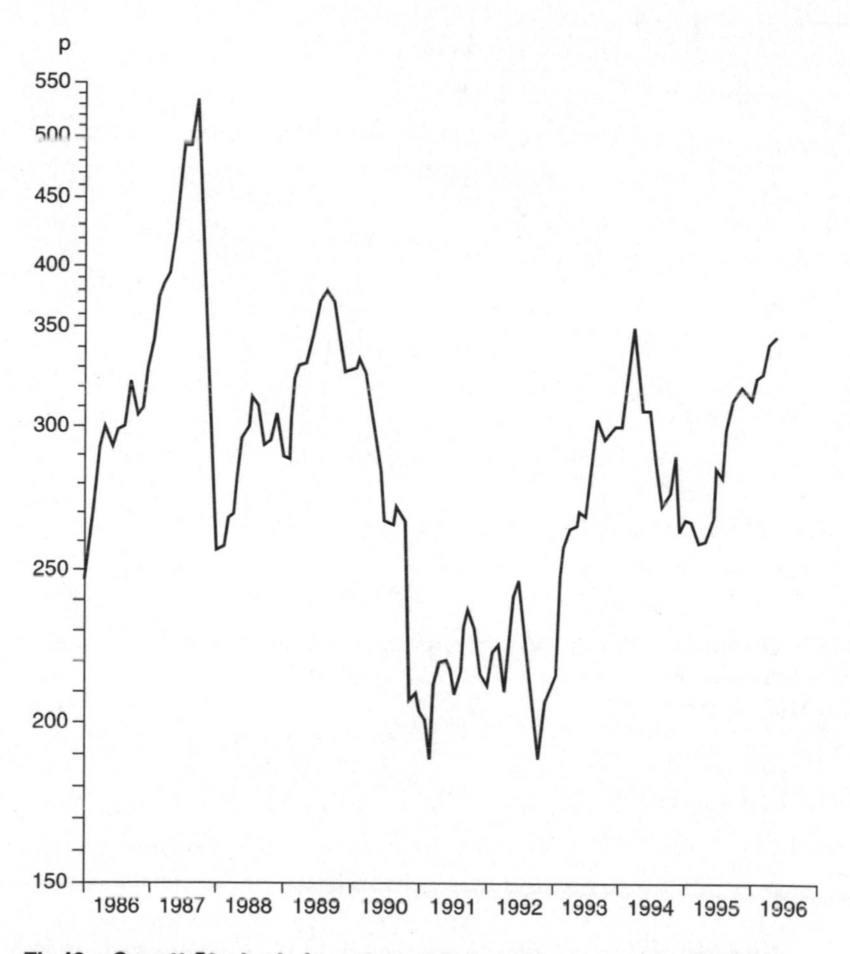

Fig I6 Govett Strategic investment trust: net asset value 1986–96
Source: Datastream

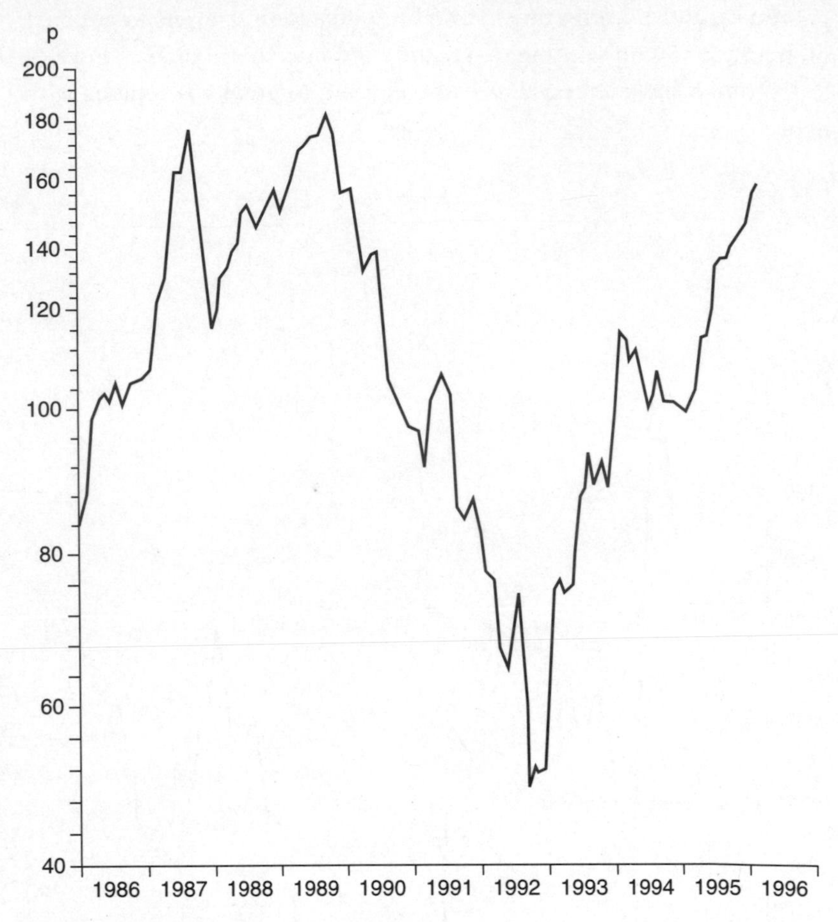

Fig I7 Invesco English and International investment trust: net asset value 1986–96

Source: Datastream

Investors in investment trusts have a further advantage over unit trust investors – they have significantly more say in the running of the fund. An investment trust company has a board of directors – answerable to shareholders – which employs a fund management company to run the fund. This arrangement is normally just as cosy as the most cynical investor would expect, and the fund management company goes about its business with little interference from the board.

However, investment trusts can face hostile takeovers by other investment trusts or hostile action by a large shareholder. In 1995 Scottish Value investment trust, a large shareholder in the Throgmorton Preferred Income Trust, rounded up enough shareholder support to sack the incumbent fund manager and transfer the contract to itself. The shareholders who supported Scottish Value hope that it will achieve better returns than the previous manager.

A unit trust, by contrast, is effectively owned by the fund manager. Unit trust investors rely on a trustee to keep the fund on track, but they have few options except to cash in their investment if the fund's performance is consistently poor.

DISCOUNTS AND PREMIUMS

Discounts and premiums always sound promising. One sends a message that you are on to a bargain, the other says you have struck quality. The *Financial Times* prints the discount or premium with the share price in its investment trust share price listings – with the other share prices in the second section of the newspaper – but you can work out a trust's discount or premium yourself. Subtract a trust's share price from its net asset value (NAV – the value of the trust's investments divided by the number of shares the trust has in issue) and express the difference as a percentage of the NAV.

To recap, a discount means the share price is less than the net asset value, a premium means it is higher. In the *Financial Times* listings a premium is indicated by a minus sign.

At the end of 1995, Foreign and Colonial, the oldest and largest of the investment trusts with an enormous and deserved following among private investors, had a share price of 162p and a net asset value of 159p. The difference between the two figures is 3p, which gives a premium of just under 2 per cent.

However, the discount on one trust means little until you compare it to some other trusts in the list. Foreign and Colonial is an international general trust. Its premium reflects its popularity with investors and its outstanding investment record. Bankers Investment Trust, which has an even better record than Foreign & Colonial, traded at a premium of 3 per cent at the same time. However, Witan, a large trust with a respectable record traded at a discount of 8 per cent. Arguably, a good trust trading at a discount can be better value than an outstanding trust trading at a premium.

Box 13 **Discounts and premiums – why do they matter?**

Supply and demand are the main factors in making discounts widen, narrow or disappear. Many investment trusts have narrowed their discounts by running monthly savings schemes – the constant flow of money into the trust keeps up demand for the shares. A solid record of asset growth, and dividend growth if that is part of the trust's investment brief, will also narrow the discount. Pure fashion, such as a sudden enthusiasm for emerging markets, can also affect the discount in some investment trust niches. For example, discounts on emerging markets investment trusts widened in the wake of the Mexican debt crisis in 1995. International investors panicked about the strength of the developing economies and switched to safer investments.

In summary, buying investment trusts at a discount means you are getting more shares for your money. And in theory, a trend to narrowing discounts will add an extra kick to your shares' performance. However, a change in fashion or a prolonged downturn in the stockmarket will make discounts widen, as with the emerging markets funds. Also, buying for a wide discount alone can mean you are left with shares no-one else wants to buy – that is why they were cheap in the first place.

'... a discount means the share price is lower than the net asset value, a premium means it is higher.'

Some types of trust, such as high income trusts, are more likely to trade at a premium, particularly in times of low interest rates. Dartmoor High Income trust was trading at a 16 per cent premium at the end of 1995. Venture Capital trusts are at the other extreme. They are risky by nature and the discount to NAV reflects that. Kleinwort Development was trading at a huge 26 per cent discount to NAV at the end of 1995. However, each trust may have its own little wrinkles, unconnected with its sector, to explain a discount or premium.

SPLIT-CAPITAL TRUSTS

Split-capital investment trusts began in the 1960s as an antidote to high rates of income tax. The simplest type of split-capital trust offers two types of shares – capital shares benefit from all the capital growth achieved by the trust but receive no income and income shares receive all the income, but show no capital growth. Shares in such trusts can be extremely attractive to particular groups of investors, such as retired people wanting as much income as possible, or high earners paying higher rate tax and wanting only capital growth. Even if the tax advantages have faded now that capital gains and income are taxed at the same rate, it is still easier to control capital gains tax liabilities than those for income tax. Also, split capital trusts have built-in gearing. If a market is rising, capital shareholders will earn an extra kick, because the income shareholders' cash is working for them as well as their own capital.

Split-capital trusts have fixed lives. They are normally wound up, and the assets distributed to shareholders after a predetermined number of years. The point of having a fixed life is that investors can be confident of being able to realise their investment at a specific date. The value of shares in a split trust will vary according to how much time the trust has left to run before the shares can be redeemed, as well as the type of share, interest rate expectations and the market's perception of risk in the trust. For example, capital shares tend to trade at a big discount to their net asset value. This reflects uncertainty about how good a return the fund manager will achieve, but the discount tends to narrow as the time to cash in the shares – their redemption date – draws closer. That is because investors know there is less time left for stockmarkets to go horribly wrong. However, income shares tend to trade at a premium which drops away as the redemption date closes in – some income shares receive very little at redemption because they have already enjoyed a solid income stream.

Split-capital trusts soon evolved more variations on income and capital shares. A summary of the basic six, with an explanation of the key statistics to use in assessing the shares is given below. The Association of Investment Trust Companies (see below) supplies all this information and more in a *Monthly Information Service* (MIS) aimed at private investors and their advisers. It is always important to check how long a trust has to run before it winds up.

Capital shares

Capital shares receive no dividends, but get all the assets left over once the trust has repaid the other classes of share. A rising market works wonders for capital shareholders because of the gearing effect, but they carry more risk if the market is sluggish. Look for the 'gross redemption yield'. It tells you the total return on the shares, as an annual percentage, if you were to hold the shares to redemption. The shares do not have a pre-set payout on redemption, so you will find a range of gross redemption yields showing the return you would get according to different rates of growth. It is up to the investor to judge what the trust can achieve.

Scottish National capital shares have been highly volatile since the trust launched in 1987, as comparison with the FT-SE-A All Share shows (see Figure I8). The AITC's hurdle rate shows the trust will have to grow its assets at 3 per cent a year if it is to repay the shares at their current share price of 25p. However, if the assets grow at 5 per cent a year investors who buy the capital shares at this price will get 38 per cent return. Investors could lose their whole investment if the trust fails to grow at all in the coming two years and seven months.

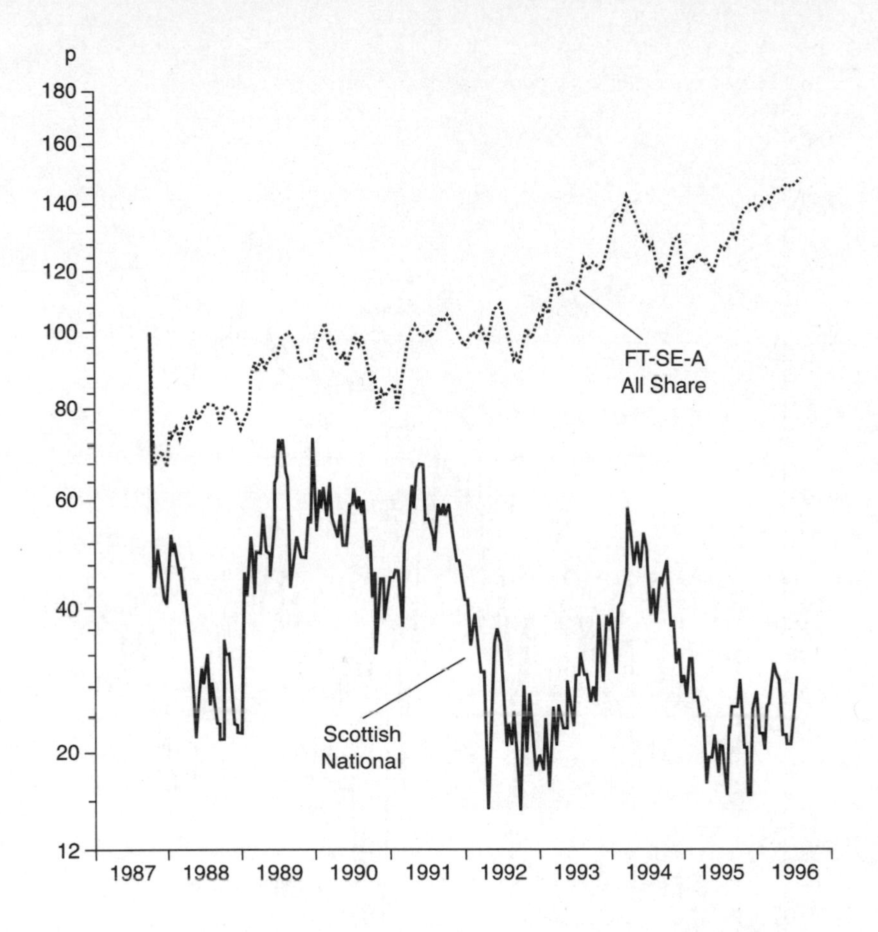

Fig I8 Scottish National capital shares versus the FT-SE-A All-Share Index 1987–96

Source: Datastream

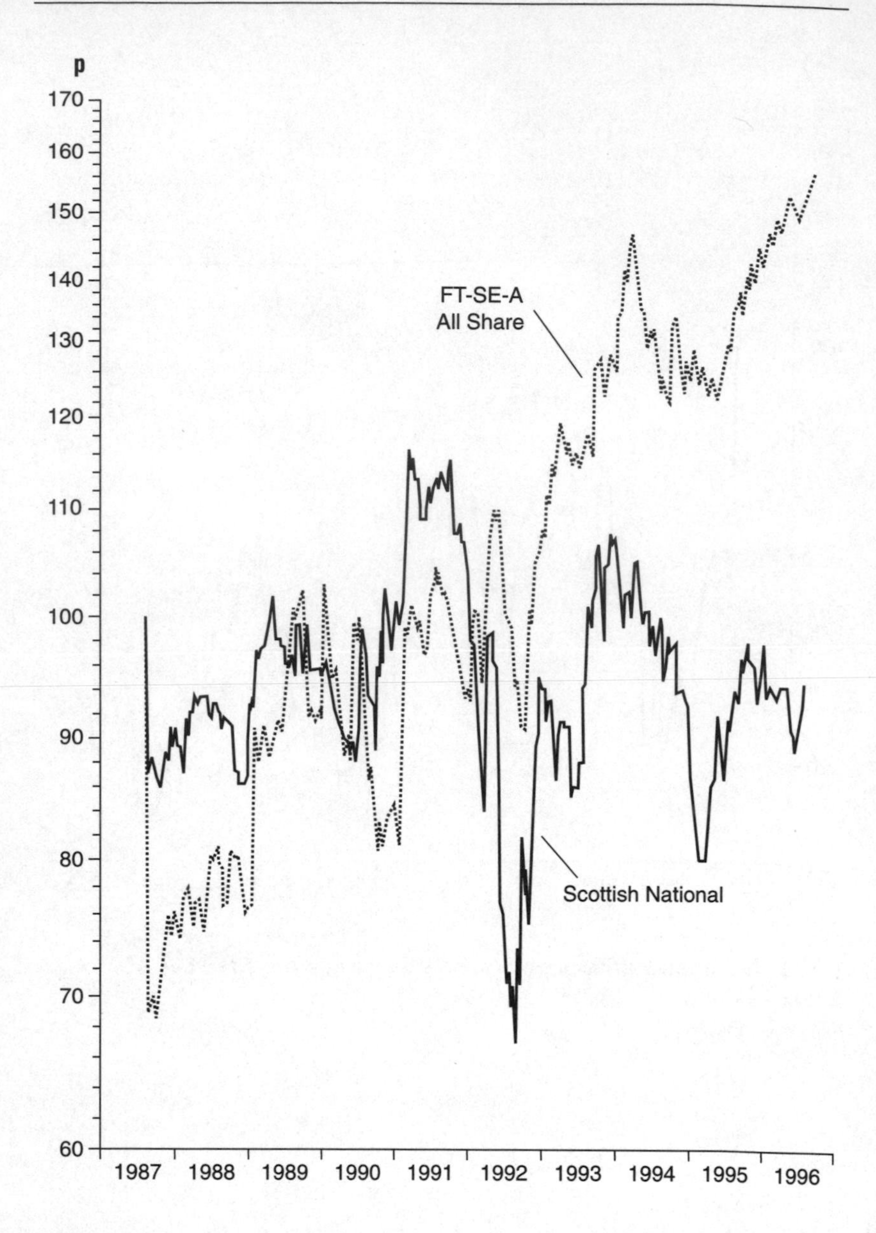

Fig I9 Scottish National income shares versus the FT-SE-A All-Share Index 1987–96

Source: Datastream

Income shares

Income shares receive all the income earned by the trust, but no capital growth when the trust winds up and the shares are repaid. Some income shares do not even repay the investor's original capital sum, just a nominal penny a share. This type of share is sometimes called an annuity share, because all it does is pay an income. Look for the hurdle rate and for the gross redemption yields.

The income shares of Scottish National (see Figure I9) have also been volatile, but they have held their value better than the capital shares. The AITC figures reveal that investors can look forward to a payment of 100p per share from the company's assets when it winds up. The market price of the income shares should climb to match that value in the coming two and a half years. However, the asset cover figure shows that in early 1996 the trust's assets are enough to cover just 90 per cent of the redemption value. Note that the share price is 89p, in line with the trust's asset cover.

Income and residual capital shares

Highly geared ordinary shares have recently been renamed by the AITC, **'Income and residual capital shares'**. They offer high income but you will only get your money back if the assets do well enough to cover the zero dividend preference shares first and have more left over to pay you as an income and residual shareholder. Whether or not you receive a payment will depend on the structure of the trust, and how well its investments have done. The hurdle rate and the gross redemption yield are key statistics in considering these shares.

The City of Oxford ordinary shares fall into this camp (see Figure I10). It has almost four years to redemption and the trust's assets have to grow 7.5 per cent a year for investors to get a return at the current price. However, the income yield is over 30 per cent and even if the assets fail to grow, investors still get an 11 per cent return, thanks to the dividend income.

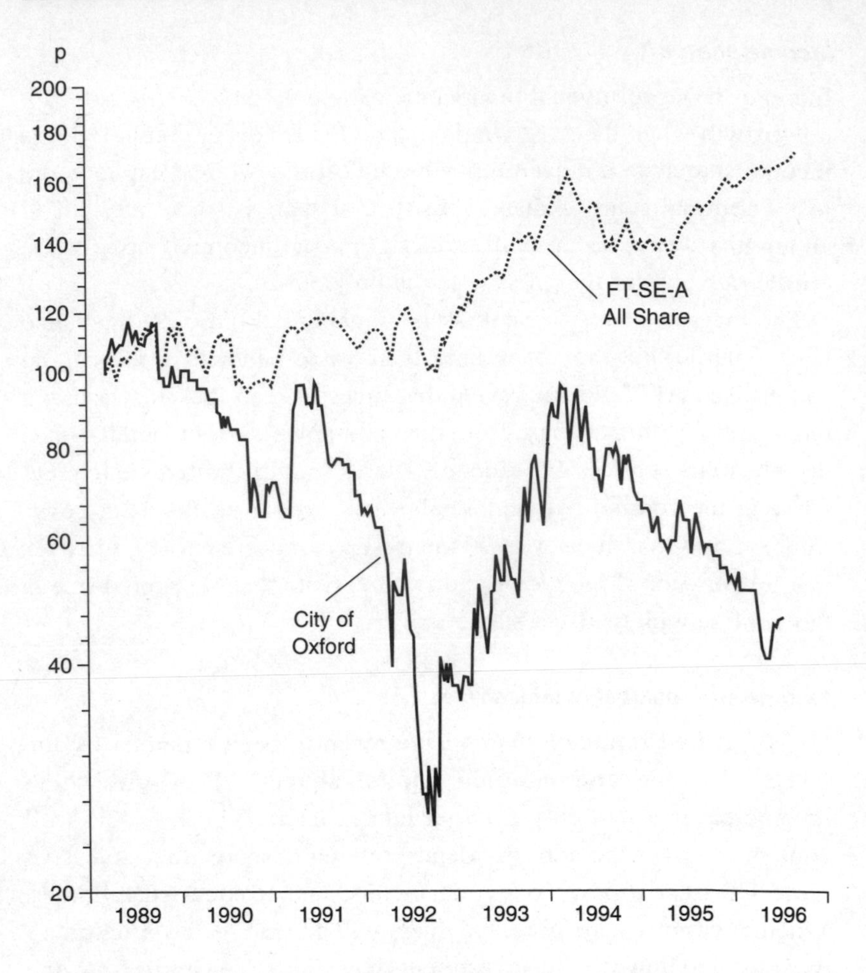

Fig I10 City of Oxford ordinary shares versus the FT-SE-A All-Share Index 1989–96

Source: Datastream

Zero dividend preference shares

Zero dividend preference shares pay no income, but offer a predetermined capital sum when the trust winds up. Look for the hurdle rate and the gross redemption yield. Look too for the trust's 'asset cover' – this ratio tell you how far the existing assets of the trust currently cover the promised payout on redemption.

Scottish National zeros have clocked up steady growth since 1987 (see Figure I11). The shares are considered a low-risk investment because they were normally repaid first among the classes of share issued by the trust. The AITC's hurdle rate shows that the trust's assets can shrink 14 per cent a year and still be enough to repay the zeros at 325p.

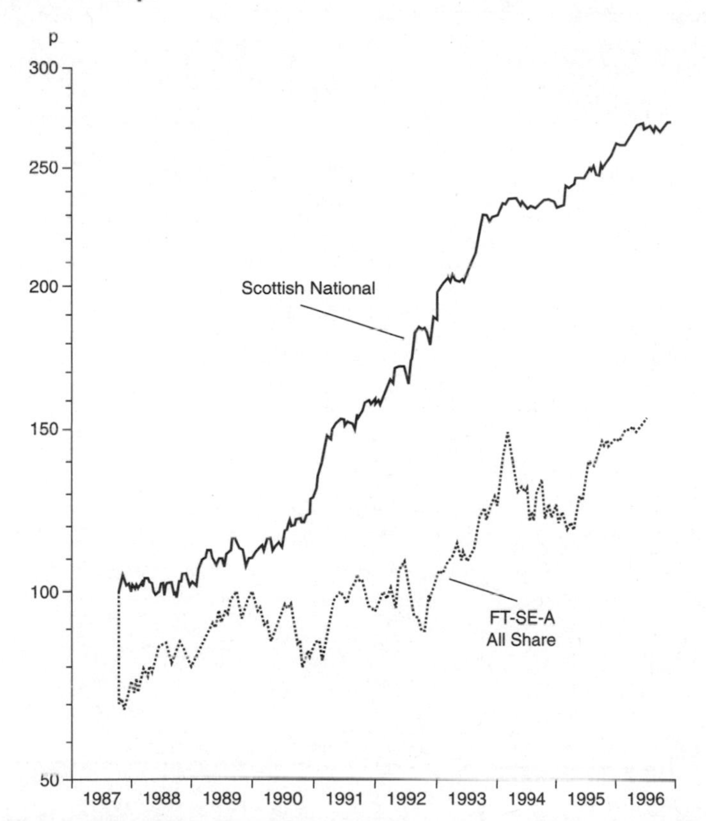

Fig I11 Scottish National zero dividend preference shares versus the FT-SE All-Share Index 1987–96

Source: Datastream

Stepped preference shares

Stepped preference shares have growth built in for income and capital. Few in number – well under a dozen trusts have issued them – they pay a predetermined dividend which increases by a given amount throughout each year of the trust's life. Again, look for the hurdle rate, the gross redemption yield and the asset cover in assessing these shares. Normally paid before most other classes of share, these shares are relatively low risk.

Scottish National's stepped prefs have shown steady growth, like the zeros (see Figure I12). Again this reflects its growing income and the fact that the trust will repay them at a fixed price and its robust asset cover of over seven times shows it can easily meet the obligation.

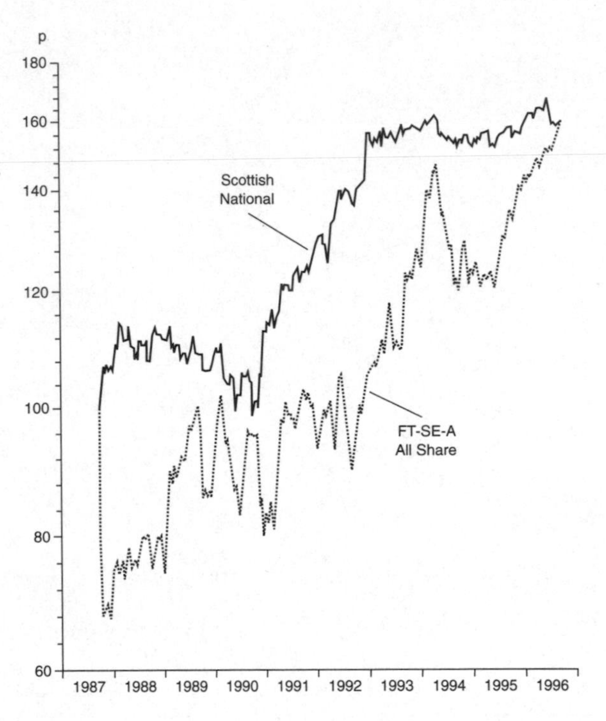

Fig I12 Scottish National stepped preference shares versus the FT-SE-A All-Share Index 1987–96

Source: Datastream

Capital indexed shares

Capital indexed shares are rare. Similar to the equity loan stock issued by some conventional trusts, the shares are linked to the performance of a share index, such as the FT-SE 100. On redemption they are supposed to make a capital payment in line with the growth in the index during the life of the trust.

The different types of share will have little wrinkles according to the structure of their trust. The trust will always spell out the terms of the shares, but split-capital trusts are complex. It is worth taking advice before you invest in split-capital investment trust shares.

ZERO DIVIDEND PREFERENCE SHARES

A zero dividend preference share is a share that has a predetermined rate of capital growth

Market Capitalisation (£m)	Share Price (pence)	NAV (pence)	Company	Years-months to wind-up	Redemption Price (pence)	Gross Redemption Yield (% p.a.)	Asset Cover (at wind-up)	Hurdle Rate (% p.a.)
25	248.5	222.6	OLIM Convertible	3.3	327.14	8.8	1.0	–0.2
14	136.5	127.0	River & Mercantile Extra Income	4.7	191.20	7.6	2.8	–26.2
38	96.0	92.7	River Plate & General	0.8	100.00	6.3	2.9	–79.7
49	129.5	109.3	Schroder Split Fund	5-11	203.00	7.9	1.5	–6.9
171	267.0	246.6	**Scottish National**	2-7	325.00	7.9	1.7	–14.1
4	60.00	58.7	SR Pan European	5-8	90.83	7.6	2.0	–11.8

CAPITAL SHARES

The capital share is the share that is entitled to the surplus assets on wind-up after repayment of other share classes

Market Capitalisation (£m)	Share Price (pence)	NAV (pence)	Discount/ +Premium (%)	Company	Years-months to wind-up	Gross Redemption Yield (% p.a.) assuming annual growth rates of 0%	5%	7.5%	10%	Hurdle rate % p.a.
16	25.0	84.4	70	**Scottish National**	2-7	–100.00	38.3	74.5	102.5	3.2
7	168.0	259.8	35	St David's	2-9	2.6	20.8	28.8	36.3	–0.6

STEPPED PREFERENCE SHARES

A stepped preference share is a share with a predetermined growth in both income and capital

Market Capitalisation (£m)	Share Price (pence)	NAQV (pence)	Dividend (net pence per share)	Gross Yield (%)	Company	Years-months to wind-up	Redemption Price (pence)	Gross Redemption Yield (% p.a.	Asset Cover (at wind-up)	Hurdle Rate (% p.a.	Annual Step (%)
27	161.5	120.4	13.3000	10.3	Fleming Geared Income & Assets'	11-11	100.00	11.5	2.0	–11.5	–
51	187.5	178.4	4.6365	3.1	General Consolidated	1-10	203.60	8.0	2.3	–35.8	+7.5
64	165.5	156.4	6.5157	4.9	River & Mercantile Trust	4-2	188.60	8.4	–22.4	+5.0	
51	161.0	150.8	7.3874	5.7	**Scottish National**	2-7	171.00	8.3	7.4	–47.4	+5.0
56	154.5	145.3	7.0355	5.7	TR Technology	2-2	161.20	8.8	2.6	–13.6	+5.0

Fig I13 Split-capital trusts – classes of share

Source: AITC 29 February 1996 MIS

INCOME AND RESIDUAL CAPITAL SHARES

An income & residual capital share is a share in a company with wind-up date designed to give shareholders a highly geared return both in term of capital and income

Market Capitalisation (£m)	Share Price (pence)	NAV (pence)	Discount/ +Premium (%)	Dividend (net pence per share)	Gross Yield (%)	Company	Years-months to wind-up	Gross Redemption Yield (% p.a.) assuming annual growth rates of 0%	5%	7.5%	10%	3yr div. growth %	Hurdle rate % p.a.
17	90.0	78.9	+14	13.0000	18.1	Abtrust Preferred Inc	2-3	–2.3	12.7	19.7	26.4	9.4	9.4
6	20.5	26.9	24	5.5000	33.5	**City of Oxford**	3-7	11.7	29.1	45.0	57.6	2.0	7.5
5	32.0	44.7	28	4.0000	15.6	Edinburgh Income	4-3	–0.9	21.1	29.4	36.8	–6.4	4.8
1	10.0	17.1	41	1.1200	14.0	Exmoor Dual	5-6	–5.3	–2.4	–0.9	36.2	–4.9	8.8

INCOME SHARES

An income share is the share that is entitled to the surplus income after expenses and after the income requirement of any prior charge has been met

Market Capitalisation (£m)	Share Price (pence)	Dividend (net pence per share)	Gross Yield (%)	Years-months to wind-up	Redemption Price (pence)	Company	Gross Redemption Yield (% p.a.) Assuming annual growth rates of 0%	5%	7.5%	10%	5yr div. growth (% p.a.	Asset Cover (at wind-up)	Hurdle Rate (% p.a.)
54	96.0	7.8500	10.2	5-11	100.00	Schroder Split Fund	6.7	13.8	16.4	19.0	–	0.5	2.3
142	89.0	7.9500	11.2	2-7	100.00	**Scottish National**	10.8	16.5	16.8	17.0	–1.6	0.9	1.8
9	111.0	16.0000	18.0	2-9	90.00	St David's	11.2	13.0	13.9	14.9	3.9	2.0	–10.0
9	38.0	7.1000	23.4	3-5	23.44	Throgmorton Dual	12.6	19.1	20.1	21.1	–	0.8	0.9

Fig I13 Contd.

'C' SHARE ISSUES

Sometimes investment trusts decide they need to raise more money and a 'C' share issue is their way of tapping existing and new investors for fresh funds. It is roughly comparable with a rights issue (see FUND-RAISING, page 73), but should not dilute existing shareholdings.

Box I4 **Top tips for choosing an investment trust**

- Look for a simple trust with one class of share
- Make sure you know what your investment objective is before you go shopping
- Use the AITC categorisation of trust to make whittling down the choices easier
- Most importantly, look at the asset value performance over a good range of time periods and make sure the trust outperforms its benchmark index
- Then look at the share price performance over the same time periods and check that it is broadly in line with the asset performance
- Do not buy a trust if it is standing at a premium of more than 2 or 3 per cent.

Source: Bridget Cleverly, Schroders Investment Management

One year	**Five years**	**10 years**
Larger groups Henderson Touche Remnant 3i Kleinwort Benson	Henderson Touche Remnant Foreign & Colonial Murray Johnstone	Foreign & Colonial Henderson Touche Remnant Edinburgh
Smaller groups Templeton Aberforth Cazenove	JO Hambro M&G Finsbury	M&G (out of five) – –

Remember that the annual awards are only a snapshot of performance. Look for firms that appear in the award tables year in, year out.

Fig I14 Award-winning investment trust managers, 1995

Source: Micropal/Planned Savings

MAKING THE MOST OF INVESTMENT TRUSTS

- Know what you want from your trust – income, capital growth, investment in the UK or internationally, or both, or exposure to the excitement of emerging markets in the Far East or Latin America.
- Decide how much you can invest – choosing between a lump sum of £1,500 or regular savings of £20 a month will narrow the number of trusts you need to consider.
- Look at the trust's discount or premium in the context of other trusts in the same sector and consider how the discount or premium has changed over a number of years. The Association of Investment Trust Companies (AITC) is the best source of information for private investors – its Monthly Information Service divides trusts into their sectors, gives the key statistics on net asset value and share price performance and full details of which ones are 'pepable', or have savings schemes. Anyone can get a free sample copy of the AITC's monthly bulletin and a year's UK subscription costs £35, from the AITC, 8–13 Chiswell Street, London EC1Y 4YY.
- Avoid buying potential fashion victim investment trusts at a premium. These include any of the niche areas such as single country or emerging market trusts.
- Be wary of investment trust new issues. Once the marketing campaign by the fund manager dries up, the shares may well go to a discount.
- Do not count on paying less commission when you buy shares through a savings scheme. A few savings schemes also charge commission for financial advisers on top of their own charges, whether or not the investor uses an adviser. Some schemes waive charges for buying, but charge for selling or for issuing a share certificate. There is also stamp duty, as on all share purchases.

Further reading

Money Management, owned by the same group as *Investors Chronicle*, and *Planned Savings* magazines, published monthly and sold in newsagents, also give full investment trust share price performance statistics. *Investment Trusts*, a quarterly magazine also available in newsagents, focuses exclusively on investment trusts. And *Investors Chronicle* reviews all investment trust accounts as they are published.

J

JARGON

Definition: **Technical language used by experts, or aspiring experts, in a specialist field.**

All investors complain about jargon and claim to avoid it at all costs, but it creeps in just the same. Arguably, investment jargon is an essential shorthand and investors should be suspicious only when they feel someone is using jargon as a way to dodge the important questions about an issue, or to hide a lack of knowledge. Here is a summary of the investment shorthand that crops up regularly in the financial Press or in talking to investment advisers. You will find some of these words and phrases – and others – explained throughout the book.

Basis point: A percentage point has 100 basis points. Investors tend to talk about interest rate movements, for example, in terms of basis points.

Bonus: With-profits policies are a form of stockmarket investment sold by life insurance companies (see LIFE INSURANCE, page 140). Investors in with-profits policies are buying a stake in a life company's with-profits fund, and they receive their investment returns as annual, or reversionary, bonuses and terminal bonuses. The point is that the bonuses should smooth out the peaks and troughs of stockmarket performance over the life of the policy, which can be from 10 to 30 years. The annual bonus will be less than the underlying asset growth in good years and more in bad years. Once the annual

'...investors should be suspicious when they feel someone is using jargon as a way to dodge the important questions about an issue, or to hide a lack of knowledge.'

bonus is added to the value of the policy, it cannot normally be taken away as long as you hold the policy for its full term. But the terminal bonus is far more volatile and can make up a sizeable chunk of the final payout. It reflects stockmarket conditions at the time and any gains which have still to be paid out.

Bulldog: A form of sterling bond issued by foreign borrowers. They are not 'pepable'.

Call options carry the right to buy something at a fixed price.

Crest is the electronic settlement system replacing the Stock Exchange's Talisman system from July 1996. 'Settlement' is the name for the exchange of money and share certificates and changes to companies' share registers that happen when people buy and sell shares. Having an electronic settlement system should remove most of the paper and speed up the system. Investors can still use share certificates under Crest if they choose. Crest, developed by the Bank of England, followed a failed Stock Exchange attempt to develop an electronic settlement system called Taurus.

Cycle: Why do the wood pulp cycle or the steel cycle matter to investors? The basic answer is that in times of rising demand for a product, manufacturers will expand their factory capacity to meet demand and take full advantage of the rising prices. They open too many new mills, supply outpaces demand, prices fall and the manufacturers start closing mills to cut capacity.

Margin is the collateral that an investor puts down to support his position if he is writing options or dealing in futures. When a broker makes a margin call he is looking for more collateral.

Nominees: Nominee companies are a familiar part of the investment scene. Stockbrokers, banks and investing institutions set up nominee companies to ease administration, but UK private investors tend to dislike allowing their shares to be put 'in a nominee'. It means that the shares are held in the name of the nominee company. The investor is the beneficial owner of the shares, but he has to arrange with the nominee company to receive annual reports and any shareholder perks. There may also be administration charges for using the nominee company and for transfers in and out of it. There also remain nagging doubts about the security of investments held in nominee accounts. However, all Pep investments are held in nominee accounts and modern share settlement systems (see **Crest**) often require shares to be held in nominee names or work more efficiently for shares held in nominee names.

OEICs: Open-ended investment companies (OEICs) are a form of pooled investment fund like unit trusts and investment trusts. They are already commonly used in the rest of Europe and, like companies, have a board of directors and can issue different classes of share. However, they are called 'open-ended' because their share capital is not fixed. Like unit trusts they can shrink or grow according to the amount of money they attract from investors. In the UK they will come under basically the same tax rules as unit trusts, and it is likely that many unit trusts will convert themselves into OEICs in order to attract funds from private investors outside the UK. In spring 1996, the financial watchdogs had still to finalise the rules for setting up OEICs.

Offshore investments tend to be based in places like Bermuda and the Cayman Islands, but Jersey, Guernsey and Dublin count as offshore as well. Tax is the main reason for moving offshore. In offshore roll-up funds you can postpone paying tax until you cash in the investment. Some investments, such as some types of futures funds, are not allowed in the UK and investors move offshore for the sake of a wider choice. Look out for surprisingly high charges, for custodian fees, for example, and always check whether you stand in line for any compensation if your investment goes wrong. You may be completely outside the UK financial services umbrella.

Pibs, or permanent interest bearing shares, are bonds issued by building societies. They pay a fixed rate of annual interest but are irredeemable – the building society will never buy them back under normal circumstances. It is possible to buy and sell Pibs through a stockbroker and the prices are published weekly in the *Financial Times* and some other newspapers.

Put options carry the right to sell something at a fixed price.

Volumes: The stockmarket's health relies heavily on the number of shares being traded – the more shares traded, the more money is going through the system. Investors will see volume measured by the number of shares changing hands, the value of the shares and the number of bargains, i.e., deals, completed. Steadily falling volumes mean falling profits for stockbrokers and job cuts in the City.

KICKBACKS

Definition: **A kickback is a payment to someone who has some influence in a deal or transaction in return for their help for arranging the deal. It is not always illegal, although it has that connotation.**

Within living memory, financial journalism was automatically considered to be corrupt. Journalists could easily profit from having information in advance of their readers. You could say it was a form of free sample from the companies they covered.

In theory however, investment still lends itself to shady dealing and much of it is legal. Here are the areas to beware.

Vast changes in communications technology have levelled the playing field by making financial information more freely and widely available. Once the Stock Exchange notices any unusual dealings – and it is reasonably easy to pick these up, given modern computing power – it can easily trace deals back through the stockbroker to the investor. In theory, however, investment still lends itself to shady dealing and much of it is legal. Here are the areas to beware.

COMMISSION AND CHARGES

The financial services industry uses commission to motivate financial advisers and their own salesforces to sell their products. Changes in the way the insurance companies must explain their charges should make it much easier for investors to see how much they are paying in commission to their adviser. So far, it remains complicated. If in doubt, ask your adviser what proportion of your investment will go in charges and commission to the adviser and the company.

Box K1

The Watchdogs

The Financial Services Act 1986, for all its faults, transformed the financial services industry and has made it much harder for crooks to thrive unhindered and for investors to stumble into trouble. It set up a group of regulators, since streamlined, to provide rule books for particular groups and to monitor their activities. Always check whether your adviser is authorised by one of the watchdogs, if not you are outside the rules for compensation. The Securities and Investments Board runs a helpline (telephone: 0171-929 3652) which will check whether a firm's name is on its list of authorised advisers. If you have a complaint, your first stop should be the firm's compliance officer. If you are still unhappy, contact the appropriate regulator.

Stockbrokers
The Securities and Futures Authority (SFA)
Cottons Centre, Cottons Lane, London SE1 2QB
Telephone: 0171-378 9000

Fund managers
The Investment Management Regulatory Organisation (Imro)
Lloyds Chambers, 1 Portsoken Street, London E1 8BT
Telephone: 0171-390 5000

Financial services companies selling to the public
The Personal Investment Authority (PIA)
1 Canada Square, Canary Wharf, London E14 5AZ
Telephone: 0171-538 8860

Chief watchdog
The Securities and Investments Board (SIB)
Gavrelle House, 2–14 Bunhill Row, London EC1 8RA
Telephone: 0171-638 1240

Note: The PIA has now taken over most of the work of two former watchdogs Fimbra and Lautro. However, lawyers and accountants tend to be regulated by their professional bodies such as the Law Society and the Institutes of Chartered Accountants. It remains unclear that the 'recognised professional bodies' are wholly effective in regulating their members.

The unit and investment trust industry has fought off plans to change the way trusts reveal charges and commission, but they can be absurdly high. Advisers may also receive a slice of the annual management fee as renewal commission. Over half of a 5 per cent upfront fee on a unit trust will go on commission, and if you buy your trust directly from the unit trust company, it may still charge the full fee. Ask for a rebate or discount, or consider using one of the discount unit trust dealers featured regularly in the personal finance Press.

CHURNING

An easy way for an adviser paid by commission on transactions to bump up his income is to roll over an investor's portfolio as frequently as possible, even if it is unnecessary. This is churning and the financial watchdogs have outlawed it. Look for fee-based advice. Stockbrokers are gradually switching to fee-based services and *Money Management*, a sister magazine of the *Investors Chronicle*, runs a register of fee-based financial advisers. However commission remains an element of advisers' income and it is important to find out why your investments are being bought and sold if it looks excessive.

EXECUTIVE SHARE OPTIONS

Long-running discontent about executive pay erupted in the row about Cedric Brown's pay as chief executive of British Gas. Share options also came under the spotlight, and the government removed some of the tax benefits that had made share options so attractive. Share options give the right to buy new shares in company at a fixed price, normally the market price at the time the options are issued. The principle is that company directors will do a better a job of growing profits and, as a result, the share price, if they have the prospect of an equity stake in the company. The problem is that sometimes it has been far too easy for directors to earn their share options. You can check the details of directors' share options in companies' annual accounts.

INSIDER DEALING

Insider dealing is benefiting from share deals where you have significant information about a company's prospects which has not been revealed to the whole market. Having inside knowledge, such as advance warning of a takeover bid or a large acquisition or a damaging court action, is only illegal if you deal on the back of that information.

CROOKERY

The main warning sign that an investment may be in the twilight zone will be exceptionally good returns. The 50 per cent annual return promised by some of the ostrich farming businesses in 1995–96 amounted to a large danger sign over the investment. Always compare promised returns with returns available on other investments or savings. It is easy to find out the bank base rate: just ask a local bank or building society, and the financial pages of newspapers will normally quote the current yield on shares and bonds. A call to a firm of private client stockbrokers should be enough to find out the current capital returns on shares and bonds. Any investment paying more than the general returns available means it is at least more risky than other investments and may be a fraud.

Box K2 Compensation schemes and ombudsmen

The Investors Compensation Scheme (ICS)
Gavrelle House, 2–14 Bunhill Row, London EC1Y 8RA
Telephone: 0171-628 8820

The ICS is the safety net for clients of failed investment companies. If a company that has misled, badly advised or defrauded investors is still in business, it has to compensate its clients itself. However, many firms collapse without assets and the ICS has to step in. It can only help investors who have a claim against firms that are regulated under the Financial Services Act. That is why it is so important to make sure your adviser or investment manager is authorised. Also, the ICS can normally only handle claims relating to events after 28 August 1988, the date it was set up.

Stocks and shares, unit trusts, futures and options, personal pensions and some long-term insurance plans all come under the ICS umbrella. However, it does not cover investments such as coins or antiques.

The maximum compensation paid by the ICS is £48,000. It pays the first £30,000 of an agreed claim in full and 90 per cent of the next £20,000.

Banks, building societies and insurance companies have their own compensation schemes and ombudsmen.

The banking, building society and insurance ombudsmen handle complaints once a customer has exhausted the complaints system of the bank or building society. The ombudsmen can order the bank or society to compensate customers.

The Office of the Banking Ombudsman
70 Gray's Inn Road, London WC1X 8NB
Telephone: 0345 660902

The Insurance Ombudsman Bureau
City Gate One, 135 Park Street, London SE1 9EA
Telephone: 0171-928 7600

K

K2 **The Building Societies' Ombudsmen**
Millbank Tower, Millbank, London SW1P 4XS
Telephone: 0171-931 0044

The compensation schemes step in if a bank, building society or insurance company goes under. However, like the ICS, they only pay a proportion of the sum lost by investors. It is important to spread savings across a number of banks and building societies to avoid falling outside the compensation limits.

The **Deposit Protection Board's** scheme pays 90 per cent of your loss up to £18,000.
19 Old Jewry, London EC2R 8HA
Telephone: 0171-601 3050

The **Building Societies' Commission**'s scheme pays 90 per cent of the sum lost in a building society collapse, subject to a maximum of £18,000.
15 Great Marlborough Street, London W1V 2LL
Telephone: 0171-437 9992

The **Policyholders' Protection Board**'s scheme pays 90 per cent of the value of funds in life insurance or pensions investments on the day the insurer went under, with no ceiling on the amount of compensation. It will pay 90 per cent of the money in claims under general insurance policies, as long as it decides they are valid.
51 Gresham Street, London EC2V 7HQ
Telephone: 0171-600 3333

LOSING THE LEAST ON KICKBACKS

- Understand the investment you are buying. There is no need to be offensively sceptical about the financial services industry. Many financial advisers and financial services firms set high standards of integrity and most investors expect to pay for a good service.

But you are vulnerable to misunderstanding if the investment is complicated and sold in a hurry.

- Avoid shares where the price yo-yos violently. Too often this is fuelled by market rumour where someone is making money from spreading gossip over-enthusiastically. Private investors are unlikely to be able to profit from volatile shares.
- Spread your investments, even cash. The high interest rate paid on large amounts and by small banks is a premium for risk. Even where compensation schemes cover a loss, they can take months, if not years, to settle claims and repay investors.
- Check the background of your adviser. The watchdogs will not be able to give an opinion on whether a firm is good or bad at giving advice, but they can tell you whether the firm is authorised. A surprising number of advisers operate outside the financial services rules.

L

LIFE INSURANCE

Definition: **Some life insurance is used as an investment as well as financial protection against death. In particular, an endowment is an insurance policy that links investment with life insurance. It will pay out whether or not you die within its term, and thousands of people in the UK have used endowment policies to repay their mortgages. Endowments are pooled investments, like unit trusts and investment trusts. Investors' money is pooled to cut risk and cost. However, endowments have a more complicated charging system than unit trusts or investment trusts. Term life assurance is pure insurance, and has no investment value. None of the criticisms of life insurance as an investment apply to term insurance, and it is to be recommended.**

A maturing endowment policy is a beautiful thing – years of monthly payments finally come good. The problem is that endowments, like all insurance-based investments, are costly and inflexible. Too much of the money put into an insurance-based investment goes into charges. Failing to hold the investment for its full term, which can be anything from 10 to 30 years, can mean swingeing penalties. What is more, cuts in bonuses over the last few years mean that some home-owners who bought during the 1980s housing boom will find the payment from the endowment covering their mortgage is too little to meet the mortgage debt.

Here are the main types of endowment:

- With-profits policies pay a return based on bonuses added to the original sum assured. There are annual bonuses and a terminal bonus. Look out for different types of annual bonus – sometimes it will be a percentage of the sum assured, and sometimes only a percentage of the bonuses already paid. Until the early 1990s, terminal bonuses had climbed to absurd heights, sometimes making up almost 50 per cent of the final payout. The system of bonuses, fixed by the life insurance company, should mean your investment builds up steadily over the life of the policy. In practice, with-profits payouts became relatively unpredictable as terminal bonuses grew in size compared with the annual bonuses.

- Unit-linked policies have a more direct link to the stockmarket than with-profits policies. Premiums buy units in stockmarket funds run by the life insurance company. As in unit trusts, the units grow – or shrink – in value along with the investments in the fund.

The charges on lump sum investments in insurance funds – such as with-profits bonds – are straightforward. Investors pay upfront charges and annual management charges. The charging system bites far harder on policies requiring regular monthly payments. On unit-linked policies, investors may pay premiums, but receive hardly any units in the investment fund. For example, in the early 1990s an investor paying £60 a month on a 25-year policy may only have had 70 per cent of the monthly payment buying units. The rest was going on charges.

Identifying the charges on with-profits funds is even harder than it is with unit-linked policies. Charges are deducted before the with-profits bonus is worked out. Investors rely on a calculation called annual reduction-in-yield. It can also be used to measure the effect of charges on unit-linked policies.

For example, the rate of return, or yield, on an investment is 10 per cent. An investor is paying £100 a month into an insurance fund. Over 25 years the charges can mean a reduction-in-yield of 1.7 per cent, says the insurance company's literature. That may not soud much, but over 25 years it comes to almost £30,000.

The worst effect of the insurance companies' charging system is that cashing in a policy early, even one year before the end of a 30-year policy, has a disproportionately large effect on the value of the investment. However, a large number of people do cash in early because they need the money unexpectedly.

Box L1

Second-hand endowments

You can sell your endowment policy rather than surrender it to the insurance company, and the market for second-hand endowments normally pays a far better rate than the insurer. The market is for with-profits endowments, and they must be at least a third of their way to maturity or be five years old, whichever is greater. The buyers of second-hand endowments still have plenty of scope to make money on their investment. They pay a better rate to the original investor than the insurer would pay, but it is still at a discount to the policy's true value. The buyer then continues the payments on the policy until it matures. The Association of Policy Market Makers (telephone: 0171-739 3949) will give you a list of firms that can deal in endowments. The main firms include:

Beale Dobie (telephone: 01621 851133)
Foster & Cranfield (telephone: 0171 608 1941)
Policy Portfolio (telephone: 0181-343 4567)
Securitised Endowment Contracts (telephone: 0181-207 1666).

Pressure on insurance companies to make their charges and the effect of cashing in early more explicit mounted with the crisis in the housing market. Homeowners, unable to cope with their mortgage payments, wanted to sell their houses and cash in their endowments. But they found their endowments were worth far less than they imagined. Insurance companies now have to spell out how much a salesman receives in commission, and the cash cost of ending a policy early.

Insurance companies now have to spell out how much a salesman receives in commission, and the cash cost of ending a policy early.

Insurance policies used to have significant tax advantages which partly made up for their fundamentally unfair charging structure. However, most of these advantages have been dismantled. Here are the main tax features of insurance-based investments.

- Life insurance policies bought before 14 March 1984 carry tax relief on the premiums. The tax relief is a further reason to hold the policy to maturity as it boosts the return on the investment.
- Returns on life insurance investments bought from friendly societies – the best-known include Family, Tunbridge Wells, Liverpool Victoria and Homeowners – are tax-free. The most you can invest in a tax-free plan is £270 a year or £25 a month, although the friendly societies always lobby for this to be increased.
- The insurance company pays basic-rate income tax and capital gains tax before the investor receives his return. As with other investments higher-rate taxpayers have to pay a further 20 per cent in tax. With lump sum insurance investments – called single premium bonds – the tax rules do allow investors to take an annual income worth 5 per cent of the original sum invested without having to pay the higher-rate tax right away. The tax bill is worked out when the bond matures. This is highly attractive to investors due to retire who expect to have dropped down a rung on the tax ladder by the time they cash in their investment.

MAKING THE MOST OF INSURANCE-BASED INVESTMENTS

- Try to avoid investing through insurance policies, whether it is through regular savings or through insurance bonds.
- If you must buy an insurance-based investment, keep the charges to a minimum by opting for a lump sum investment.
- Make sure you hold any existing insurance-based investments to maturity.
- If you want to cash in your policy early, find out how much it is worth on the second-hand endowment market (see box L1) before you surrender it to your life company.
- Remember that the returns on most insurance-based investments are not tax-free, it is just that you have no further tax to pay unless you are a higher-rate taxpayer.

- Look at the past performance of life insurers' funds – there can be huge differences.
- If you do want an endowment mortgage, go for a with-profits policy which at least carries less risk than a pure stockmarket investment. Avoid unit-linked endowments at all costs.

LLOYD'S

Definition: **Lloyd's of London dates from the 17th century and is the world's oldest insurance market. Underwriters, on behalf of their names, accept liability for specific losses in return for a premium. Until 1993, investors in Lloyd's, known as Names, were individual members organised through a system of agents. The Names had unlimited liability and could be asked to part with their 'last cufflink' to meet insurance claims. The agents arranged Names' investment in a range of syndicates. Now private investors in Lloyd's invest through companies with limited liability, although there is still some unlimited liability investment. Lloyd's losses finally tipped it into public crisis in 1993. By late August 1996 it believed it had reached a lasting solution to its problems.**

L

Lloyd's reputation is based on meeting all insurance needs, however risky or bizarre. It can still trumpet a spotless record on meeting all valid claims. However, in five underwriting years from 1987 to 1992, the market clocked up serious losses. By early 1996, the losses came to £7.9bn. Two main factors seem to have fuelled these losses: first, the so-called 'long-tail' liabilities in the US on long-running issues such as asbestosis, the effects of pollution and health risks, and secondly, a cluster of disasters within a short period, including the Piper Alpha oil rig disaster in 1988, hurricanes and the 1992 Los Angeles riots. The losses were compounded because syndicates and companies had reinsured themselves with each other.

Lloyd's reputation is based on meeting all insurance needs, however risky or bizarre.

Box L2

What's in a Name?

Lloyd's Names had held on to their reputation for great wealth, but many had in fact little capital backing. The wealth threshold for becoming a name in the 1980s was £100,000, excluding your house. However, investors found they could get bank guarantees based on the value of their houses. With hindsight, this was most unwise.

The threshold for Names has been £250,000 since 1990, and bank guarantees must not include your house. Names must also deposit funds worth 30 per cent of the business they are doing at Lloyd's. Wealthy individuals with assets of at least £500,000 can qualify to do larger-scale business if they meet further financial guarantees. Investors can also opt to turn themselves into a limited-liability company and use that route to invest, but Lloyd's investment trusts will be a good route for the majority of small investors. Traded on the UK stockmarket and classified under insurance in the share price listings, the trusts are more risky than conventional investment trusts. After all, they are specialists. Some invest in syndicates run by a range of managing agents, other stick to syndicates run by just one agent. The main trusts on the market in early 1996 are as follows:

Abtrust Lloyd's Insurance Trust
Angerstein Underwriting Trust
CLM Insurance Fund
Euclidian
Finsbury Underwriting Investment Trust
HCG Lloyd's Investment Trust
Hiscox Select Insurance Fund
Kiln Capital
London Insurance Market Investment Trust
Masthead Insurance Underwriting
Matheson
New London Capital
Premium Underwriting
Syndicate Capital Trust
Wellington Underwriting

Note that these trusts carry more risk than conventional investment trusts. It is important to research a potential investment carefully and to take advice before investing.

In 1993 the Names, many claiming they were unable as well as unwilling to meet their liabilities, revolted, arguing that some agents and syndicates had bent the rules and their malpractice had contributed to the losses. Some of the Names settled their claims, but in late August 1996, with the deadline for a solution closing fast, Lloyd's had to scramble to pull a deal together. At the time of this book going to press, Lloyd's had claimed success.

The main planks of the solution at that stage were:

- Separating the pre-1993 Lloyd's claims liabilities into another company, Equitas.
- Settling the legal claims – Lloyd's offered £800m and £2bn of debt credits to bail out people who cannot meet their share of the bill for closing the pre-1993 books. The debt credits effectively waive that part of the debt.

Box L3

Lloyd's – the phrasebook

Syndicates: Forming syndicates means Names have enough funds between them to spread their risk. Syndicates tend to follow one class of business – marine, non-marine, aviation or motor. Composites, a mix of these classes of business, are becoming more common.

Underwriters: Underwriting agents fall into two main groups. Members' agents run a Name's underwriting affairs. They place him on syndicates and allocate premium limits, i.e., the total premium income a Name is allowed to accept. Managing agents handle the underwriting of syndicates. They accept insurance risks and invest the premium income.

MAKING THE MOST OF LLOYD'S

- Do not invest in Lloyd's just because it sounds good. The social statement of being a Lloyd's Name no longer applies.
- The best way for investors to buy a stake in Lloyd's may well be to go through one of the Lloyd's investment trusts, or to buy shares directly in a Lloyd's managing agent. AJ Archer and Ockham are both listed on the main stockmarket. However, these trusts carry their own risks. Take advice.

Further reading

The annual reports of the stockmarket-listed underwriters are very helpful – contact the company secretaries of AJ Archer and Ockham.

MARGIN TRADING

***Definition:* Margin trading is the practice of borrowing to invest in the stockmarket.**

Margin trading is slowly establishing itself in the UK. It makes sense for experienced investors, with portfolios big enough to survive possible losses, to borrow money to invest. The bulk of private investors are best advised to steer clear for the present, however.

The principles of margin trading are simple. You pay a proportion, perhaps 50 per cent, of the cost of your share buying upfront. That is your margin. The rest of the cost comes from a loan facility you have set up with your broker. The loan is secured on the shares you are buying. However, it is possible for an investor to secure loans on shares he already owns in his own right.

You normally have to repay the loan within a certain time, and this is where margin trading comes into its own for serious traders. If you buy and sell the shares quickly enough, in theory at a profit, you never have to put up fresh capital of your own. You just keep rolling over the investment. Being able to 'gear up' your portfolio in this way means you have the chance of making more money. But if gearing pushes up the gains, it also pushes up the losses.

Brokers, the people lending the money or arranging the loan, protect themselves by having the right to make a margin call – asking you to put up more cash or further security if the price of the shares covered by your loan is falling. If you cannot meet the margin call, you have to sell the shares. In theory, that protects the investor and the broker. The investor should lose only the margin he put up in the first place, the broker does not lose at all.

So far in the UK, margin trading is out of bounds for most private investors. The stockbrokers who do lend or arrange loans to investors limit the service to those with very large portfolios. However, a new

'So far in the UK, margin trading is out of bounds for most private investors.'

pressure for change comes with the start in 1996 of Crest, the long-awaited electronic share settlement system. Crest will greatly increase the use of nominees, a system where individual shareholders keep their holdings under their stockbroker's name. Margin trading, or its equivalent, has been common in the United States for many years. Its popularity was a factor in the Wall Street Crash when margin trading was unregulated. Arguably, however, it was the arrival of the US equivalent of Crest (see JARGON, page 129) in the 1970s and better regulation that triggered the most recent growth in margin trading in the United States.

Bank accounts run by stockbrokers for clients are a logical next step after nominee accounts. The end-result should be that stockbrokers, who are also having to upgrade their systems to cope with Crest, will have a better grasp of their clients' true financial position. Their improved knowledge and access to clients' assets mean they will be more likely to consider margin trading or a general loan, perhaps for purposes other than buying more shares, such as to fund a car or a holiday.

MAKING THE MOST OF MARGIN TRADING

The whole point of margin trading is being able to borrow cheaply in order to invest, so it will always pay to shop around for competitive interest rates. However, other issues should be beyond haggling. So far there are no explicit rules governing margin trading in the UK, but stockbrokers hope that the financial watchdogs will step in eventually. Matthew Orr, of private client stockbrokers Killik & Co, argues that investors need clear guidelines on:

- the type of assets suitable as a basis for margin trading, i.e., would it be appropriate to lend money against a portfolio of highly volatile, hard to trade, small company shares – probably not;

- the point at which the stockbroker should make an additional margin call when share prices have fallen, for example;
- the point at which an investor should close out his position or put in more cash: this could be when the balance of debt to equity has reached 75/25.

Avoid dealing with any stockbroker – or any other type of financial adviser – who offers a margin trading facility without covering these three issues.

Further reading

The Great Crash 1929, JK Galbraith (Penguin)

N

NEW ISSUES

***Definition:* An issue of new shares in a company which is going to list its shares on the stockmarket for the first time. The company can be newly established, or previously privately or State-owned. Strictly, the term 'ne w issue' can also apply to issues of new shares in companies already on the stockmarket (see FUND-RAISING, page 73).**

Privatisation fever in the 1980s gave the UK investor a sugar-sweet introduction to share ownership. It was the heyday of the new issue, and private investors flocked to buy into established businesses like British Telecom and British Gas. Sid, the mythical private investor dreamed up by the British Gas advisers, was born.

On the whole the Sids did very nicely in the 1980s. Politics influenced the way the privatisation issues were priced – low enough to trigger an immediate profit for short-term investors, but with a generous dividend yield to make the shares attractive as a long-term holding. Sometimes it was a give-away. Investors who bought shares in British Telecom at the partly-paid new issue price of 50p in 1984 enjoyed an instant profit of 86 per cent, just 24 hours after the shares started trading on the stockmarket. But there are plenty of new issue sob stories to counter the contented BT investors. Here are the mechanics of new issues and tips for spotting the winners and the duds.

Companies can bring their shares to the market for the first time in five ways: an offer for sale, an offer for subscription, a placing, an intermediaries offer, or an introduction.

An **offer for sale** means the company employs an adviser, such as a merchant bank or its sponsoring broker, to buy shares in the company and sell them on to the public at a fixed price.

An **offer for subscription** means the company or its adviser invites the public to buy shares not yet in issue.

'... there are plenty of new-issue sob stories to counter the contented BIT investors.'

A **placing** means the company, assisted by its advisers, sells all or some of its shares to specific investors, rather than to the general public or existing investors in the company. It is most unusual for private investors to be able to buy shares in a placing, although some brokers may be able to break into the magic circle on your behalf. Institutions, with more money to spend, tend to be first in the queue.

An **intermediaries offer** means the company sells shares to an intermediary, i.e., a stockbroker or financial adviser, so that the intermediary can sell them on to its clients.

An **introduction** happens when the shares are already held by large numbers of investors. The difference is that now the shares will be listed on the stockmarket for the first time. This is how many companies formerly traded under Stock Exchange rule 4.2 – a matched bargain facility where buyers and sellers had to find each other to do the deal – graduated to the Alternative Investment Market in 1995 and 1996 (see ACCOUNTS ANALYSIS, page 15).

Sometimes companies use an **offer for sale** or **for subscription by tender** to list. Here potential investors bid for the shares, with the issuing house setting a minimum issue price. The shares are all sold at a striking price – normally the best price offered, or slightly lower – once all the applications are in. This practice is well-established in the United States, where companies and advisers issue a 'red herring', or pathfinder prospectus in advance to gauge interest. Pathfinder prospectuses are familiar in the UK, and the idea is increasingly gaining ground for all types of fund-raising.

Assuming a company satisfies the exchange's conditions of listing (see *Box N2*), it will issue a prospectus. This document gives as much information about the company as it is ever likely to publish – far more than any annual report.

Box N1

Sock Shop

Sock Shop, the UK hosiery retailer, came to the stockmarket in May 1987 to raise almost £5m. It issued 3.9m shares at 125p, but it received applications for 206.3m shares – it was 53 times oversubscribed. The shares more than doubled to 257p on the first day of trading and climbed to 330p in 1988. Less than three years later, in February 1990, the shares were suspended at 34p and the banks sent in the administrators. Its market capitalisation of £7.5m was less than half its debt. The company went into liquidation in August and the business was bought by another company.

To be fair, hindsight makes everyone an expert. Yes, Sock Shop floated on an ambitious forward PE ratio of 24 (see ACCOUNTS ANALYSIS, page 1), but in summer 1987 the stockmarket was going like a train. Ambitious PE ratios were considered normal. Sock Shop had a record of fast profits growth, and its rapid expansion had given it a high profile. Investors who bought on flotation made a 164 per cent profit if they sold at the 330p share price peak. The trick was to spot that the story had turned sour, and sell the shares before the banks stepped in.

Box N2

Why can't my cat have a listing?

Businesses usually opt for a flotation, listing, or quotation – all names for the same process – because they want to raise money to expand the business, and perhaps because the owners want to cash in some of the capital they have built up in the company. It also puts a firm value on the company. The Stock Exchange has some demanding rules for companies which want to be listed. Companies must find a financial adviser prepared to act as its sponsor, but they must also have:

- published or filed accounts for at least three years which have had a completely clean bill of health from the company's independent auditors;

N2
- had continuity of management throughout the three years covered by the accounts;
- have directors who have between them appropriate expertise and experience for the business, and no conflicts of interest with their duties to the company;
- have sufficient working capital for its present needs;
- be capable of making decisions independently of any controlling shareholder, i.e., someone with 30 per cent or more of the voting rights in the company, or able to control a majority of the company directors.

Companies must also expect to have a minimum market capitalisation of £700,000, and at least 25 per cent of their shares should be in public hands. If the percentage in public hands falls below 25 per cent, the exchange reserves the right to suspend the shares from trading.

USING A PROSPECTUS WELL

The prospectus tells investors how much money the company is raising, in what way and with what purpose. It gives details of the company's history – including its financial record – the nature of its business and its markets, its current trading position and its prospects. There will be descriptions of the directors' background and the senior management. It supplies letters from the company's advisers vouching for the accuracy of the figures in the prospectus, and also lists the risks entailed in buying shares in the company. These can range from statements of common sense – 'prolonged cold weather could adversely affect sales of our ice cream products' – to the outrageous. The prospectus for Optical Care (Bermuda), set up to sell low cost spectacles in Eastern Europe, and traded on the Alternative Investment Market, warned: 'No assurance can be given that organised or other crime or official corruption will not in the future have material and adverse effect on the company.'

A prospectus can be a difficult read, thanks to the wealth of information it offers. But a company is unlikely ever again to go into similar depth about its businesses and finances. It is worth reading beyond the summary page of 'key information' such as the PE ratio and dividend yield. After all, a company's advisers will have worked hard to make these figures attractive in comparison with similar businesses already on the market. Details about the directors and senior management can be very revealing, as can details of the directors' contracts. For example, how much are the directors paid, and how long a notice period must the company give directors? Directors with generous notice periods under rolling contracts can walk away with enormous pay-outs, even if they have performed badly. The prospectus also gives details of major contracts and outstanding litigation which the company would keep a lid on in normal circumstances.

Companies coming to the stockmarket also make a commitment to share information with their shareholders. A company must announce, via the Stock Exchange, any information 'necessary to enable holders of the company's listed securities and the public to appraise the position of the company and to avoid the establishment of a false market in its listed securities'. The Stock Exchange also expects companies to submit drafts of all circulars to shareholders for approval, and will block transactions which it deems inappropriate. That rule is particularly useful in preventing small companies with stockmarket listings behaving like private companies, for example, putting through deals which may benefit large shareholders or directors more than the other shareholders in the company.

Private investors have always liked new issues, even when the companies have been a far more risky investment than British Telecom or British Gas, both effective monopolies when they came to the market. Part of the attraction has been the scope for quick profits.

If you believe a new issue will be very popular, you can gamble that the shares will rise sharply in price when they start trading. The name for this type of gamble is 'stagging'. Companies invite people to subscribe for a limited supply of shares. If too many people apply for shares, i.e., the issue is oversubscribed, people will receive fewer shares than they want and are prepared to buy them in the market when the shares start trading. Strong demand and limited supply mean the price rises, and people who did get shares at the offer price can sell at a profit. However, the share price is likely to fall, if too few people have subscribed for shares and there is an 'overhang' of shares in the market.

Knowing about likely flotations is extremely useful. Companies must advertise their prospectus in at least one national newspaper. Some go further in promoting their shares to the public, running their application form as advertisements. However, some are more discreet and the prospectus, available from the stockbroker or from the company, can be the only source for an application form. It can be quite a scramble, as there is often little time for investors to get an application form, let alone post it before applications close and trading starts in the shares.

The financial Press always has stories of likely flotations, and the *Investors Chronicle* publishes a weekly table of companies due to float, or rumoured to be about to float.

It has become significantly more difficult for private investors to take part in new issues, even for keen stags. In 1996 the Stock Exchange scrapped its rule demanding that companies coming to the market with a market capitalisation of more than £50m should offer a proportion of their shares to the general public. The rule change cuts the cost of gaining a stockmarket listing – public offers are undoubtedly expensive – and in theory, companies can still choose to offer shares to the public. Companies worth more than £100m will probably continue to run public offers when they come to the market. However, the overall effect has been to limit choice and opportunity for the private investor, although some stockbrokers have stepped in to fill the gap (see *Making the most of new issues*, on page 160).

Box N3

Looking at a new issue in practice

Orange, the mobile phone company owned by Hong Kong telecoms group Hutchison Telecom and British Aerospace, came to the market in April 1996 (see Figure N1 under 'Market newcomers: recent issues'). It floated just 25 per cent of its shares, encouraging investors to believe that Hutchison and BAe had faith in Orange's prospects. Otherwise they would have sold more of their shares. The issue, which was open to the general public, was very popular. Its market value of £2.45bn was less than analysts expected, and the shares moved to a 15 per cent premium above the 205p issue price. However, the *Investors Chronicle* pointed out that the long-term prospects of Orange were less rosy than the story so far. It had grown fast since starting in 1994, but each new subscriber came at a high cost and profit were a long way off – '1999', said analysts. When Orange floated, it was still subsidising each handset by £200. Losses in 1994 and 1995 were £119m and £140m respectively. The *Investors Chronicle* advised caution – the cable television and telephone companies were also floated on the back of long-term profit forecasts, but failed to meet expectations. The Orange prospectus detailed 19 risk factors, under headings such as 'limited operating history', 'operating and net losses', 'deficiency of net assets'; 'significant competition'; 'substantial indebtedness'; 'ability to manage growth and expansion'; and 'network construction risk'.

MARKET NEWCOMERS: COMING SOON

Company	Contact	Main activity	When expected	Likely value	Likely method of issue
Gartmore Japan	Panmure Gordon 0171 638 4010	Investment trust	15 April	£25m	Placing/offer
		Gartmore's Japanese unit trust has performed well, but not as well as some existing Japanese investment trusts.			
Cliveden	Beeson Gregory 0171 488 4040	Hotel and country club owner	11 April	£30m	Placing
		Owns Cliveden, a stately home hotel in Berkshire. Raising £8m for acquisitions. See IC 29 March p86.			
FI Group	UBS 0171 901 3751 Granville 0171 488 1212	Computer services	10 April	£60m	Placing
		Raising £6m of new money. Priced at 235p putting it on a PE of 21 which looks about right. See IC 15 March p 95.			

The 'Market Newcomers' table gives the first whispers of new flotations. The Sunday newspapers, normally fed stories of new issues by the companies' public relations advisers, are also a good source of flotation gossip. Some never come to the market, however. The less information, the more speculative the story.

ON OFFER THIS WEEK

Company	Contact	Main activity	Which market	Market value £m	% equity floated	Method of issue	Price announced	Application date	First dealings	Issue price p	Prosp PE ratio	Div yield %	Date of IC comment
Xavier Computer	St James's Ptnrs 0171 439 6005	Computer services	Ofex	5.1	25	Subscription	26 Feb	Early Apr	20 Mar	10	13	–	–
			£1.3m is being raised to complete purchase of Xavier computer systems. Group is chaired by Allan Harle, ex-Formscan.										

Once companies reach the 'On Offer This Week' table, investors have to move fast to get a prospectus and subscribe for shares. Given that companies no longer have to make a retail offer, investors will probably have to go through a broker's new issues service. A low percentage of equity floated is normally a good sign – existing investors are sticking with the company. The application date – sometimes confirmed late on in the offer – is the deadline for share applications.

MARKET NEWCOMERS: RECENT ISSUES

Company	Main activity	Market	% floated	Market Makers	Method	Issue price p	First dealings	Market value £m	Price on 25.03.96	% change since Issue	Prosp PE ratio	Div yield %	Last comment
Orange	Mobile phone operator	Main	25	–	Placing/offer	205	2 Apr	2447.0	–	–	–	–	15 Mar p95
		The retail offer has been oversubscribed which suggests the shares should get off to a brisk start. But profits are a long way off.											

Applications for shares in companies in the Market Newcomers table have closed, but investors can see whether they went to a premium when trading started and, by the number of market makers, how easy it will be to trade the shares. Two market makers is the minimum for companies on the main market.

Fig N1 Extracts from 'New Issues' section, *Investors Chronicle*, 29 March and 5 April 1996

MAKING THE MOST OF NEW ISSUES

- Dealing-only stockbrokers offering a new issue service include the Share Centre (telephone: 01442 890800), ShareLink (telephone: 0121-200 2474) and Barclays Stockbrokers, which also has an advisory arm, (telephone: 0800 551177). The services are not perfect, and as ever, investors should shop around.
- Ask your stockbroker to approach the broker – known as the issuer – running a placing. The issuer cannot deal with you directly, but can deal with your stockbroker. A good private client stockbroker will have existing relationships with firms that regularly handle new issues.
- Only a minority of each year's new issues turn out to be a good investment at the issue price. Even if the price rises once the shares start trading – this is known as going to a premium – it may well slip back later. Watch out for opportunities to buy in the market at a better price.

O

OPTIONS

Definition: **An option gives the right, but not the obligation, to buy or sell something at a given price and time. Investors will encounter two types of option – traditional and traded. A put option gives the right to sell and a call option gives the right to buy. (See Box O1 below for more definitions.)**

Box O1

Options – the phrasebook

A **call option** carries the right to buy something at a fixed price. A **put option** carries the right to sell something at a fixed price.

In-the-money options have some intrinsic value – on a call option this means the strike price is less than the price of the underlying goods. **Out-of-the-money** options have no intrinsic value – on a call option this means the strike price is more than the price of the underlying goods.

Margin is the collateral that an investor puts down to support his position if he is writing options. When a broker makes a margin call he is looking for more collateral.

The **premium** is the price of an option, and the strike price or exercise price is the fixed price at which you have the right to buy or sell.

Volatility reflects how much the price of the underlying goods is likely to bounce around.

Writing or **selling** options means that someone accepts the riskier side of an options contract. He accepts an obligation to buy or sell shares at a fixed price.

Options, despite their reputation for complexity and high risk, can give a refreshingly different slant on stockmarket investment. Dealing in options means taking a view on whether a share is going to move up or down in price, by how much and how quickly. Valuing options intelligently requires a view on the market as a whole, the economy, interest rates and the volatility of the individual share as well as an opinion of the share's underlying value.

TRADED OPTIONS

If an option gives an investor the right to buy or sell a share at a given price, traded options allow you to buy and sell the right itself. The holder of an option has no obligation to buy the share, and the option runs out after nine months, leaving the investor with a profit or having lost his investment. The immediate appeal of traded options is that investors need to put up far less cash to buy an option than they would to buy the equivalent number of shares. As a result they can make far larger percentage gains, as the very basic cost comparison in *Box O2* (opposite) shows. But it is also significant that throughout the nine-month life of a traded option investors have a choice about exercising their right to buy or sell the share and they can sell the option itself.

Options, despite their reputation for complexity and high risk, can give a refreshingly different slant on stockmarket investment.

Box 02 **Cost comparison: options versus shares**

Reuters shares are 767p and you expect them to rise to £10. For £1,000 you can buy rights over 100,000 Reuters shares.

1 Price behaves as you hoped and rises to £10

	Buying 100,000 Reuters shares £	**Buying 100,000 Reuters options £**
Initial cost	767,000	1,000
Cost of exercising option	–	850,000
Proceeds of sale	1,000,000	1,000,000
Profit	**233,000**	**150,000**
Return	**30%**	**150%**

2 Price moves in the wrong direction and falls to 700p. You do not exercise your option.

	Buying 100,000 Reuters shares £	**Buying 100,000 Reuters options £**
Initial cost	767,000	1,000
Cost of exercising option	–	–
Proceeds of sale	700,000	–
Loss	**67,000**	**1,000**
Return	**–9%**	**–100%**

Depending on how you use options, it is possible to limit your risk to losing small sums or to lose an infinite amount. The authorities' suspicion of options trading led them to ban it in the UK between 1734 and 1860, and again between 1939 and 1958. The practical appeal of options lies in their capacity, when properly used, to give investors some insurance against falling share values. The more you pay, the more insurance you get. Experienced options investors can also use options to generate income from their existing portfolios and to take limited bets on share price movements.

SO YOU WANT TO BUY AN OPTION ...

1 Choose your investment.
2 What direction is that investment going to follow?
3 By how much is it going to move?
4 How long will it take to make that move?

Shares in Reuters, the information systems and media group, stand at 767p in early April 1996. You decide that shares in Reuters are going up. (The numbers are deliberately unrealistic to keep the example simple.)

Route 1

You think Reuters shares are going to rise dramatically – going up to £10 within a month. An out-of-the-money call option will give you maximum gearing – a relatively small outlay opens up the chance of very large returns. The 850p April call option costs 1p. You have to acquire rights over at least 1,000 shares – a contract, or lot, so that is a minimum investment of £10. But dealing costs mean that a larger investment, such as £1,000, makes more sense. Investing £1,000 buys control of 100,000 shares worth £767,000. If you are right you will be able to exercise your option to buy the shares at 850p. Selling them at £10 will bring a profit of £150,000. The risk – quite a big risk, as you can imagine – is that Reuters shares stay well below 850p, your option expires worthless and you lose your £1,000. The key is to remember that you can cut your losses by selling the option in the market before it expires.

Route 2

You still think Reuters shares are going to rise, but slowly. You buy an in-the-money call option – the October 700p call for 103p. It has 67p of intrinsic value – the difference between 700p and 767p – and 36p of time value, allowing for the possible rise in the shares between April and October. The intrinsic value of your call option will grow as long as the shares rise in value, but the time value will decay as the months pass. The ideal situation is to be able to sell your option –

close your position – and take a profit before the time value goes altogether. The worst situation is to forget to do anything with the option before it expires – you will lose the money you invested upfront.

Options become seriously risky for investors when they move from buying options to selling, or writing them. When you sell an option – except when you are reversing out of an earlier deal – you are accepting an obligation to buy or sell the security underlying that option. The risks are obvious, particularly with hindsight. You write a put option on 1,000 shares in a food manufacturer, for example. At some time in the nine months before the option expires, a scare about salmonella in chickens wipes 20 per cent off the value of the manufacturer's shares, and the person who bought your option decides to exercise it. If you have the cash to buy the shares, this is merely unfortunate. If not, you are in trouble. Either way you end up out of pocket. In short, selling options is an altogether more difficult business than buying them, and private investors interested in this route will find a number of obstacles in their way. Some stockbrokers are reluctant to accept deals of this type, and investors need to put down more money upfront than in other types of option trade.

There is more to say on writing options, but first, here is an introduction to the basic mechanics of traded options. Private investors should find it reasonably easy to find information on traded options and to deal in them. They are easily available for the FT-SE 100 Index, and for most of the leading UK companies. Figure O1 lists the companies for which it is possible to buy and sell options.

LANGUAGE

The language of options can be a difficult barrier for options newcomers, but there is plenty of help on hand (see details of the Liffe literature in *Box O3,* on page 168). The holder of a call option has the right to buy shares. The holder of a put option has the right to sell shares. In each case a fixed price will apply – the strike price or exercise price – and when an investor puts his right to buy or sell into action he is exercising his option. The price of an option is called the

Share	Expiry cycle	Share	Expiry cycle
Abbey National	J	Lasmo	F
Allied Domecq	J	Lonrho	M
Amstrad	M	Lloyds TSB	M
Asda	J	Lucas Industries	F
BAA	J	Marks & Spencer	J
Barclays Bank	M	National Power	J
Bass	J	NatWest	J
BAT	J	Orange	M
Blue Circle	F	P&O	F
Boots	J	Pilkington	F
BP	J	PowerGen	J
British Aerospace	F	Prudential	F
British Airways	J	Railtrack	M
British Gas	M	Redland	F
BSkyB	M	Reuters	J
British Steel	J	Rolls Royce	F
British Telecom	F	Royal and Sun Alliance	J
BTR	F	RTZ	F
Cable & Wireless	J	J. Sainsbury	J
Cadbury Schweppes	F	Scottish Power	M
Commercial Union	J	Sears	M
Courtaulds	J	Shell	J
Dixons	M	SmithKline Beecham	J
GEC	F	Standard Chartered	J
Glaxo Wellcome	J	Storehouse	J
Granada	M	Tarmac	M
Grand Met	F	Tesco	F
Guinness	F	Thames Water	J
Hanson	F	Thorn EMI	M
Hillsdown	M	Tomkins	M
HSBC	J	Trafalgar House	J
ICI	J	Unilever	J
Kingfisher	F	United Biscuits	F
Ladbroke	F	Vodafone	F
Land Securities	J	Williams Holdings	F
		Zeneca	J

Expiry cycles: J – January, April, July, October; F – February, May, August, November; M – March, June, September, December.

Fig O1 Traded options: the companies (at August 1996)
Source: LIFFE

premium, and investors normally buy options in units of 1,000. So if the price of an option is 10p, the minimum investment is £100.

Remember that, like shares, options have bid/offer spreads and you have to pay brokers' commission on your traded options deals. Even execution-only dealing costs are high enough to mean investors have to commit relatively large sums for the deals to make cash sense. Expect to pay a minimum of £25 to open a trade (i.e., buy your option) and £15 to close it (i.e., sell your option before it expires). The commission rates are 1.25 per cent of the premium to open and 1 per cent to close. Investors also pay £2 per contract, or lot, of 1,000 options.

PRICE MECHANICS

All the jargon makes sense once investors have become used to the way traded options work. Two main elements make up the price of an option – intrinsic value and time value. An option will be in or out of the money according to whether or not it has intrinsic value.

A call option has intrinsic value if its strike price is lower than the price of the underlying shares. For example, on 30 March 1996, United Biscuits had a share price of 233p. The *Financial Times* showed call options for United Biscits with an exercise price of 220p. They had 13p of intrinsic value because they gave the right to buy shares more cheaply than in the market. They are referred to as in-the-money. The FT also showed call options with an exercise price of 240p. They had no intrinsic value – why pay more than in the market? They are out-of-the-money.

The 240p call option premium is therefore made up solely of time value. The longer the options have to run, the greater their time value, because there is more time for the United Biscuits share price to change. The prices of the options for different months of expiry illustrate very clearly how the value of an option falls as the expiry date approaches – options expiring in May have less time value than options expiring in November. The time value of options falls particularly fast in the last few weeks before expiry.

With the put options for United Biscuits, the reverse is true. Here there was an option to sell United Biscuits at 240p. It had intrinsic value – it is in the money – because in the market a seller would receive just 233p a share.

Box 03

Traded options: the first stop

Liffe, the London International Financial Futures and Options Exchange, provides and regulates the UK market for financial futures and options. It also provides an excellent range of information and training for private investors. Information from Liffe includes:

- free introductory material explaining traded options;
- a reading list, which includes the books mentioned in *Further reading*, page 180;
- a traded options workbook costing £5 and introductory video costing £10;
- training courses costing £60 for a half-day and run throughout the year in London and a number of regional centres;
- a free newsletter for private investors, published twice a year;
- details of stockbrokers who deal in traded options.

The Liffe contact number for private investors is 0171-379 2486.

'Time value' depends on more than just the passage of time. Among other things it reflects the volatility of a share price. If the share price tends to fall and rise sharply across a wide range, the person selling an option to buy or sell the shares faces more risk. The option price will change to reflect changes in the market's perception of a share's future volatility. The greater the movement in the underlying share price the greater the option premium. All that is happening is that the market is adjusting the option price to suit the level of risk. It is like a bookmaker shortening or lengthening his odds as people change their opinion of a horse's prospects.

Option prices are affected by two further factors – dividends and interest rates. Holders of options for shares in a company do not receive dividends. After all, they do not have a direct stake in the business. But movements in the share price related to dividend payments will knock on to the option price. Changes in interest rates can also make a small difference to the prices of options.

The pricing of options can be fascinating for some investors and the Black–Scholes model is the best-known mathematical model for valuing an option. Investors with time, inclination and the appropriate computer software can use models very effectively to reach judgements about their trading strategy. *Further reading* (see page 180) suggests some books which discuss the Black–Scholes model and options theory in some depth. However, the average successful options trader does not have to be a rocket scientist.

PUTTING OPTIONS INTO ACTION

Investors develop their option trading skills by experience – do not be surprised if your alarmingly youthful broker started trading on the stockmarket when he was still at primary school. There are basic rules of thumb to guide investors in the right direction, and some option strategies follow, but the most important rules are to know what you want from your investment before you start and to be ruthless about cutting your losses. *Box O4*, on pages 173–177, summarises some traded option strategies; here are some examples of options in action.

- Making money out of your belief that a share or the market is going to rise or fall.

At the end of 1995, Abbey National shares had risen to over 640p, having started the year at under 450p. Many analysts were still keen on Abbey's prospects, but in late November you believed the shares would fall in the next six months and bought a March 600 put option for 19p when the shares were 633p. The shares fell steeply in early 1996, hitting 562p in March (see Figure O2) and your option more than doubled in value.

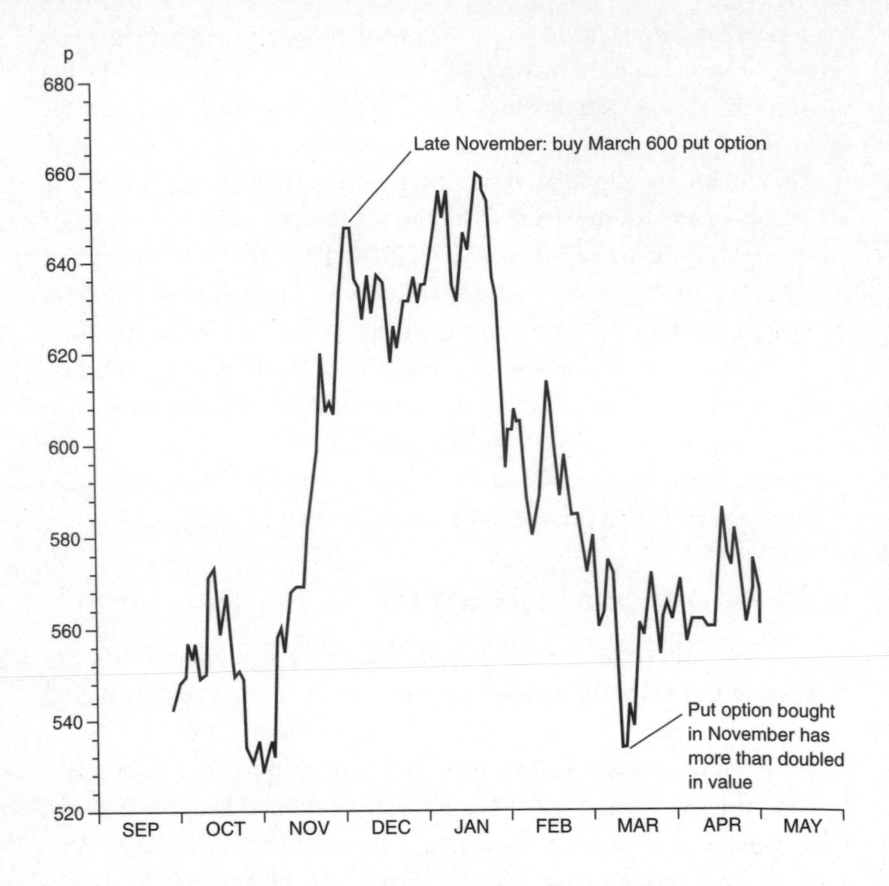

Fig O2 Abbey National share price performance 1995–96
Source: Datastream

- Locking in a good purchase price for a share – sometimes you know you want to buy shares at a given price, but the cash is not to hand. This is important for private investors as well as institutional fund managers and is a useful fallback if you need to give notice to withdraw cash from a savings account, for example.

Shares in Dixons, the electrical retailer, stood at 277p in July 1995. You liked the story revealed by the group's 1994–95 results, but lacked the cash to buy the shares. You bought two February 260 call option contracts at 32p. The cost, excluding commission, was £640. By November you had the cash and the

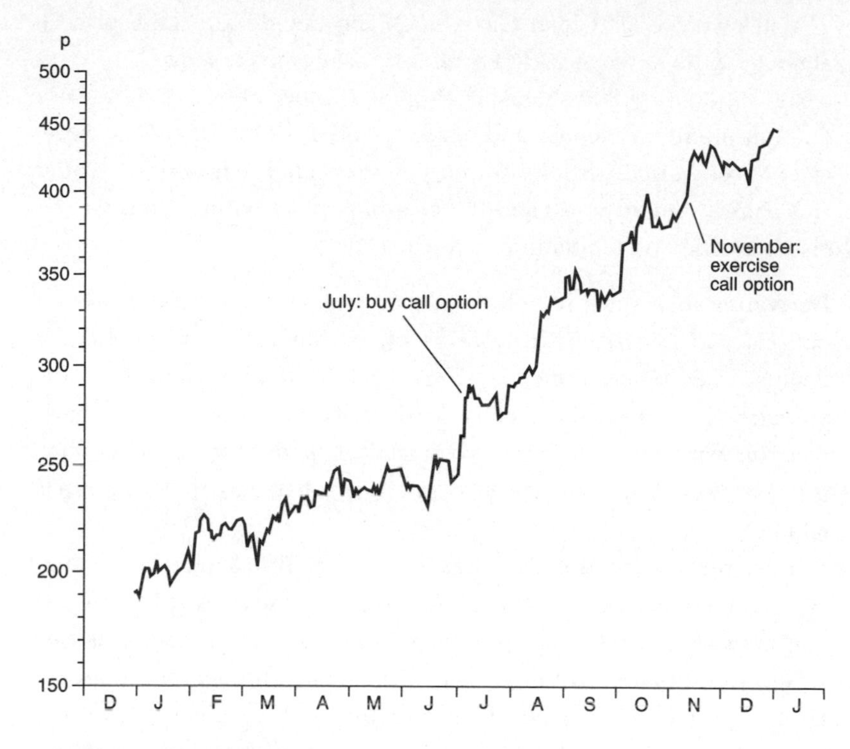

Fig O3 Dixons share price performance 1995–96
Source: Datastream

shares were 406p. Exercising your call option, covering 2,000 shares, cost £5,200. The total cost for the shares and the option was £5,840 compared with a cost of buying the shares in the market at 406p of £8,120. The saving was 28 per cent.

- Taking a view on the stockmarket – investors brave enough to take a view on whether the market is going to rise or fall can buy FT-SE 100 index options. This can also be a way to protect a diversified portfolio from share price falls.
- Boosting the return from your portfolio – it is possible to write call options with some confidence if the option is covered, i.e., you own the underlying shares already and are prepared to sell them if necessary.

You own 5,000 British Gas shares and decide the share price is about to settle down at 230p for next three months at least. You write a call option on 1,000 shares at 240p at 10p per option. You receive £100 in premium income and agree to sell 1,000 British Gas shares at 240p if required. As it turns out, your expectation is correct. British Gas shares remain static and the option expires without being exercised. You keep the premium and the shares.

Derivative specialists advise private investors to steer clear of writing options and of trading in options on currencies, commodities, or interest rates. There are exceptions, such as writing calls on shares you already own (covered calls, as described above), puts on shares that you want to buy anyhow or even taking a view on short-term UK interest rates. But there are also practical obstacles to serious risk-taking.

Investors writing options must put up an initial margin payment and each day thereafter, according to the way the market has moved, you may be asked to put up more margin to cover potential losses. Liffe, the London International Financial Futures and Options Exchange, and the London Clearing House have clear rules about how much margin investors must provide. 'Inappropriate for private investors' may sound glib, but these are investments for people who spend their days keeping track of prices and news on real-time news services. It is a business where companies can make or lose fortunes before the rest of us have eaten breakfast.

Box 04

Straddling and strangling

Long call: buy call option

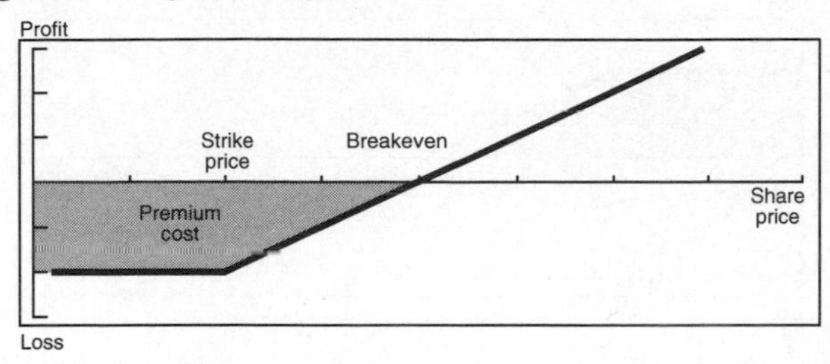

Fig O4 Long call

Source: London Commodity Exchange

When to use: Appropriate when you have a very bullish view of the market

Profit potential: Unlimited in a rising market. The greatest returns are usually made as a long call moves from out of the money to in the money

Risk: Limited to the premium paid for the option. The maximum loss is incurred if you hold the option and let it expire out of the money.

Long put: buy put option

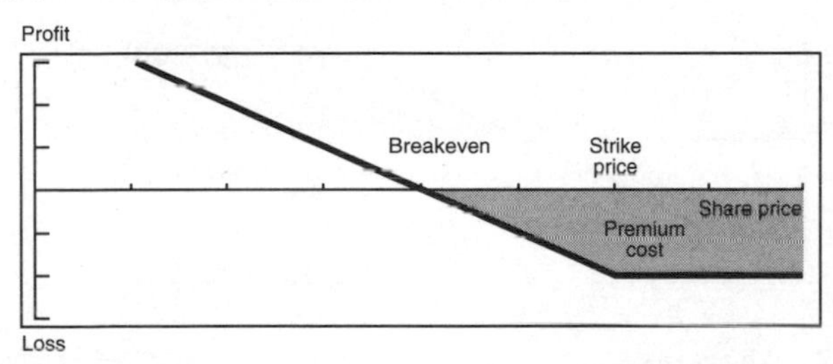

Fig O5 Long put

Source: London Commodity Exchange

When to use: Appropriate when you have a very bearish view of the market.

Profit potential: Unlimited in a falling market. The greatest returns are usually made as a long put moves from out of the money to in the money.

Risk: Limited to the premium paid for the option. The maximum loss is incurred if you hold the option and let it expire out of the money.

04 Short call: sell a call option

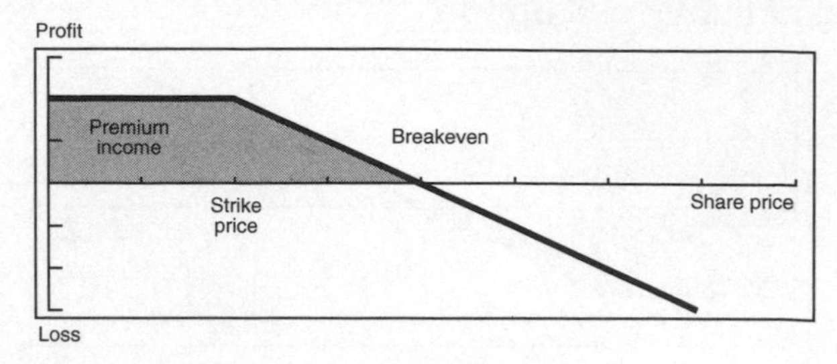

Fig O6 Short call

Source: London Commodity Exchange

When to use: Not appropriate for private investors unless they already own the underlying shares. Use when you expect sideways or falling price movements.
Profit potential: Limited to the premium income.
Risk: Unlimited in a rising market.

Short put: sell a put option

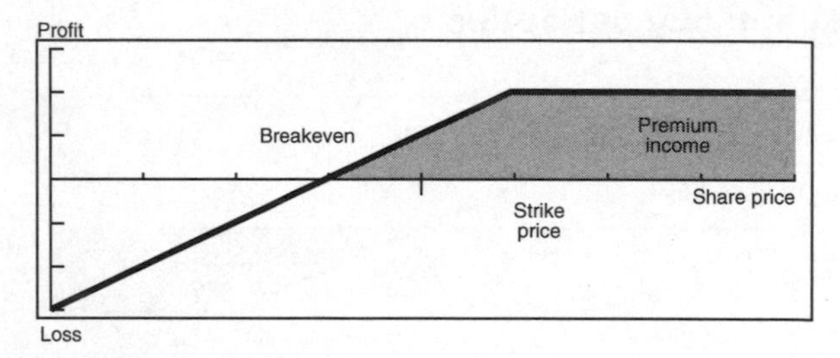

Fig O7 Short put

Source: London Commodity Exchange

When to use: Not appropriate for private investors unless they want to buy the underlying shares. Use when you expect sideways or rising price movements.
Profit potential: Limited to the premium income.
Risk: Unlimited in a falling market.

04

Bull call spread

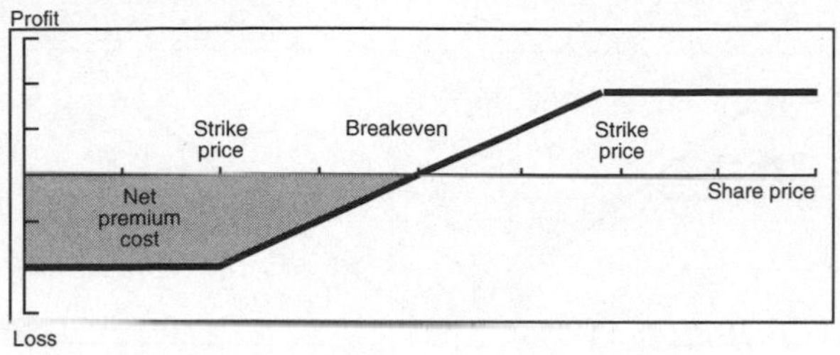

Fig O8 Bull call spread

Source: London Commodity Exchange

Buy a call option at a low strike price and sell a call option at a high strike price

When to use: When you have a moderately bullish view of the market, in effect it will cut the cost of buying a call.

Profit potential: Limited to the difference between the two strike prices minus the net premium cost.

Risk: If prices fall, the maximum loss is limited to the net premium cost.

Bear put spread

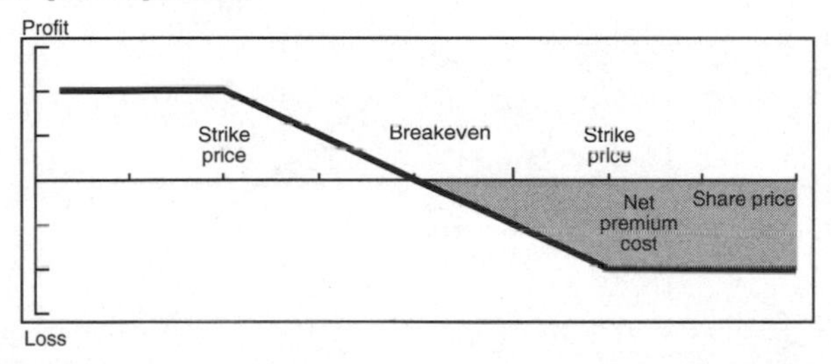

Fig O9 Bear put spread

Source: London Commodity Exchange

Buy a put option at a high strike price and sell a put option at a low strike price

When to use: When you have a moderately bearish view of the market, in effect it will cut the cost of buying a put.

Profit potential: Limited to the difference between the two strike prices minus the net premium cost.

Risk: If prices rise, the maximum loss is limited to the net premium cost.

04

Long straddle

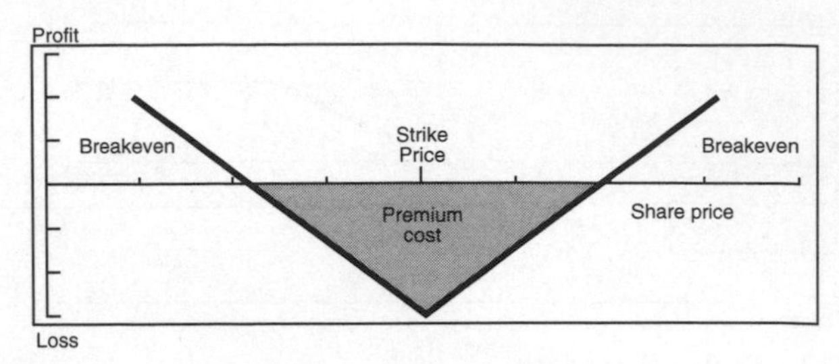

Fig O10 Long straddle

Source: London Commodity Exchange

Buy a put option and buy a call option with the same strike price
When to use: Appropriate when you expect a sudden movement in prices, higher or lower, and rising volatility.
Profit potential: Unlimited
Risk: Maximum loss is limited to the premium cost of buying the call and buying the put.

Short straddle

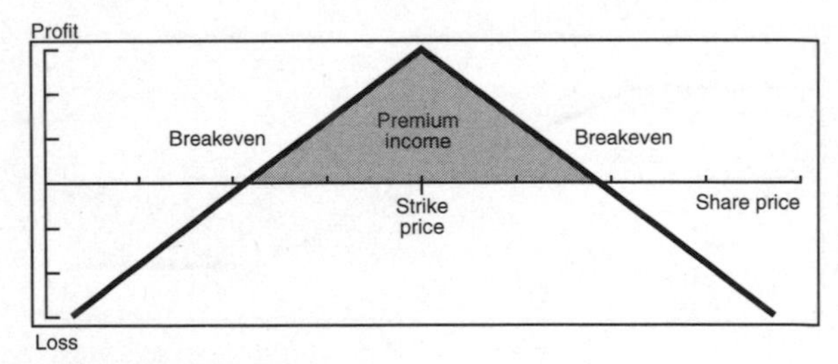

Fig O11 Short straddle

Source: London Commodity Exchange

Sell a call option and sell a put option with the same strike price
When to use: Not appropriate for private investors. Used when you expect a sideways movement in prices, and possibly lower volatility.
Profit potential: Limited to the premium income
Risk: Unlimited

04

Long strangle

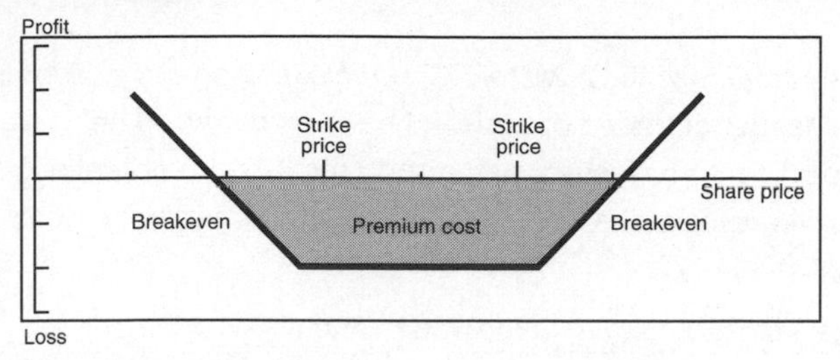

Fig O12 Long strangle
Source: London Commodity Exchange

Buy a put option with a lower strike price than the underlying share and buy a call option with a higher strike price
When to use: Appropriate when you expect a sharp movement in prices, up or down, and rising volatility. The strategy is similar to a long straddle, but needs larger price movements to become profitable.
Profit potential: Unlimited
Risk: Limited to the cost of the premiums.

Short strangle

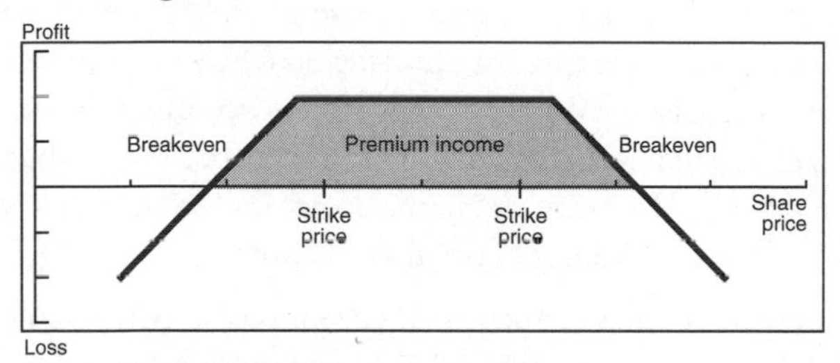

Fig O13 Short strangle
Source: London Commodity Exchange

Sell a call option with a higher strike price than the underlying share and sell a put option with a lower strike price
When to use: Not appropriate for private investors. Used when you expect sideways price movements, possibly with falling volatility. The strategy is similar to a long straddle, but raises less premium income and needs larger price movements to become profitable.
Profit potential: Limited to the premium income.
Risk: Unlimited.

Box 05

Top tips from the trader

My weekly column in the *Investors Chronicle* is hedged with warnings as to the danger of traded options. If I have managed to help readers make money, and to weave a path round most of the potential disasters for several years, the key must lie in never forgetting: momentum and stop limits.

You must have momentum in the underlying share price on your side. That is where energy must be concentrated before buying a call or a put. If the shares fail to move in the direction you want immediately after buying your option, then you should not have bought. Time value is running against your position the second after you buy. So do develop a system (charts, company analysis, studying sunspots) and stick to it. I then favour using stop limits as a discipline. If you decide not to use any particular one, then it is your money, but at least you will have forced yourself to question whether your original strategy has failed, as your theoretical stop is hit.

For readers of my column, I concentrate on buying calls or puts. I have nothing against private investors using more complex strategies, but you must remember that professional traders refer to many of those as 'crocodile trades'. The costs will eat up your profits as well as chunks of your capital. so be sure before you trade what your cost and potential for profits really are. If you do not understand clearly and precisely what you are about to do, then do not trade.

Traded options offer the chance of excellent profits when you make the right decision. But it is vital to nail down small losses quickly (the first loss is invariably the smallest), and let profits run. Also, do not be in a hurry to start with real money. Trade for a few months on paper and see how you get on. Then divide your capital into 10 and never risk more than one unit on a particular trade. That will be enough if you are correct in your purchase. When the market crashed in October 1987, puts rose by enormous amounts in a few hours. Good profits can be won over time from the market, but you must get those underlying share movements right. Good luck with your trading.

Source: *The Trader*.

TRADITIONAL OPTIONS

Traded options only cover shares that are commonly traded, such as FT-SE 100 shares, so investors who want to take a view on shares in medium-sized and smaller companies need to use traditional options. These have several differences from traded options.

- You can buy a traditional option, but only with a view to exercising it. Unlike a traded option, you cannot sell a traditional option in the market.
- The maximum life of a traditional option is three months. You can buy traded options with expiry dates ranging from three months to nine months.
- The exercise, or strike price of a traditional option is usually the current share price. You can buy traded options with exercise prices above or below the current share price.

Example

You want to buy a call option on Reuters shares. The Reuter share price, as in the example for traded options, is 767p. You 'give for a call' at 767p for three months – bought in April, the option would expire in June. The cost of the option, or premium, is roughly 7 1/2 per cent of the exercise price, in this case 57p. If the Reuters share price rises, as you expect, you will be able to exercise your option to stand to make a profit. You buy the Reuters shares in June below the market price and sell in the market. If the share price falls, you allow your option to expire.

You can keep track of the most popular traditional options in the *Financial Times* – it lists them on the same page as its traded options coverage. Only two London brokers handle traditional options – K&H and BZW – and your stockbroker should be able to deal through them on your behalf. The two firms also publish guides to traditional options, which they will supply through your stockbroker.

MAKING THE MOST OF OPTIONS

- Commit only a proportion of your investment funds to options trading – some experts suggest 10 per cent, others talk in terms of the number of shares you would normally have bought.
- Use a stockbroker who will give you advice when you start trading options rather than an execution-only service. The execution-only services cannot legally give you advice, even if you want it.
- Remember that options lose time value as they age and eventually will expire – you must be able to keep track of your options investments if you are going to invest profitably.
- Work out the best and worst outcomes before you trade and set a stop-loss – a point where you will sell out if the investment is moving the wrong way. It is better to cut losses by selling your option than to allow the option to expire worthless. One form of stop-loss is to measure losses on a position as a percentage of your capital, say 2 per cent.

Further reading

Traded Options – A Private Investor's Guide, Peter Temple (Rushmere Wynne)

Options Pricing – An International Perspective, Gordon Gemmell (McGraw-Hill)

P

PERSONAL EQUITY PLANS

Definition: **A tax-free wrapper for UK and European Union shares, some types of corporate bond, preference shares and convertibles, qualifying unit and investment trusts. Plan managers make the investments on behalf of investors and handle all administration. Investments in a Pep escape income tax and capital gains tax. The maximum annual Pep investment for an individual is £6,000 in a general Pep and £3,000 in a single-company Pep.**

Personal equity plans (Peps) have become a mainstay of financial planning in the UK, despite their limited value for many investors. The fact is that Peps work best for higher-rate taxpayers, who make up just 10 per cent of UK taxpayers. If you normally pay 40 per cent tax, your tax savings in a Pep can rapidly overtake the Pep charges. But it is all too easy for investors to believe that Peps are the best possible investment route for all.

To be fair to Peps, even some non-taxpayers may pay less in charges by investing in unit trusts via a Pep than they would pay in the same fund without the Pep wrapper. Also, only pension schemes offer better tax perks than personal equity plans and, arguably, many young investors who are basic-rate taxpayers now will become higher-rate taxpayers. Building up Pep investments now could save them tax in later life. It is still sensible to remain highly selective in considering Peps, however.

Within the framework of the Pep rules (see *Box P1*) a wide range of Peps have developed. The main categories are general, single company, corporate bond and self-select Peps. It makes sense to split these categories into two broad types – managed and self-select. Most Peps are managed, i.e., the investor either chooses a trust with a ready-made Pep wrapper or chooses a Pep manager who selects the investments as well as administering the Pep. Investors who want to make their own decisions have to use self-select Peps.

Box P1

Peps – the rules

- Individuals living in the UK can invest up to £6,000 each tax year through a general Pep. Investments in a general Pep can include UK shares, corporate bonds, qualifying unit and investment trusts. They can also hold some shares in European Union companies.
- Individuals can invest a further £3,000 each tax year through a single company Pep, which as its name implies, can hold the shares of one company only.
- The Inland Revenue splits unit and investment trusts into qualifying and non-qualifying. In simple terms non-qualifying trusts are those with less than half their investments in UK or European Union shares. Within the £6,000 general Pep allowance, investors can have up to £1,500 in a non-qualifying trust. It's always worth double-checking a trust's Pep status.
- Investors make cash payments to Inland Revenue-approved personal equity plan managers. The plan managers make the investments for the Peps and hold them on behalf of investors. Investors must arrange with the plan manager about receiving annual reports and shareholder benefits. Some plan managers refuse to arrange this.
- It is possible to hold cash in a Pep for a limited time – it must eventually be invested, or it will be subject to tax when the investor withdraws it. The ceiling for interest withdrawn in a tax-year is £180. Withdraw more than £180 of interest, and the Revenue will tax the whole sum withdrawn.
- If investors want to switch existing holdings into Peps, they need to sell the shares and instruct the plan manager to repurchase them.
- Investors can transfer shares from approved employee share schemes into single company Peps without triggering a capital gains tax (CGT) charge. They must transfer the shares within 90 days of exercising rights under the share scheme.

P1

- Peps cannot be held jointly. Each investor must set up a separate Pep. The tax-free status ends on the death of the Pep-holder – only existing gains and income are locked in tax-free.
- Investors subscribing for new issue shares can transfer the shares into a Pep within 30 days of the announcement of the share allocations in the new issue (see page 152).
- Investors can take up rights issues by using cash already in their Pep or putting in further cash up to the Pep limits.
- Unused Pep allowances cannot be carried forward to later tax years.
- To be 'Pepable', corporate bonds must have a fixed rate of interest, have at least five years to run and be issued by a UK company – not a bank or similar credit institution.

Unit trust or investment trust Peps, now the majority of the Pep population, are general Peps. General Peps can hold a range of investments, including unit trusts and shares. General Pep investors can also put up to £1,500 a year into non-qualifying trusts, i.e., trusts with less than half their holdings in UK or European Union shares.

Single-company Peps, as the name implies, hold shares in just one company, and many companies run their own low-cost Peps – known as company-sponsored Peps – for their shareholders. Some advisers call single company Peps 'the forgotten tax shelter'. About £2bn is invested in single company Peps, compared with £20bn in general Peps. Investment trust companies are not eligible for single company Peps.

Corporate bond Peps, introduced in 1995, broke Pep tradition and allowed investors to buy up to £6,000 of bonds through a Pep. The bond Peps generate a higher income than building society or bank savings, and at relatively low risk, as long as the funds underlying the Peps are well-managed. Note that only corporate bonds qualify under the Pep rules, not gilts. The choice of corporate bond Peps ran to over 100 by 1996, barely a year after they started.

By contrast, under 100 – less than 10 per cent – of the Peps available in early 1996 were self-select Peps. The relative lack of competition has made self-select an expensive route, even to the point of wiping out the tax savings. For example, re-investing dividends can be enormously expensive because of the minimum dealing costs. The Pep managers have responded to investors' unhappiness with the high charges to some extent. Some Pep managers have capped fees. For example Fidelity Brokerage's fee cap in early 1996 was £150 a year, and Sharelink's maximum dealing charge at the same time was £37.50 per deal. Both companies are execution-only stockbrokers, i.e., they offer no advice on which shares to buy.

The Pep costs to look out for on self-select Peps are fees for:

- arranging attendance and voting rights at company annual general meetings;
- dividend collection;
- providing company reports and accounts.

All these can come on top of a Pep administration fee. The cheapest self-select Peps tend to come from among the company-sponsored single-company Peps – some allow multiple shareholdings (see Figure P1).

Company	Minimum investment
BAA	£1,500
BBA	300 BBA shares
BET	£1,000
BNB Resources	700 BNB shares
British Aerospace	200 BAe shares
British Airways	200 BA shares
British Land	1,000 BL shares
Hays	200 Hays shares
Hickman International	250 Hickman shares
Iceland	200 Iceland shares
Marston Thompson & Evershed	200 Marston shares
Meggitt	1,000 Meggitt shares
Redland	200 Redland shares
Transport Development Corporation	200 TDC shares
Williams Holdings	1,000 Williams shares

Barclays Stockbroker is plan manager for all the Peps listed here.

Fig P1 Multi-stock company-sponsored Peps

Source: Chase de Vere PEPGUIDE 1996

P

Example: The low cost Pep route

For example, compare and contrast the British Airways Privatisation Pep, sponsored by British Airways, and run by Barclays Stockbrokers, with a typical self-select Pep.

The British Airways Pep allows investors to hold whatever shares they like in the Pep as long as they have at least 200 British Airways shares. It has no initial charge, an annual charge of 0.5 per cent plus VAT, with a £15 minimum, and dealing costs are 0.5 per cent (minimum £5) for British Airways or other privatisation shares, and 1 per cent (minimum £10) for other shares. Investors receive half-yearly statements and valuations, annual reports and all shareholder benefits without further charges.

The self-select Pep offered by a well-established firm of regional stockbrokers is significantly more expensive. It has no initial charge, but the annual charge is 1 per cent plus VAT, the dealing costs are 1.25 per cent plus £30, and investors have to pay £10 plus VAT if they want to go to annual meetings. The calculation in Box P2 shows how even a higher-rate taxpayer would be out-of-pocket in the first year of running the Pep. The cost/benefit equation improves in later years, particularly as tax-free capital gains clock up. The execution-only self-select plans offer a relatively good deal. But even in 1996, nine years into the Pep story, the corporate multi-stock Peps are the best bet for small investors who want to Pep their direct stock-market holdings. No wonder small investors have flocked into unit trust Peps.

PEPS – THE CHARGE SHEET

Low charges are less important than good investment performance and Pep charges have fallen steeply in the last few year, but investors still need to beware:

- Upfront Pep charges on top of charges for the underlying investment vary. Few plan managers levy extra upfront charges any longer, but the upfront charges on unit trusts will often still apply. Investors in shares should expect to pay dealing charges, but commission over 1.5 per cent is steep, unless you are getting excellent advice and a full range of shareholder services.

- Annual charges on top of the charges on the underlying investment fund. These are increasingly rare for unit trust or investment trust Peps. Expect mainstream Pep managers to charge at least 0.5 per cent plus VAT for share Peps. Charges will normally be higher among small Pep managers. Paying more than 1.5 per cent plus VAT a year will mean your investments must work extra hard to grow. The same applies to share Peps.

- Look for extra charges for cashing in your Pep before the year is out or for withdrawing some of the funds.

- Some Pep managers charge for accepting shares transferred from another Pep manager, or for allowing you to transfer out. This can be as much as £25 per holding. Enough Pep managers have no charge for transfers for investors to be able to avoid having to pay for choice.

- A dwindling number of Pep managers charge for collecting dividends for investors or for arranging investors' access to annual general meetings or shareholder perks. These are valuable shareholder rights. Some AGMs are great days out – EMAP, Stanley Leisure, Hazelwood Foods, Northern Foods and St Modwen Property all have reputations for fine food at their AGMs. Perks can include discounts for wine and food – at restaurant groups Chez Gerard and My Kinda Town – or clothes – Austin Reed, Sears.

P

Box P2

Peps – expensive to start

Two private investors, Mrs Murphy and Mr Smith, buy shares in three companies through two different self-select Peps. They both buy:

400 British Airways at 540p, yielding 3 per cent gross
200 Granada at 750p, yielding 2 per cent gross
400 Marks & Spencer at 420p, yielding 3.1 per cent gross

Mrs Murphy uses a multi-stock company-sponsored Pep and Mr Smith uses a self-select Pep run by a highly-respected firm of private client stockbrokers. Both are higher-rate taxpayers. Here is how much they pay in the first year, ignoring any capital gains.

	Mrs Murphy	**Mr Smith**
	£	**£**
Dealing costs	37	67
Dealing charge	–	90
Annual Pep charge (including VAT)	31	63
Attendance at meeting	–	35
Total	68	255
Less Tax saving*	59	59
Cost in Pep Year 1	**9**	**196**

*Assuming dividend income before tax of £147, the tax saving for a 40 per cent taxpayer would be £59.

MAKING THE MOST OF PEPS

- Know your tax status. If you are a higher-rate taxpayer, the odds are that Pepping your investments will pay off from early on in the life of your Pep. If you are a basic-rate or lower-rate taxpayer, your main benefit from a Pep will be over the long-term, and it is particularly important that you find a Pep with low charges. If you are a non-taxpayer, there is little benefit to you from investing through a Pep, unless you find that it is cheaper to invest in your chosen unit or investment trust with a Pep wrapper than without. Higher-rate tax is 40 per cent, basic-rate 24 per cent, and lower-rate 20 per cent.

- Remember that above and beyond Peps, each individual has an annual capital gains tax allowance of £6,300 in 1996–97 – any gains you realise within that figure are tax-free.
- Make your Pep investments for the long-term to gain the full benefit of the tax perks. Allowing your capital to build up should mean the gains within the Pep will be greater than your normal CGT allowance. As a rule of thumb, it makes sense to Pep shares likely to trigger a high income tax charge. For example, it makes more sense to Pep a share with a high dividend income than one with low dividends.

Example: When to Pep

A higher-rate taxpayer has £5,000 split between two shares. Share A yields 10 per cent, or £500 a year before tax. Share B yields 3 per cent or £150 a year. The investor could saves £200 in tax by Pepping share A, or £60 in tax by Pepping share B. Share A belongs in the Pep. (Of course, if an unexpected takeover bid means share B trebles in value, hindsight will tell a different story.)

- Investors with existing portfolios can transfer their holdings into Peps gradually, even if they have no desire to make fresh Pep investments. Someone who had been moving into Peps since they started in 1987, would have had almost £65,000 invested in an onshore tax shelter by April 1996.
- You can transfer Peps without losing the tax benefits. It is as important to review your fund manager's performance with Pepped funds as with any other investment.
- Investment performance will always be more important than tax perks or charges, but with Peps it is essential to know the rules (see *Box P1*) and to know the charges (see *Box P2*). Otherwise you risk finding that you will have to pay tax because your invest-

ments have not been properly Pepped or being clobbered with unexpected charges.

- Few first-time investors are lucky enough to have a lump sum ready to put into the stockmarket. The brave, or foolhardy, borrow the money, but a regular savings plan is an effective and sensible way to build up capital and can be a cracking investment.
- Ignore the Pep panic at the end of the tax year. Investing in a hurry is a bad idea. However, even if you do not want to invest your full Pep allowance right away, investors in self-select Peps can use it up by moving cash into the plan. Just remember to invest it, or the Inland Revenue will tax it.

Further reading

The Chase de Vere *PEPGUIDE* is the most comprehensive guide to Pep charges, minimum investment levels and performance. Independent financial advisers Chase de Vere publish the guide annually. It costs £12.95, which Chase de Vere refunds if you buy a Pep through them. Contact 0800 526092, or write to 63 Lincoln's Inn Fields, London WC2A 3BR.

Look out for the annual Pep surveys published by newspapers and magazines. They may be vehicles for advertising, but they are a mine of information.

Q

QUANTITATIVE FUND MANAGEMENT

***Definition:* Quantitative fund management is the use of mathematical modelling in making investment decisions. Fund managers analyse enormous quantities of information about stocks and invest in assets that seem to produce unusually good returns.**

A handful of UK pension funds switched out of shares before the October 1987 stockmarket crash, thanks to advice from US pioneers of quantitative fund management. The result, an investment performance 20 per cent better than the funds which had failed to switch out of shares, opened the door to the quants. Now most UK fund managers use some form of computer modelling to help their investment decisions, but few if any rely on it. Traditional, more intuitive methods, still hold sway in the City.

Computer modelling allows investors to squash information into a manageable form. Then they can identify a pattern, for example the behaviour of share prices in the UK, and the reasons behind that pattern. In theory, once they know why UK share prices have moved in the past, it is possible to predict how they will react to the same events or changes in the future. Professional investors in the 1990s have a glut of information thanks to global communications and they have the computer power to use it.

In 1987 the quantitative analysts decided shares were overvalued and due to fall because they had analysed past share price movements. Other investors realised intuitively, or from other indicators, that shares were overvalued, but could convince themselves that this time something was different about the stockmarket. The results of the computer model showed that nothing was different. It was a form of proof that the quantitative analysts and fund managers believed, and events proved them to be right.

Box Q1

Portfolio theory in action

Portfolio theory is the mathematical proof that shows why it is less risky to hold a portfolio of shares than to hold just one (see RISK, page 195). It started – or at least reached a wider audience – when a US academic pointed out that the risk of an investment portfolio depends on the co-variance of its holdings. Co-variance is the extent that prices move together. Applying portfolio theory should help an investor to reach an 'efficient' portfolio, i.e., one that gives the best returns for the risk taken on by the investor. In the 1960s, another US academic decided that the market itself is an efficient portfolio. He had developed a model which related the returns on an asset with its propensity to move in line with the market. The next step was to measure risk for individual assets, so that you could create more efficient, less risky portfolios. However, investment experts still disagree about whether people beat the market by luck or by design. The belief that you cannot beat the market has led to the creation of tracker funds which follow a market index (see INDICES, page 104). Conventional fund managers know and apply the lessons of portfolio theory, but they would rarely use it in practice. Increasing computer power has made it practical to select securities more carefully in order to 'diversify away' as much risk as possible. As a result, quantitative fund managers can afford the time and effort to take portfolio theory literally. The mathematical formulae of portfolio theory can easily deter investors who are more at home with intuitive investment analysis, but some surprising people, who would have called themselves wholly innumerate, become addicted.

The fund managers in 1987 were using computer models to help them choose the right investment market – bonds, cash, shares. It was tactical asset allocation, and fund managers are still happy using computer models, at least to help decide how to allocate assets. They are less happy using models to help in choosing individual shares. The simple explanation for this is that markets are an average of all the bonds or companies within them, and overall they are influenced by major events such as interest rates. An individual company can be buffeted by any number of events, inside and outside the company.

It is relatively easy to keep track of worldwide interest rates, and to write a computer model that factors in perhaps half a dozen key economic and financial indicators. It would be much harder to include factors that may be critical for a company or even an entire industry, for example the retirement of a powerful chief executive or the price of paper. The same factors would barely move the market as a whole, if at all.

Box Q2

Modelling – not just a glamour job

Emanuel Derman, an analyst at US investment bank Goldman Sachs, has spotlighted seven main types of model risk.

- Modelling may be inapplicable in the first place.
- The assumptions behind the model may not apply to current market conditions.
- The data driving the model may be inaccurate.
- The model may be all right, but the model solution is wrong (remember, this is mathematics).
- A correct model may be used beyond its domain of applicability.
- The numerical solution of the model may be badly approximated.
- There may be hardware or software bugs; or the historical data may be unstable.

Source: Goldman Sachs

As a result, fund managers may well have models for stockpicking, but how much they use them is debatable. Modelling sounds scientific and therefore to many people either incomprehensible or infallible, but computer modellers can make mistakes. Modelling is all about regression – measuring the relationship between two events. A model can give the right result only if its equation is written correctly, and if it is told to measure the right information. Told to measure the link between share price movements and *Investors Chronicle* journalists' cake consumption over 30 years, it would come up with an answer. The skill of quantitative analysis is to write the equation correctly and to identify the right factors for the model to measure.

Scepticism, after an early burst of enthusiasm in the late 1980s, has slowed the progress of quantitative fund management. How often can computer models, used on their own, give the right answers? Tracker funds, a basic form of quantitative fund management, have become its most common use in the UK. They set out to track stockmarket indices, either by buying a sample of the shares in the index or by replicating the index exactly, and have proved an enormous success with investors. Relatively low charges have helped win over investors to tracker funds. After all, goes the argument, tracker funds should be cheap because they are effectively run by computer.

MAKING THE MOST OF QUANTITATIVE FUND MANAGEMENT

- Most fund managers use quantitative techniques in some form. BZW and Legal & General are known as the biggest quantitative fund managers in the UK, largely because of their tracker funds (see INDICES, page 104). Tracker funds are a form of passive quantitative fund management – it is passive, because the skill is to follow an index. Pure active 'quant', where the skill is using quantitative techniques to pick stocks is rare in the UK, even among pension fund managers.
- Do not expect quantitative fund managers always to make the right decisions – computer modelling can go wrong or the managers can make mistakes.

Further reading

Capital Ideas, Peter Bernstein (Free Press)

RISK

Definition: **Risk is the chance that you may suffer misfortune. In investment, it is the possibility that your investment will fall in value.**

Rows between financial advisers and their clients often stem from misunderstandings about each other's definitions of risk. It is so obvious with hindsight, but investors do forget that a low-risk investment to one person may seem wildly reckless to another.

It is an absurd situation, given the time spent discussing, refining and writing about risk. The textbooks will tell you that all investors are risk averse, it is just that they make different decisions when they have to match risk and reward. Crudely, a 25-year-old millionaire will worry less about losing £5,000 than a 65-year-old investing a £50,000 pension lump sum. Professional investors have used mathematics to refine this analysis of risk and reward (see QUANTITATIVE FUND MANAGEMENT, page 191) and have developed a number of useful lessons for private investors. In practice, private investors should be able to manage risk successfully without quadratic equations.

R

STOCKMARKET UPS AND DOWNS

The stock financial warning, 'the value of your investment may fall as well as rise', and the advice to hold any stockmarket investment for five to ten years to earn a good return, reflect the volatility, or uncertainty, of stockmarkets compared with a building society savings account. Volatility is measured by the standard deviation, i.e., how much the trust's performance has differed from the long-term investment average. Investors can check the volatility of a unit trust, for example, when they look up its investment record (see UNIT

TRUST, page 229). The performance statistics often quote the standard deviation of the unit trust – a low figure implies low volatility. For example, the average UK growth unit trust in early 1996 had a standard deviation of just over 3. The average gold and mining unit trust had a standard deviation of over 6, and the average cash unit trust measured just over zero.

Knowing the past volatility of your investment helps in building your portfolio, but you cannot know what will happen next. That is why pooling and diversifying investments can be helpful. Portfolio theory (see QUANTITATIVE FUND MANAGEMENT, page 191) tells investors that it pays to hold a mixed bag of investments. Mathematicians call it looking for investments with a low correlation. For example, if you have two investments A and B, ideally you want investment A to go up when investment B loses value. That way one compensates for the other's loss. In practice that may mean holding overseas unit or investment trusts to diversify a mainly UK-based share portfolio. Portfolio theory also tells private investors that relatively small portfolios should have about 10 to 15 different shares spread across different markets, and industries. Adding more shares will not diversify away any more risk, but will add to the expense of running your portfolio.

The theory is helpful, but for many private investors the simple, practical tool of stop-loss levels will be still more useful. All serious investors keep track of their holdings from week to week. A stop-loss is a signal to review the holding and decide whether to sell it. You can set the stop-loss at any level you like, 10 per cent, 20 per cent or more. But if a share falls 10 per cent it is worth investigating the reasons behind the fall. Some investors always sell if the price has halved, whatever the outlook. The point is to set a discipline and keep to it.

'... pooling and diversifying investments can be helpful.'

There will be times when a share price recovers after you have sold up, but it is equally possible that the company is heading for disaster.

Even if a share has fallen 70 per cent since you bought it, it can be worth selling to save just 30 per cent of your investment. Hanging on for good news may lose the whole lot.

MAKING THE MOST OF RISK

- Spread your portfolio across different markets. Consider using unit or investment trusts to diversify your portfolio away from the UK.
- Monitor the prices of holdings in your portfolio and set levels where you will sell rather than soak up further losses.

Further reading

An Introduction to Risk and Return, RA Brealey (Basil Blackwell)

A Random Walk Down Wall Street, Burton G Malkiel (Norton)

S

SHARES

Definition: **Companies divide their capital into equal units called shares. Buying the shares brings rights – a stake in the business, and risks – of losing your investment. Shareholders are last in the queue when the assets are shared out if a company goes out of business. Lenders and trade creditors will receive their share of the cash first. All limited companies have shares, but only public limited companies have the right to offer those shares to the general public through a listing on the Stock Exchange.**

'Investing profits in the business should, in theory, make the shares more valuable.'

Shareholders own their company, and in theory can do what they like with it. In practice it does not work that way. Yes, managers work for the shareholders, but they do not give shareholders many opportunities to throw their weight around.

Investors buy ordinary shares in a company to share in its profits, they can normally assume that they will have the right to vote on motions at the company's annual general meetings (AGMs), and at extraordinary general meetings (EGMs), when the owners of the company have to approve large or unusual transactions.

Successful companies can pay out their profits in dividends or put them back into the business. Investing profits in the business should, in theory, make the shares more valuable. The market price of the shares should rise to reflect the growing assets and profits of the company. The more profitable a company is, the greater the scope for paying dividends. Shareholders tend to like receiving chunky dividends more than management enjoys paying them, but some companies have a policy of paying relatively generous dividends. For example, property tiddler Cleveland Trust makes a point of paying out most of its rental income in dividends, so that its dividend yield is generous, even by the standards of property companies.

A glance at the share price listings in the newspapers shows that companies issue several different types of share apart from plain vanilla ordinary shares.

- Voting and non-voting ordinary shares. Some companies, normally because they are still family-dominated, have 'two-tier share structures'. This means the company has two types of ordinary share in issue. Both should have equal rights to receive dividends and a share in the profits, but one type will carry all or most of the voting rights in the company. You can normally spot companies with this two-tier structure because they will have 'A' and ordinary shares in issue. The share structure can be even more complicated – satellite broadcaster BSkyB has 'A', 'B', 'C' and 'D' shares in issue, for example. Big companies began to drop the voting/non-voting structure in the 1960s – Marks & Spencer was the first to enfranchise its voting shares. Great Universal Stores, the mail order group, and leisure group Whitbread dropped their two-tier structures only in 1993 (see *Box S1* below).

Box S1

Clinging to independence

Some companies still cling to the two-tier structure, although it can undermine the whole point of being a listed company – attracting fresh outside investment. Institutional investors tend to steer well clear of companies where the voting shares are concentrated in a small group of shareholders. Eldridge Pope, the regional brewer and pub company, is one of the best-known small companies with a two-tier structure. Here the Pope family control the board and the voting shares. The chart of the company's share price reflects the market's hope that Eldridge Pope is about to drop its two-tier voting habit as much as better trading by the brewer. The two-tier structure blocks takeovers and the rise in value is really a takeover premium – present in most share prices.

S1 Scrapping the two-tier structure – known as enfranchising the non-voting shares – normally causes the shares to leap in value. That is because institutions are more likely to invest in companies where they can have a say and the expectation of increased demand for the shares pushes up their price. Big companies which have clung to the two-tier structure include brewer Young & Co and the Savoy Hotel company. The Savoy has survived as an independent company only because of its share structure.

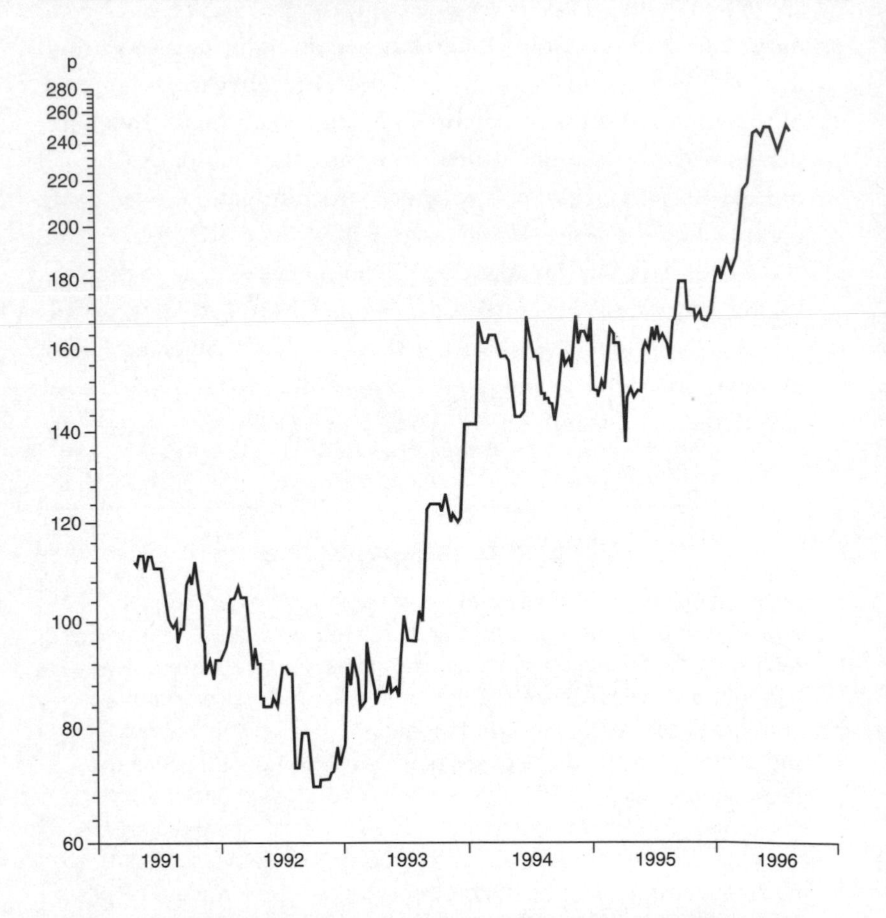

Fig S1 'Hoping for bid excitement': Eldridge Pope 'A' share price performance 1991–96

Source: Datastream

SHOWING A PREFERENCE

Ordinary shares, voting or not, count as equity share capital. However, non-equity share capital – preference shares – is also a common feature in company balance sheets.

Preference shareholders are preferred in that they rank before ordinary shareholders in getting their share of the business. Preference dividends will be paid out before ordinary dividends and preference shareholders will receive their share of the assets before ordinary shareholders if the company is wound up. Some types of preference share capital are very like bank debt. However, preference share dividends are almost always fixed, and will often be repaid at a pre-determined time, so they are more like bonds than shares. It makes them more predictable and less risky than ordinary shares, but it also cuts them out of most of the capital growth ordinary shareholders can expect.

Preference shares can fall into several types, even several at the same time. They can be cumulative – unpaid dividends will build up as a liability to preference shareholders. They can be convertible – holders have the right to convert the preference shares into ordinary shares at a given date (see CONVERTIBLES, page 52). They can be redeemable – the company will repay the shareholders at a certain date, sometimes at the company's discretion. They can be participating – the shareholders will usually receive a profit-related element with the fixed dividend.

It is easy to ignore preference share capital. 'Cumulative redeem-able convertible preference shares' sound off-puttingly complex. However, it is important for several reasons.

First, ordinary shareholders can lose out to preference shareholders. Money going in dividends to preference shareholders is cash that could be going back into the business or going into ordinary shareholders' dividends. True, preference shareholders have paid for the privilege, but sometimes the effect of preference shares is more like bank interest than dividends. Also, ordinary shareholders' entitlement to the company's profits can drop sharply if large numbers of preference shares are converted. The 'fully diluted earnings per share' figure quoted in accounts is supposed to reflect this effect on shareholders' rights.

Secondly, preference shareholders can have serious clout with the company. If preference dividends are unpaid, the preference shareholders can win voting rights and force management in a certain direction. Ordinary shareholders may not gain from the preference shareholders' action.

Example: I'd prefer cash

Investors in the Signet jewellery retail chain, formerly known as Ratners, had a bumpy 1995 after a group of US preference shareholders requisitioned an extraordinary general meeting with a view to forcing the company to change strategy and sell off large chunks of the group, which had only just returned to profit. They were entitled to call the meeting because their dividends were seriously in arrears. The preference shareholders failed to win enough votes to push through their strategy. Selling off the businesses would have raised enough to repay the preference shareholders, but would have left relatively little for the ordinary shareholders. However, the rebels succeeded in rattling the cage of the Signet board, which was probably their main intention from the start. And in January 1996, the Signet board announced that it wanted to sell its UK jewellery businesses, Ernest Jones and H Samuel.

SHARE AND SHARE ALIKE

Deferred shares are a bit of a red herring. Companies in trouble and having to rebuild their balance sheet, a process known as restructuring or refinancing, often use them to wipe out accumulated past losses – called a deficit on the profit and loss account. It is illegal to pay dividends, unless the company has enough distributable reserves in the balance sheet. Companies who wipe out deficits in this way have to go to the High Court to cancel the deferred shares.

Warrants can also be considered as a type of share capital – they are considered in detail under warrants (see WARRANTS, page 235).

Bearer shares are very unusual in the UK, although a number of Swiss companies – Roche, UBS and Swiss Bank for example – have bearer shares in issue. A number of UK companies, such as insurance group Commercial Union and leisure conglomerate Granada, have issued Eurosterling bonds. These are bearer bonds and holders of such bonds have to use a coupon to claim their interest payments. Holders of the shares are not registered as owners in the company's share register, but use the share certificate as proof of ownership.

In the UK a share certificate on its own does not prove that you own the shares – your name, or the name of your nominee company (see JARGON, page 129) must appear on the company's share register. Share certificates are set to become increasingly unusual in the UK as it moves to electronic share settlement with Crest (see JARGON, page 129).

Companies sometimes tidy up their share capital using share splits and consolidations. A company's share price will shrink dramatically if the board decides to split each share into, say, two. This can happen if a company decides its share price has become unwieldy. In the UK it used to be convention that few companies had a share price of over £5, for example.

Share consolidations are more common and a consolidation is often behind what looks like an enormous rise in a company share price. For example, in 1996 surveyor Conrad Ritblat consolidated its 136m shares into just 13.6m – it was a 10 into one consolidation. 'The directors consider that a reduction in the number of ordinary shares in issue and corresponding increase in market price of each shares will serve to enhance market perception of the group,' said the company. But to investors who missed the announcement, it looked as if the share price had risen 900 per cent overnight. In fact shareholders had the same stake in the business.

Box S2

Ten into one won't go

Sometimes a company's share consolidation can harm investors' interests. Say that a company's shares are trading at 3p and the company consolidates them on basis of one-for-10. As a result the share price jumps to 30p. If the company is out of favour, the shares may well slip badly from their new price. Shares in Queensborough, a leisure company formerly known as Flagstone, put through a 50 into one consolidation, which in theory should have meant an equivalent share price of over 60p. But at the same time it raised £12m in a placing at 25p a share. The shares dropped straight down to the placing price. The main problem here was the placing – the market saw the placing price as the true measure of the company's value – not the consolidation. But it did not feel like that to the investors who had bought shares before the consolidation and placing, only to find their investment halved in a trice. Another problem is that penny share companies end up with billions of shares in issue and a huge shareholder list. That means hundreds of annual reports to be printed and sent out.

MAKING THE MOST OF SHARE CAPITAL

- Find out who owns shares in companies which interest you – the company's annual report should tell you who owns 3 per cent or more of the shares and Extel cards or the Hemmington Scott Company Refs series – available in business libraries – can give you information on this.
- Beware of companies with two-tier voting structures or very large directors' holdings unless you have total faith in the management's ability to keep the business moving in the right direction. Companies which consider themselves invulnerable to takeover or even mild shareholder pressure can prove a poor investment.

- Check whether the company has preference share capital and how much cash the preference dividends are taking out of the business – should you consider the preference shares as debt, or do they not have to be repaid? If they are redeemable preference shares, when are they due to be repaid and do you think the company will be able to meet that debt? And why did the company issue preference shares in the first place? Was it because they were struggling for cash and the business was too risky for potential investors in new ordinary shares?
- Think twice when you think a company's share price is completely bombed out. Apart from the fact that it can have drifted down to a couple of pence for good reason – it is about to go out of business – there is always the risk that the shares would go lower if they could. A share consolidation – possible if the company has a large number of shares in issue – can give the shares space to fall further.

SOFTWARE

***Definition:* Computer software has opened any number of previously locked doors for the private investor. Relatively complex portfolio analysis and charting that had been the domain of the professionals can now happen in the front room. Packages cost from £50 to £1,000.**

Investment software offers two main benefits. The most basic packages do little more than help investors keep on top of their bookkeeping. You still have to record the information about your transactions in the system, but the package can run the calculations – including indexation – to prepare a capital gains tax statement suitable for your tax return.

Box S3 **Software suppliers – a snapshot**

The investment software packages available to investors change so rapidly that there is little point in suggesting particular products – they will be out of date by the time you read this. However, the *Investors Chronicle* carries regular reviews of the software packages available and coming on to the market and below are some of the established names in the investment software field. Most of these should offer you a demonstration disc or a trial package.

Fairshares Software
56a High Street, Epsom, Surrey, KT19 8AP
Telephone: 01372 741969

Financial Systems Software
Royex House, 13th Floor, Aldermanbury Square, London EC2V 7HR
Telephone: 0171-600 6033

Indexia Research
121 High Street, Berkhamsted, Herts HP4 2DJ
Telephone: 01442 878015

S3

NUMA Financial Systems
PO Box 1736, Bradford-on-Avon, Wilts BA15 2LY
Telephone: 01225 723072

SEPAL
1 Wood Farm Cote, Mill Green, Hatfield, Herts AL9 5NU
Telephone: 01707 276156

Synergy Software
Britannic House, 20 Dunstable Rd, Luton LU1 1ED
Telephone: 01582 424282

Updata Software
Updata House, Old York Road, London, SW18 1TG
Telephone: 0181 874 1747

David Winrow Marketing
PO Box 9, Northwich, Cheshire CW9 7TP
Telephone: 01606 41241

Bear in mind that appearing in this list is not a recommendation. You will still need to shop around and make your own judgement.

The real advantage of the packages, however, is that they make it easier to keep track of the shares in your portfolio, and at least in theory, to stick to your portfolio disciplines such as stop-losses. The packages allow investors to use historical share price information to track the progress of individual shares and identify trends. At its simplest, investors may just check the graph of a share price over the last 12 months to see how far the share price is from its 12-month peak and low. But many packages also allow investors to value options and to calculate the moving averages needed to draw charts for technical analysis. Some on-line packages – admittedly among the most expensive – even plug you into earnings forecasts, information on directors' dealings and historical profits figures.

Box S4

Internet addresses for investors

The Internet is a low-cost source of an enormous range of information. True, some of it is useless, but some is highly valuable to investors, particularly those researching companies. Here is a snapshot of the Internet web sites open in early 1996.

Wall Street Direct (a US list of software suppliers)
http://www.wsdinc.com/

Updata Software (software company)
http://www.demon.co.uk/updata

Financial Times (business newspaper)
http://www.ft.com

Daily Telegraph (UK newspaper)
http://telegraph.co.uk

Bloomberg (financial news service)
http://www.bloomberg.com/

Hemmington Scott (financial publisher)
http://www.hemscott.co.uk/hemscott

Interactive Investor (investment and unit trust information)
http://www.iii.co.uk

MAKING THE MOST OF INVESTMENT SOFTWARE

- Check whether your computer is up to it. Most investment software packages are IBM-compatible, and need at least a 386 processor. It can be hard to get software for Apple Macs.
- You need upwards of 10 megabytes of hard-drive memory and at least four megabytes of system memory. Experts advise having as big a hard disc as you can afford.

- Insist on receiving a demonstration disc: it is the best way to make sure the package suits.
- Software suppliers may be able to offer you a choice between DOS or Windows software. Calculations can run more quickly in DOS than Windows. However, Windows is easier to use, and PCs have got so powerful that Windows should no longer be considered slow.

'The real advantage of the packages is that they make it easier to keep track of the shares in your portfolio, and at least in theory, to stick to your portfolio disciplines such as stop-losses.'

- You need to link your package to a source of share price information. The main choices are plugging into a teletext service – you buy a teletext circuit card for about £200 and connect your computer to the television aerial; receiving weekly or monthly updates on disc; or downloading information via a modem? Taking information via the Internet – for which you need a modem – is one of the cheapest options.
- Make sure your software company can offer the help-desk facilities you expect to need, upgrades at a reasonable price and beware of hidden extra charges.

S

Further reading

The *Investors Chronicle* runs regular surveys on investment software and reviews new packages.

Profit from your PC, David Linton (Rushmere Wynne) – David Linton runs Updata, an investment software group, but the book is a balanced and informed look at the best way to use your investment software.

TAKEOVERS

Definition: **An offer to buy the share capital of a company. Many takeovers are agreed with the management of the target company, but some companies opt to slug it out for control.**

> ***'The moral is that takeover speculation on its own is normally a bad reason to buy a share.'***

Investors normally stand to make money from a takeover bid. The whisper of a bid for a company will send its price shooting upwards – bid speculation added 20 per cent to the share price of electricals and media group Thorn-EMI in 1996. Rumours of a bid from a large electronics group such as Sony or Acclaim for the troubled computer games specialist CentreGold sent its share price bouncing back up to 80p in autumn 1995 (see Figure T1). As things turned out, Eidos, another small UK computer games group, made a bid at just 40p a share. CentreGold's management had agreed the bid and pledged their shares to Eidos.

The moral is that takeover speculation on its own is normally a bad reason to buy a share. Too often it turns out, for example, that the company's financial position is even worse than outsiders imagined and the bidder finds a let-out clause to drop the deal. However, spotting takeovers in advance is part of the fun of investment, particularly if you can have your own reasons for thinking a company is a good takeover target – perhaps you work in the same industry and understand the direction it is taking.

Also, bids can turn sour. In 1989 a group of investors mustered a £700m bid for the stationery group DRG – it was one of the biggest takeovers seen on the stockmarket. Analysts reckoned the bid undervalued DRG, but a setback in share prices helped the bid go through.

The plan was to break up DRG and sell it off, but the UK economy slid into recession and the new DRG owners sold the parts of the group for far less than they had expected. However, a share offer can be attractive if you like the bidder or if you believe you can sell the shares in the market at a good price.

In practice, few investors ever get round to buying shares in their favourite takeover targets. They are far more likely to end up considering takeovers as they happen, which can be equally difficult. Companies pile the pressure on shareholders to jump one way or the other in a hurry, when shareholders' best option is to take their time. Also,

Fig T1 CentreGold share price performance 1993–96
Source: Datastream

Fickle' may supposedly be every fund manager's middle name, but institutional investors can turn down bids for reasons that never reach the public. Giant building materials group Redland bid for Ennemix, a tiny quarry company with a very poor record but a high net asset value compared with the bid price, in 1996. Redland started with a 29.99 per cent stake and ended up with just 43 per cent of the shares. Investors were flummoxed as to why, despite the net asset strength, Redland had failed to win over enough shareholders. Later in 1996, French building materials group Lafarge took control of Ennemix, but Redland remained as a large minority shareholder.

TAKEOVERS – THE TIMETABLE

- What are the key dates in the bid timetable? Once someone announces a firm intention of making a bid they have 28 days to post their bid or offer document. Day 0 is the day the bidder posts the document and the bid timetable runs on a 60-day clock. If a rival bidder steps in the clock returns to zero. The bid target has 14 days in which to post its defence document. Day 39 is the last day on which a bid target can publish important new information about itself – namely trading results, profit or dividend forecasts, asset values or a proposed dividend. Day 46 is the last day the bidder can announce new terms. And the bid must close on Day 60.

  Confusingly, there can be several closing dates. The first is at least 21 days after the offer document is posted, and the bidder can halt the bid then. Bidders tend to set an early closing date – it must be at least 21 days – and then extend it. The bidder tots up the number of shares pledged to accept its offer – the acceptances – at each closing date and may extend its bid as it wishes up to Day 60. The bid must be unconditional as to acceptances or lapse by Day 60. Day 81 is the last day on which a bid can go wholly unconditional.
- How big a stake can a shareholder own before it has to bid for the company? Takeover rules force a shareholder who owns 30 per cent or more of a company's shares to offer to buy all the other

shares. It can be an existing shareholder who acquires shares taking them over 30 per cent. This is known as a mandatory bid and very occasionally the bidder has no intention of taking over the company, it is just going through the motions.

Companies where a potential bidder has a large stake carry a bid premium in the price. The bidder is obliged to pay cash and it must pay the highest price paid in the last 12 months. Some investors hover at 29.99 per cent without ever trying to buy the whole company. Once a shareholder hits 30 per cent it must bid immediately for the whole company.

- How much of a company must the bidder have to win the bid? Bidders set their own conditions for winning bids, building in protection such as saying the bid will lapse if it is referred to the Office of Fair Trading. The key number in a takeover is 50 per cent. Once the bidder has acceptances for 50 per cent of the target's shares, it can declare the bid unconditional as to acceptances. The offer remains open for at least 14 days to allow other shareholders to accept. Once the bidder has over 90 per cent of the shares, it can compulsorily buy out the shareholder rump.
- If I accept the bid, can I change my mind? Yes. Investors can withdraw their acceptances from Day 42 onwards, if not earlier, and the bidder will send back their title documents for the shares.
- What happens if I accept the bid, but it does not go through? The bidder will return your certificate of title.
- What happens if I do nothing – effectively reject the bid – but it succeeds? You have at least 14 days in which to accept the bid after it goes unconditional as to acceptances. Bidders can keep their offer open for months. Or you can stay a minority shareholder until the bidder has 90 per cent of the shares. At that point the bidder can legally oblige you to sell, but it will be at the same terms as the takeover offer. Minority shareholders are in a very weak position as regards dividends and so on.

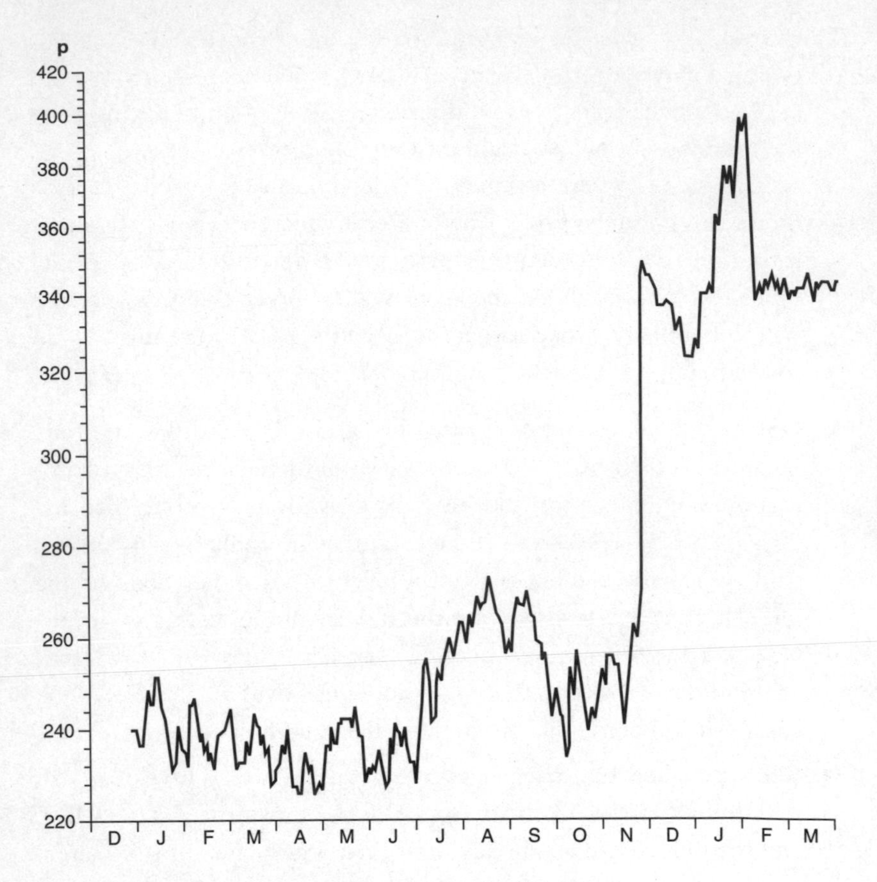

Fig T2 Forte share price performance 1995–96

Source: Datastream

Box T1

Forte – Little Chef changes hands

One of the most exciting takeovers of 1995–96 was the Granada bid for Forte. Here it was all too easy to be distracted by the personalities – gritty charmer Gerry Robinson from Granada, a motorway-services-to-television group, against first-generation aristo Sir Rocco Forte. Figure T2 shows the progress of Forte's share price over the 12 months leading to the bid. It was 275p when the bid started in late November and hit 384p on 23 January 1996, the day the bid went unconditional.

The *Investors Chronicle* keeps track of announced takeover bids in its 'Mergers and Adquisitions' pages. Figure T2 shows an extract from the takeovers table at 19 January 1996, well into the Forte bid. Here is a summary of the *Investors Chronicle*'s coverage during the bid.

1 December 1995 Granada had bid £3.4bn for Forte, offering four Granada shares and £23.25 per 15 Forte shares, effectively 339p a share.

'Granada wants to balance out its cash generating and capital intensive businesses and reckons Forte's assets can work harder. Sit tight.'

8 December 1995 Forte had hit back with a scheme that could force Granada to increase its offer.

'Forte's plan to sell off assets puts ball firmly back in Granada's court. Sit tight.'

12 January 1996 By the New Year Forte had mustered a still stronger defence.

'Forte's strong defence document offers an £800m share buyback alongside Savoy shares worth 23p per share. Await a higher Granada offer.'

19 January 1996 Decision time. Granada has promised a 47p per share special dividend on top of its existing offer, valuing Forte at £3.8bn. The bid timetable had reached Day 56. Investors had four days to accept or reject the bid or sell their shares in the market before the bid closed. Granada had increased its bid making it worth 386p per share with a cash alternative of 362p a share.

T1 But the *Investors Chronicle* had its doubts. Forte's record was dismal, but management had come good in the course of the bid and Granada's management record was perhaps less sparkling than it appeared. The *Investors Chronicle* argued that Granada had mainly grown by acquisition and what's more, had paid too much in 1994 for London Weekend Television.

'On balance, Granada's offer is not big enough, nor its strategy sufficiently convincing for us to recommend acceptance – reject the bid. Those who are especially doubtful about Forte's strategy should sell in the market ... A Granada win seems likely. But the fact that some shareholders can be persuaded to sell their shares cheaply is not a recommendation to do it.'

Granada won. The bid went unconditional as to acceptances on 23 January, but only closed on 9 April 1996.

TAKEOVER BIDS

Target	Activity	Bidder	Activity	Value £m	Terms	Bid Timetable	Closing date
Hobson	Food manufacturer	Hillsdown	Food producer	121	31p cash per Hobson share	na	na
	88.9% acceptances. Hillsdown's purchase of Nager gives it another 2.2%. Offer is unconditional.						
South Wales Electricity	Electricity distributor	Welsh Water	Water utility	872	1 Welsh + £40.25 cash for 5 Swalec	Day 32	29/1
	Welsh Water has received 46.1% acceptances on top of the 12.9% it already owns. **Accept.**						
Forte	Hotelier	Granada	TV & rental	3,800	4 shares + £23.25 cash for 15 Forte shares*	Day 56	23/1
	*Granada has also promised a 47p per share special dividend. **Reject bid. See page 20 for full details.**						
Seeboard	Electricity distributor	Central & SW	US eletricity utility	1,600	*	Day 58	21/1
	*Revised to 535.4p cash on 15/12 after distribution of National Grid shares. CSW now owns 30% and has acceptances for another 47%. **Accept.**						

Investors Chronicle keeps track of announced takeover bids in its Mergers and Acquisitions pages. This table shows an extract from the takeovers table at 19 January, well into the Forte bid.

Fig T3 Table of takeover bids

Source: Investors Chronicle

T

MAKING THE MOST OF TAKEOVERS

- Keep an eye on what the market thinks – watch how the share prices of the bidder and the target are moving. If the share price of the target stays at a discount to the bid price, that tells you the market thinks it is a fair offer. A share price above the bid price implies a better offer or a rival bid should be in the pipeline.
- Remember capital gains tax. Taking the cash offer means a disposal for capital gains tax purposes; taking the shares does not.
- The terms of the takeover tell you how much the bidder is offering for your shares. If the bid is agreed by the two managements, it is more likely to go through.
- Always wait to see what the takeover target says in its defence. If it can convince its shareholders that the bid is too low, it may force a higher bid.
- Depending on how long the bid has been running, the *Investors Chronicle* table (Figure T3) will tell you how many other shareholders have accepted the bid. Once more than 30 per cent of the shares are pledged to the bidder it becomes unlikely that another bidder will step in at a higher price and it is more likely that the rest of the shareholders will accept the offer.
- The number of acceptances should rise quite quickly after the first closing date if the bid is going well. Low levels of acceptances could force a higher offer. Wait as long as possible to decide. Investors do not have to accept a takeover bid, but once the bidder has more than 50 per cent of the shares, it has won.
- If you are concerned by the size of a bid and something happens to hold it up – perhaps a referral to the Monopolies and Mergers Commission – consider selling in the market.

TESSAS

***Definition:* Tessas, tax exempt special savings accounts, pay tax-free interest to savers who keep the Tessa open for five years without withdrawing any capital. The maximum Tessa investment is £9,000 over the full-term – up to £3,000 in Year 1, followed by up to £1,800 in each of the next four years.**

Tessa have been a cracking success for most savers. Started in 1991, the best Tessas have offered respectable rates of interest to short-term and long-term savers. Moreover, competition among banks and building societies has largely kept fees and penalties under control.

Anyone aged 18 or over can open a Tessa. Anyone who keeps their Tessa going for five years will pay no tax on the interest their money earns. The minimum investment varies between the banks and building societies. They pay their highest rates on the large lump sums, but people with small sums to save each month can do very well from a Tessa.

A basic-rate taxpayer would normally pay tax on interest from savings at 20 per cent, deducted at source by the bank or building society. That represents a recent concession by the government – the basic rate of tax paid on earnings is 25 per cent. Banks and building societies advertise their interest rates before deducting tax – gross. That is because people pay different rates of tax. But a savings account paying 5 per cent gross, in fact pays just 4 per cent in the hand – net of basic rate tax. The way round this is to bump up the gross rate in line with your tax rate. So 5 per cent on a Tessa is equivalent to a taxed savings account paying 6.25 per cent to a basic-rate taxpayer (5 per cent divided by 0.8) and 10.4 per cent (5 per cent divided by 0.6) to a higher-rate taxpayer.

'... competition among banks and building societies has largely kept fees and penalties under control.'

Comparing savings rates

Savings rates on tax-free savings accounts such as Tessas and some of the products offered by National Savings need tweaking to make them easy to compare with competing, taxed savings products.

A Tessa pays 10 per cent tax-free, for example. The competing accounts pay 10 per cent gross, i.e., before tax is deducted. A higher-rate taxpayer, paying 40 per cent tax, can adjust the tax-free rate to see how it compares with the other rates.

Divide 10 per cent by 0.6, the proportion of interest that is left after tax at 40 per cent is deducted. That gives an equivalent 'gross' rate of 16.7 per cent.

The gains from tax-free saving are considerable, as the sums show, but withdrawing capital from the Tessa breaks the tax-free spell. All interest earned on the account becomes taxable. The saving grace is that it is possible to withdraw interest – net of tax – without losing the account's tax-free status.

Tessas have tended to pay highly competitive rates of interest. This makes them a good bet for anyone with money to save, even if they think they are unlikely to keep the account going for long enough to receive the interest tax-free. Tessas with long notice periods pay the best savings rates, but even Tessas with very short notice periods can offer competitive interest rates. And there is always the chance that you will be able to leave the cash for the full five years.

When a Tessa matures – and the first generation of Tessas has just started to hit their five-year birthdays – savers have two options. They can withdraw the money and close the Tessa or, as long as they act within six months of the first Tessa maturing, they can roll over up to £9,000 straight into a new Tessa. But the first Tessa provider needs to supply a maturity certificate to prove that the money has come from a maturing Tessa.

MAKING THE MOST OF TESSAS

- Shop around is the key piece of advice for all savers, and the record of Tessas shows why it is essential to consider a range of accounts. The best Tessa result of the accounts started in January 1991 was over £14,000 from a fixed-rate Tessa run by Bristol & West. The best variable-rate result was £12,400 from tiny building society Kent Reliance. The worst result was just over £11,400 from Clydesdale Bank, according to figures from Moneyfacts.
- Small banks or building societies tend to pay higher rates of interest to compensate for the greater risk of depositing money with them. At least two small banks offering attractive Tessa rates have gone out of business since 1991.
- Consider whether the penalties for early withdrawal or transferring to another Tessa provider are reasonable. Some banks and building societies offer free transfers, but others will charge a fee and deduct interest. Being able to transfer easily is an important feature – some Tessas start with highly competitive rates only to drop down the interest-rate league table as time passes. You want to be able to get out if you think you are no longer earning a good return. Also, loyalty bonuses for sticking with one Tessa provider for five years can act as a disguised penalty for transferring. Is the loyalty bonus really good value?
- Savers whose Tessas are with building societies set to convert to banks may do well to roll over their Tessa with the same building society even if the interest rate seems uncompetitive. The benefits of the conversion bonus could easily make up for the less attractive interest rate on the Tessa.

UNIT TRUSTS

Definition: **A unit trust allows investors to pool their money in one fund – the investors cut costs and spread their risk and, because the fund is a trust, they protect each person's investment.**

Unit trusts are a great idea, when they do their job. First, pooling resources means that investors get more shares for their money. The sums work even on a small scale – dealing costs on a £5,000 investment could take almost 2 per cent of the money. On a £25,000 investment, the dealing costs would be barely 1 per cent. A fund manager buying £500,000 of shares would barely notice the dealing costs. Institutional rates of stockbrokers' commission run at about 0.25 per cent, compared with 1.65 per cent or more for private clients dealing in small sums.

Secondly, a larger fund can hold a wider range of shares. An investor with £1,000 to put straight into the stockmarket will probably buy shares in just one company. Professional portfolio managers are deeply reluctant to manage stockmarket investments for individuals with less than £100,000 because they feel anything less exposes the client to too much risk. Schroders, the blue-chip investment bank, takes this argument to the extreme of only accepting portfolios worth £2m or more. Given the pressure on investors to steer clear of direct stockmarket investment, it is no wonder unit trusts, open to investors with as little as £30 a month to put in the market, have proved so popular.

The trust deed governing the conduct of the fund means investors have a trustee – normally a bank – which is supposed to make sure the fund's administration is sound and that it sticks to its investment brief. Unit trusts set up to invest in UK blue chip companies should not put money into Korean smaller companies. The trustee can replace the fund manager, although trustee intervention is rare. In practice, investors rely on the integrity of the fund management company itself. Even big names like Midland Bank, fined in 1992 for its failure as a trustee to a unit trust in the late 1980s, can go off the rails. Also, unlike investment trusts, unit trusts face little threat of takeover and, arguably, less incentive to snap out of patches of poor performance.

The problem is that the performance of many of the 1,600 or so unit trusts in the UK is poor. Only a minority of funds consistently match the market, let alone beat it. And the huge number of funds on offer to investors makes it difficult to find the good funds among the hundreds of mediocre funds. About 180 fund management companies run almost 1,600 unit trusts, ranging in size from tiddlers like the Bank of Ireland Capital Growth unit trust to huge billion pound funds such as the M&G Recovery fund or Mercury UK Equity.

Enthusiastic marketing by the fund management companies can make investors' task even harder, but investors stand a better chance of finding a fund with consistently good performance if they know the language of unit trusts.

HOW TO INVEST

Investors buy into unit trusts in two ways – direct from the fund management company or through a middleman, such as a financial adviser. They pay an upfront charge of up to 6 per cent of the sum invested, and an annual management charge ranging from 0.5 per cent to 2 per cent. Paradoxically, buying through a middleman such as a financial adviser will often be cheaper than going direct to the company. Three or four percentage points of the upfront charge will be commission. Your financial adviser may waive some of the commission, but the fund management company will charge the full fee except on large investments. Management groups argue that the notional commission will go towards their advertising and marketing costs instead of to a financial adviser.

Box U1

Counting the cost

Supply and demand mean that someone buying shares pays a higher price than someone selling shares will receive. The bid/offer spread is the gap between the bid or buying price and the offer or selling price. It is a well-established bugbear both for investors in shares and unit trust investors .

The difference with unit trusts is that a fund manager calculates the price of units to include factors other than simple supply and demand. The two prices reflect stamp duty and dealing costs and the manager's own charges. Most trusts have a bid/offer spread of 6–7 per cent, a little more than the initial charge on the fund.

Furthermore, funds can be quoted on either a 'bid' or an 'offer' basis. A trust where more investors want to cash in their units than want to buy units – i.e., more money is going out of the fund than is coming in – will price its fund on a bid basis, reducing the published selling price and effectively penalising investors withdrawing their cash. Specialist funds, or funds which buy and sell units infrequently can have very large spreads, sometimes as high as 11 per cent.

The result of the bid/offer spread is that you can be getting less for your money than you may think in the short-term and the investment will have to work that much harder to earn you a good return.

Increasing competition among unit trust companies means that investors can get a better deal by shopping around. The unit trust listings in the *Financial Times* show the initial charges levied by each trust and they range from zero – for cash funds, which are equivalent to a bank or building society savings account; to 3–4 per cent – typically for some gilts funds and index tracker funds; to 5–6 per cent for most unit trusts. However, some unit trust companies have slashed the upfront charges on all their funds, notably Murray Johnstone – a pioneer of low charges – Hill Samuel, Abtrust and Invesco.

Annual charges do make a difference to investment performance. Some funds can incur particularly high running costs for the manager, but as a rule of thumb, beware of funds charging more than 1 per cent a year.

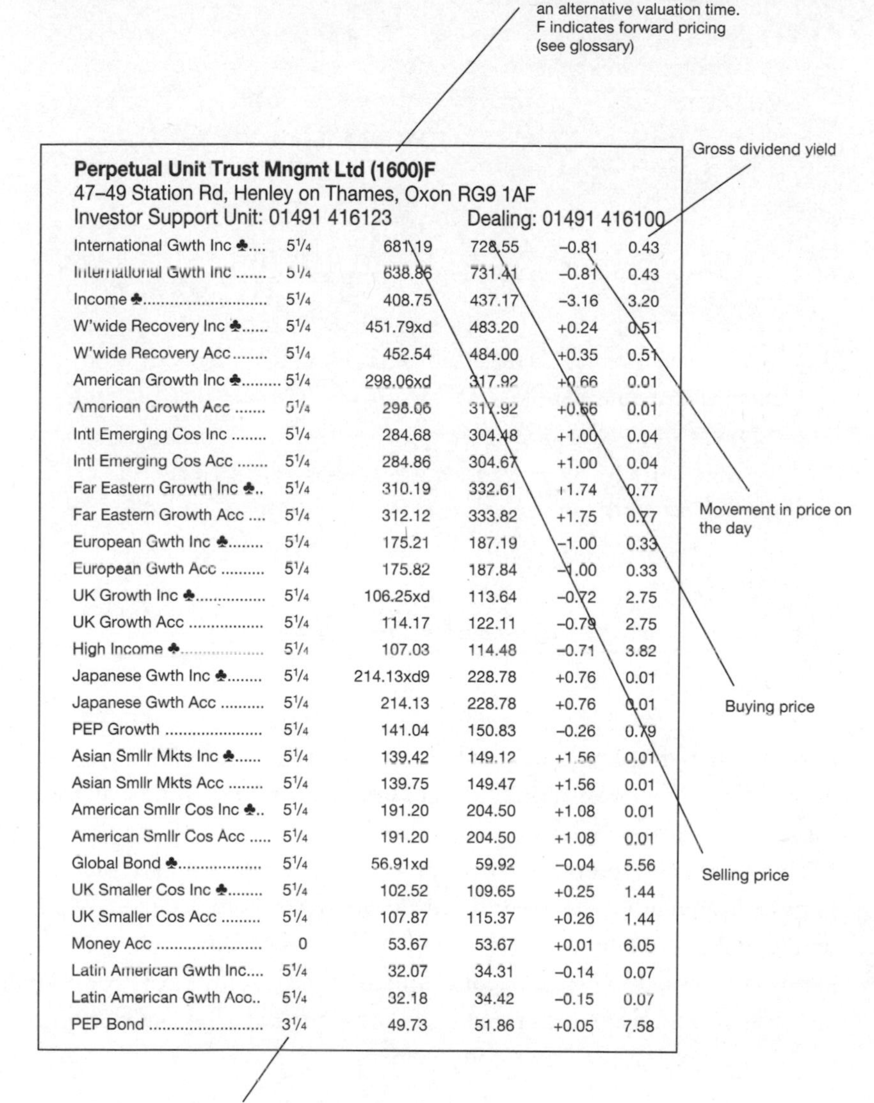

Perpetual Unit Trust Mngmt Ltd (1600)F
47–49 Station Rd, Henley on Thames, Oxon RG9 1AF
Investor Support Unit: 01491 416123 Dealing: 01491 416100

International Gwth Inc ♣....	5¼	681.19	728.55	–0.81	0.43
International Gwth Inc	5¼	638.86	731.41	–0.81	0.43
Income ♣...........................	5¼	408.75	437.17	–3.16	3.20
W'wide Recovery Inc ♣......	5¼	451.79xd	483.20	+0.24	0.51
W'wide Recovery Acc........	5¼	452.54	484.00	+0.35	0.51
American Growth Inc ♣.........	5¼	298.06xd	317.92	+0.66	0.01
American Growth Acc	5¼	298.06	317.92	+0.66	0.01
Intl Emerging Cos Inc	5¼	284.68	304.48	+1.00	0.04
Intl Emerging Cos Acc	5¼	284.86	304.67	+1.00	0.04
Far Eastern Growth Inc ♣..	5¼	310.19	332.61	+1.74	0.77
Far Eastern Growth Acc	5¼	312.12	333.82	+1.75	0.77
European Gwth Inc ♣........	5¼	175.21	187.19	–1.00	0.33
European Gwth Acc	5¼	175.82	187.84	–1.00	0.33
UK Growth Inc ♣................	5¼	106.25xd	113.64	–0.72	2.75
UK Growth Acc	5¼	114.17	122.11	–0.79	2.75
High Income ♣..................	5¼	107.03	114.48	–0.71	3.82
Japanese Gwth Inc ♣........	5¼	214.13xd9	228.78	+0.76	0.01
Japanese Gwth Acc	5¼	214.13	228.78	+0.76	0.01
PEP Growth	5¼	141.04	150.83	–0.26	0.79
Asian Smllr Mkts Inc ♣......	5¼	139.42	149.12	+1.56	0.01
Asian Smllr Mkts Acc	5¼	139.75	149.47	+1.56	0.01
American Smllr Cos Inc ♣..	5¼	191.20	204.50	+1.08	0.01
American Smllr Cos Acc	5¼	191.20	204.50	+1.08	0.01
Global Bond ♣..................	5¼	56.91xd	59.92	–0.04	5.56
UK Smaller Cos Inc ♣.......	5¼	102.52	109.65	+0.25	1.44
UK Smaller Cos Acc	5¼	107.87	115.37	+0.26	1.44
Money Acc	0	53.67	53.67	+0.01	6.05
Latin American Gwth Inc....	5¼	32.07	34.31	–0.14	0.07
Latin American Gwth Acc..	5¼	32.18	34.42	–0.15	0.07
PEP Bond	3¼	49.73	51.86	+0.05	7.58

Fig U1 Unit trust prices at 16 March 1996, listed by fund manager
Source: Financial Times

Unit trusts – the upfront cost

When you put money in shares, unit trusts or any other form of investment, you must remember that a slice of the cash will go in charges. Your money must make up the cost of the charges before you can cash in the investment at a profit. That is easy when the market is rising, far more difficult when markets are sluggish. In simple terms, here is what happens with unit trusts.

- You hand over £1,000 to a unit trust company. It immediately knocks off 5 per cent, the initial charge on the fund you have chosen. A smaller management charge will be deducted each year. The 5 per cent, or £50 in this case, pays the fund management company and commission for your adviser. Commission will probably be more than half the charge.
- Six months later you unexpectedly need your £1,000. But the market has hardly moved and your fund manager has not grown the value of the assets in the fund. You cash in your units and receive just £950.

The moral of the story is, invest for the long-term.

To recap, unit trusts are cheaper to invest in than individual shares, they cut risk, are well-regulated and are easy to buy. But investors can pay disproportionate sums in commission.

The minimum lump sum investment in a unit trust is typically £1,000. Many unit trusts offer monthly savings schemes which allow you to invest as little as £30 a month. Your money buys you units in the fund and the fund can accept as much money as investors want to put in. New money creates fresh units, which change value according to the value of the underlying investments.

Example: Excellent UK Value Fund

Excellent UK Value Fund has £100m under management at the start of 1995 and the fund is split into 100m units each worth 100p. If the value of the shares in the fund grew 10 per cent, each unit would be worth 110p.

- Past performance, even if it is one of the few guides available, can be highly misleading. Check whether your chosen fund still has the same fund manager. Also consider the reputation of the fund management group – the financial Press run several unit trust awards which give a fair idea of which fund managers are the current stars. However, do not automatically opt for the fund or fund manager at the top of the league table for one year. Look for fund managers that make regular appearances in the top 20.
- Good investment performance is more valuable than low charges, but use the *Financial Times* listings to check how the upfront charge of your chosen fund compares with the rest of the market and consider whether the fund can justify its annual management charge. If you are investing a large lump sum, ask for a discount on the initial charge. Also, check the size of the bid/offer spread when you buy and when you sell. It may be worth postponing the deal.

One year	Five years	Ten years
Larger groups		
NPI	Perpetual	M&G
Morgan Grenfell	Schroder	Fidelity
Prudential	Morgan Grenfell	Gartmore
Smaller groups		
Credit Suisse	Provident Mutual	Perpetual
Provident Mutual[1]	Credit Suisse	Schroder
Lazard	Lazard	Eagle Star

[1] Now GA Life

Remember that the annual awards are only a snapshot of performance. Look for firms that appear in the award tables year in, year out.

Fig U2 Award-winning unit trust managers, 1995

Source: Micropal/Planned Savings

Investment trusts, the main alternative to unit trusts for investors in search of a pooled investment, have a different structure (see INVESTMENT TRUSTS, page 109). They have a fixed-share capital, like any other company listed on the stock exchange, and investors who want to buy shares in an investment trust must first find someone prepared to sell to them – not normally a problem. The price of shares in an investment trust will depend on share price supply and demand and will often differ from the value per share – net asset value – of the underlying investments.

MAKING THE MOST OF UNIT TRUSTS

- Unit trusts – and investment trusts – are an ideal investment for people without time, inclination or knowledge to pursue direct stockmarket investment. They also offer private investors a way into overseas stockmarkets, particularly the emerging economies of Latin America, Asia and Eastern Europe, or higher risk investments, such as commodities.
- Know how much you can invest – remember that the bid/offer spread instantly knocks several points off your investment, so only invest money that you can afford to lock away for several years. Your disaster fund should be in a savings account with no penalties for instant cash withdrawal, not in stockmarket investments.
- Decide what you want from your investment. A bedrock invest-ment will probably be in a fund investing UK blue-chip compa nies, but you may want an investment to deliver a high income, o a more risky investment in a developing economy where there i the prospect of greater returns. Making this decision and refinin it will allow you to focus on one or two unit trust sectors.
- Use the statistics for funds' historic performance to establish ho well a fund has done. Go back at least five years. Look, too, at t short-term performance figures. A fund that has plummeted in t league tables in the last month or six months may be about to seriously off the rails, despite a good long-term performance.

V

VENTURE CAPITAL

***Definition:* Venture capital is money put into businesses without a stockmarket listing which need outside finance to start trading or expand.**

Investors enjoy a range of tax sweeteners to take the edge off investing in start-up businesses. It is only fair in most cases. The high rewards of investing in young businesses are well balanced by the risk of losing your whole investment if the business goes under.

> ***'... here are ways for private investors to put money behind growing businesses, instead of watching from the sidelines as giant venture capital investors rule the field.'***

The business expansion scheme (BES), launched in 1983, had become more of an opportunistic tax-planning vehicle than an investment route by the time it ended in January 1994. BES funding was behind many of the small pub companies that are now quoted on Aim, such as Surrey Free Inns and Cafe Inns. Its successors, venture capital trusts and enterprise investment schemes, offer significantly less juicy tax enticements. But the broad principle is the same – here are ways for private investors to put money behind growing businesses instead of watching from the sidelines as giant venture capital investors rule the field.

Box V1

BES bonanza

Business expansion schemes (BES) last for five years, so although there have been no new schemes since January 1994, investors should still see regular references to BES companies and funds. The schemes allowed an individual to invest up to £40,000 per tax year in unlisted UK trading companies. The schemes were hugely attractive to high earners as they received upfront tax relief on the cash they invested, claimed back at the higher rate of tax they paid. In terms of the pound in the hand, investors were parting with just £24,000 when they invested £40,000. Moreover, if they held the investments for five years, investors paid no capital gains tax. Failing to hold the investment for the five-year term could mean paying back some of the upfront tax relief.

Investors in BES have had mixed fortunes. Unicorn, a pub company that started as a BES and, with other pub operators, survived very difficult times in the late 1980s, was taken over in summer 1995. Investors were astounded that pub owner and brewer Morland – of Speckled Hen fame – paid 402p cash per share for the company. Morland's argument was that Unicorn's portfolio of managed pubs was well worth the price. Certainly BES investors did well. They had put 100p a share in the company in the 1980s and had seen their shares fall well below that.

Country Gardens, the garden centre group, is an example of a business expansion scheme (BES) that has moved to a stockmarket listing. Original BES investors in Country Gardens paid up to 100p per share in 1985. Like many BESs the company was heavily indebted and high interest rates brought the company to its knees in the early 1990s. In 1993, it fought off an Inland Revenue attempt to axe its BES status and investors' tax relief with it. It survived and since 1995, its shares have been quoted on the Alternative Investment Market (Aim), a junior version of the main stockmarket.

The high-risk element of the BES went by the board for some years after 1988. Schemes were allowed to invest in private rented housing under assured tenancies, some with bank guarantees built in. In 1989–90, the schemes' heyday, £129m out of the £165m raised by BES issues was for these assured tenancy companies. The schemes grew so sophisticated, investors could scoop the tax relief without exposing themselves to any risk.

VENTURE CAPITAL TRUSTS

Venture capital trusts (VCTs) arrived in 1995. They are quoted investment trusts and the trusts, as long as they invest only in companies covered by the tax rules, qualify for tax reliefs as well as investors in the trusts. The trusts offer a ready-made portfolio of high-risk, start-up holdings. Few private investors have the time, inclination or appropriate funds to spread their risk by building up a diversified basket of venture capital holdings. An investor can put up to £100,000 a year into venture capital trusts, and the trusts set up so far ask for a minimum investment of around £2,000. The tax reliefs, far less generous than those for BES investments, are:

- no income tax on dividends;
- no capital gains tax;
- 20 per cent income tax relief on investments if the trust is held for five years;
- no corporation tax on gains made by the trust;
- no curbs on property holdings by companies owned by the trust;
- investors can defer capital gains tax by re-investing realised gains into a VCT, but the gains must have been realised since 6 April 1995;
- VCTs can hand out their gains as they are realised, in the form of tax-free dividends.

The VCTs are more limited than the venture and development capital trusts already running (see INVESTMENT TRUSTS, page 109). For example, 70 per cent of their investments must be in qualifying companies, as defined by the Inland Revenue rules. Also the maximum investment in one company is £1m a year, so the projects supported by the VCTs will tend to be small-scale. Arguably, in the UK venture capital firms are looking after large-scale projects already and the small projects are the ones in need of capital. However, the investments can be in companies quoted on Aim, and if a company graduates from Aim to the main market a VCT can keep its holding for five years.

Trust	Experience ITs	Experience Ven Cap	Investments
Baronsmead VCT	Y	Y	Established profitable companies
Murray VCT	Y	Y	MBOs/development capital
Northern Venture Trust	Y	Y	Start-ups/ MBOs/expansion
Advent VCT	N	Y	Mostly established companies
British Smaller Cos VCT	N	Y	Established companies
Close Brothers VCT	N	Y	Secured loan stock or unquoted
Capital for Co's VCT	N	Y	Aim companies/MBOs
Gartmore Venture Capital	Y	Y	Established profitable companies
Hodgson Martin VCT	N	Y	Established companies
Johnson Fry Aim VCT	Y	Y	Aim companies
Pennine Aim VCT	N	Y	Aim companies
Quester VCT	N	Y	Spread of companies
Augustus Trust	Y	Y	Spread of companies
Guinness Trust	N	Y	Spread of companies

Fig V1 Venture capital trusts – a snapshot
Source: Investors Chronicle/BVCA

Investors in VCTs have a small field to choose from at the moment. The trusts were only launched in September 1995. In the early days even well-respected names had trouble attracting the sums they wanted to raise. For example the Murray VCT, run by established fund manager Murray Johnstone, set out to raise £30m but attracted only £18.4m.

ENTERPRISE INVESTMENT SCHEMES

Enterprise investment schemes, set up to encourage equity investment in smaller, private businesses, were the first successor to the BES. Their extra little wrinkle is that they encourage business angels – investors who want to take an active role in running the business as well as passive investors (see *Box V2*). Investors with no existing link to the business can put in up to £100,000 a year. The schemes can have up to half their money in property. The tax reliefs are:

- income tax relief at 20 per cent on amount subscribed for shares;
- no capital gains tax on disposals once shares have been held for five years;
- income or capital gains tax relief on losses.

Box V2

Business angels

A 'business angel' is a wealthy investor who can bring experience as well as money to a growing business. The British Venture Capital Association (BVCA) reckons that business angels are going to be interested only in firms with serious growth prospects – turnover growth of 10 per cent or more a year, and the prospect of pre-tax margins of 10–15 per cent within five years. However, business angels will often accept lower returns than an institutional venture capitalist because they have a personal, non-financial interest in the business. Potential business angels can make contact with firms through the web of business angel networks in the UK. Business angels tend to be investing less than £100,000, although the BVCA handbook of business angel information shows that investments set up through networks can range from £3,000 to £1m. The investments range from food manufacturers to biotechnology specialists. Contact the BVCA (*telephone:* 0171-240 3846) for details.

MAKING THE MOST OF VENTURE CAPITAL

- Venture capital is risk capital – only put a small part of your investment capital into this type of investment, if any. It has tended to be the preserve of the very wealthy and institutions for a good reason – they have enough money under management to be able to afford the occasional disaster.

- Fund managers running VCTs must have at least three years' experience of venture capital investment. However, pure venture capital expertise may not be enough. General equity fund management experience too, ideally in running investment trusts, can also help.
- Beware of the steep charges for VCTs. Upfront charges will be about 5 per cent, and annual charges can reach 2.5 per cent with a performance-related fee on top. Venture capital investment is time-consuming and demanding for the firm, but the fund managers will have to deliver solid results to justify such high annual charges.
- Check that funds have invested in a range of companies.
- Consider the venture and development capital investment trusts traded on the stockmarket. They lack the tax breaks of the VCTs but they have longer track records. Even if you opt for a VCT, consider the record of the fund manager in any other venture capital investment trusts it may run.
- Beware esoteric offerings such as enterprise zone trusts. They are not venture capital routes, but invest in development property in rundown areas designated by the government as enterprise zones. They normally have a 25-year term and offer upfront tax relief at the investor's top rate of tax. The risks are sky high – witness the slump in property values in the Docklands area of London.

Further reading

Background notes and handbooks are available from the British Venture Capital Association, Essex House, 12–13 Essex Street, London WC2R 3AA (*telephone:* 0171-240 3846). The EIS and BES Association (*telephone:* 0171-613 0032) is a further source of information.

BESt Investment (*telephone:* 0171-321 0100), a firm of specialist financial advisers, publishes a research on the venture capital products and will send investors sample copies of its reports.

WARRANTS

Definition: **Warrants, normally issued as an add-on to bonds or ordinary shares, give the right, but no obligation, to buy new shares in a company at a fixed price and on a fixed date.**

In a rising market, warrants can delight all concerned. Investors in a company's warrants enjoy enormous percentage gains and the company receives a low-cost cash injection. However, private investors will find relatively little investment coverage of warrants, despite the potential for enormous profits. The reason is that warrants are also an easy way to lose money for investors who fail to do their homework.

Investors need to have an opinion on the company issuing the warrants, and to know the exact terms under which a warrant investor can subscribe for shares. Here are two examples of warrants, one from an industrial company and one from an investment trust. Investment trusts are now the main source of warrants in the UK.

Example: BTR

BTR, an industrial conglomerate owning businesses ranging from tyres to transport, has issued millions of warrants. However, pressure from its institutional investors means it is unlikely to issue many more. The terms of BTR's 1995–6 warrants allow a warrant holder to convert each warrant for one share at 258p in the 30 days. The clock runs from the day after BTR posts its annual report and accounts, and from the interim results in 1995 and 1996.

The warrants started trading in 1991 at 30p. In early 1996 shares in BTR stood at 321p, and the 1995–6 warrants at 63p. In between the warrants have climbed as high as 136p, as Figure W1 shows. A warrant is 'in the money' when the underlying share price is more than the warrant's exercise price. It is 'out of the money' when the share price is lower than the exercise price. In this case, the BTR 1995–6 warrants were in the money because the exercise price of 258p was lower than the share price of 321p.

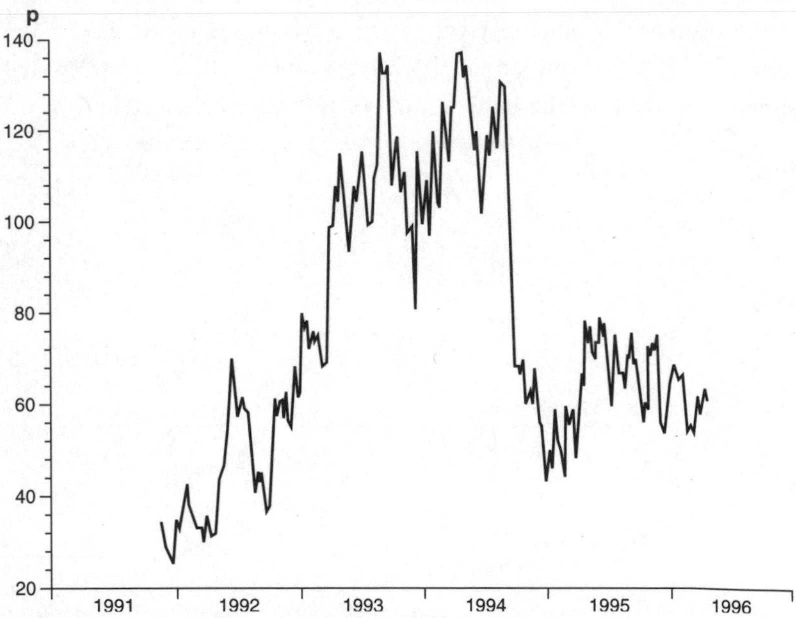

Fig W1 'Warrant ups and downs' BTR warrants

Source: Datastream

Example: Fleming Emerging Markets investment trust

Warrants in the Fleming Emerging Markets investment trust, issued in 1991 when the trust launched, allow the warrant holder to buy shares at 100p on 1 December from 1995 to 1998. Shares in the investment trust stood at 148p in early 1996 and the warrants at 59p. The warrants were in the money – the 100p exercise price was lower than the share price.

The BTR and Fleming examples show the basic principle of warrants – you buy them because you think the price of the underlying shares is going to rise and the warrant will allow you to buy the shares cheaply. In practice, investors hope to make their big gains from trading the warrants themselves rather than exercising the warrant and buying the underlying shares. As a result, it is important for warrant investors to understand the mechanics of warrant prices as well as the basic idea of warrants. Warrant prices will behave differently from share prices.

WARRANT PRICES

The price of a warrant breaks into two parts – intrinsic value and premium, or time value. A warrant has intrinsic value when its exercise price is less than the price of the underlying shares. For example, the Fleming warrants described above had intrinsic value of 48p. A warrant with intrinsic value is in the money. The BTR warrants had 63p of intrinsic value. In a rising market, the intrinsic value of warrant will rise as the warrants reach their exercise date.

Box W1

Warrants – where did they come from?

Companies issued their first warrants in the 1970s, but it was only in the 1980s that warrants took off. Some investors made particularly large profits on Japanese warrants, but the later collapse in Japanese warrant prices won warrants a bad name. Companies normally issue warrants to make a fund-raising more attractive to investors. Warrants may swing investors' opinion in favour of a takeover or acquisition that they would otherwise find hard to swallow. They can also be a very useful way of raising money.

British Biotech, a drug developer with galloping development costs and little income, raised £46m in 1994 with a rights issue at 400p a share – investors received three warrants for every four shares. The warrants gave the right to buy new shares on British Biotech at 525p in December 1995 and January 1996. If exercised in full the warrants would raise a further £48m for the company. Figure W2 and W3 show that warrant investors got a good deal.

However, for a time that £48m of extra money was in doubt. Shares in British Biotech fell 99p to 491p in February 1995, just 10 months before its warrants were due to be exercised. Trials of the company's cancer drug Batimastat had been delayed. The shares only started climbing fast again in late August, ahead of news that Lexipafant, used to treat pancreatitis, had successfully finished its key Phase II clinical trials. The trials of Batimastat restarted, and in late November, only a couple of weeks before the first exercise date of the warrants, more good news came. Another cancer drug Marimastat was on track. The exercise period of the warrants started with the shares at 1506p.

Shares in British Biotech rose from 534p in late August 1995 to 2806p in April 1996, a 971 per cent gain. Meanwhile, the warrants had climbed from 69p to 2000p before they expired in January 1996, a gain of almost 28,000 per cent for investors who sold their warrants at the peak. Later in 1996 British Biotech Shares rose still higher.

Warrants are almost taken for granted with new investment trusts and investment trust warrants make up the bulk of the warrants market. The value of investment trust shares normally falls below the value of

W1 the trust's assets, once the shares start trading – in the jargon, they 'go to an immediate discount to the underlying assets'. The warrants help compensate for this. Investment trusts often issue warrants with their shares at no extra cost to the investor.

For example, the Schroder Asia Pacific trust issued one warrant for every five shares bought at 100p at launch. The shares dropped to 95p when they started trading – recovering later as Figure W4 shows – and the warrants started at 35p. The value of the shares worked out as 95p + 35p, or 130p. The investors are happy and the trust manager can expect a further slug of new money if investors choose to exercise their warrants. They bring the right to buy shares at 100p between 1998 and 2006.

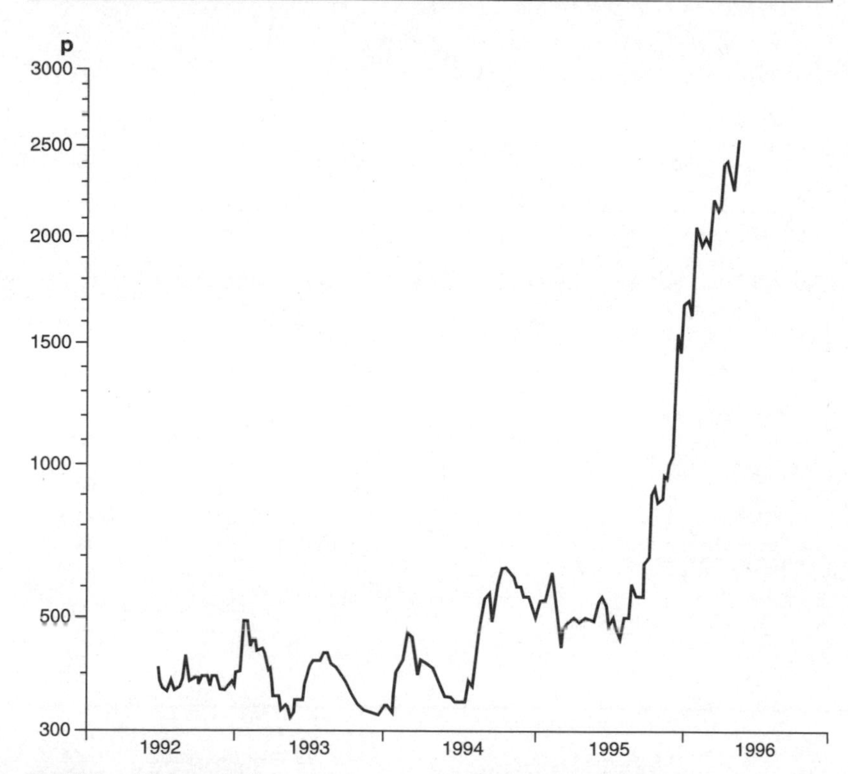

Fig W2 'A few dodgy moments ...' British Biotech shares

Source: Datastream

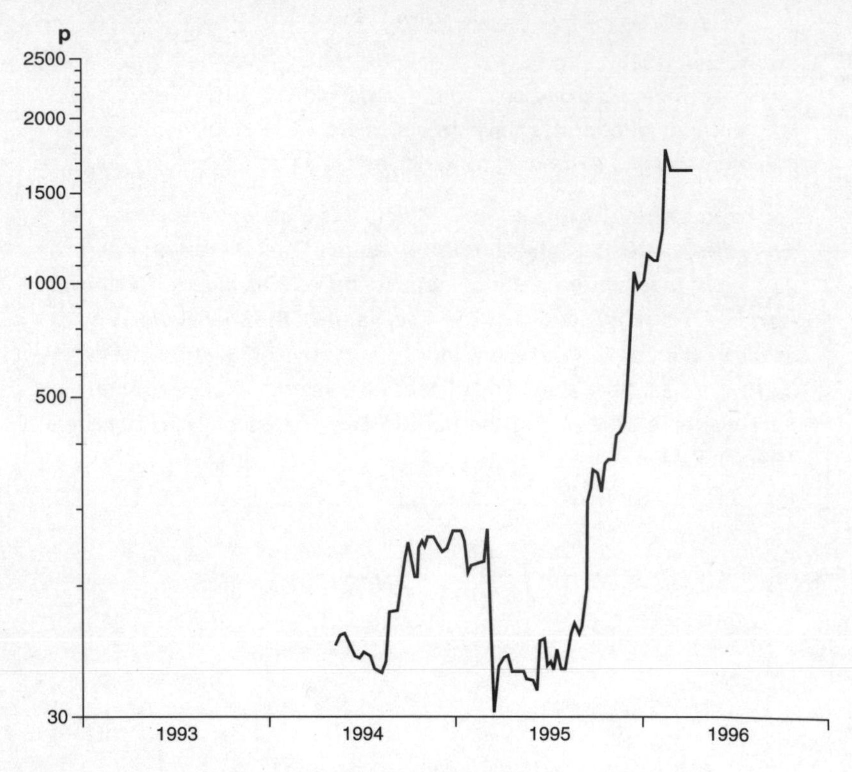

Fig W3 '... but a happy ending' British Biotech warrants

Source: Datastream

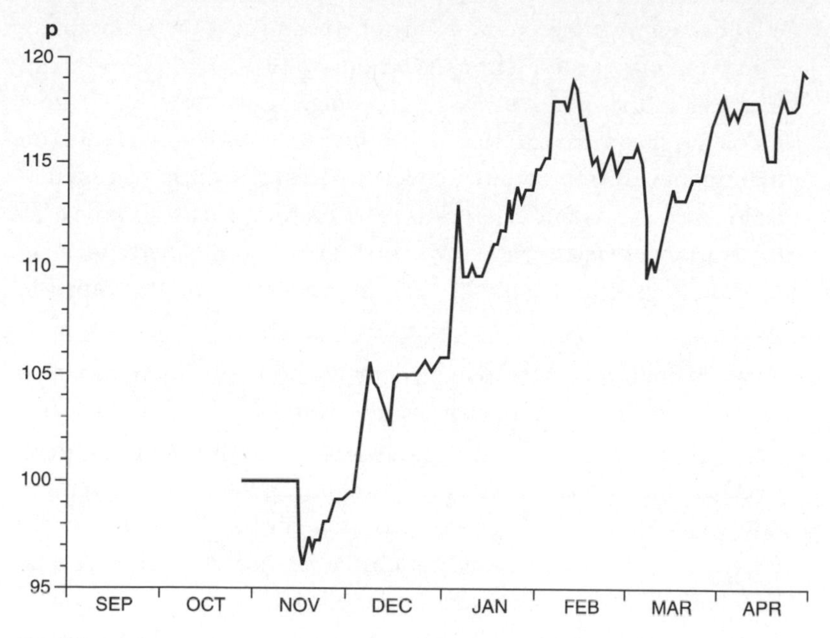

Fig W4 The sweetener in action – Schroder AsiaPacific Investment trust shares

Source: Datastream

The premium is the difference between the warrant price and the warrant's intrinsic value. The Fleming warrants have a premium of 59p less 48p, or 11p. The BTR warrants, close to their expiry, have no premium. The longer the warrants have to run, the higher the premium is likely to be because there is more time for the share price to rise and investors will pay to speculate on a share price rise. Warrants tend to have a long life, four or five years, but time decays. By the time the warrants reach the last exercise date, they will have no time value.

It is one thing to know the textbook reason for the price of a warrant. It is more difficult to decide whether the price is good value. It boils down to one thing. How much must the shares rise in value for the warrants investor to recover his money and make a profit? Here are the main points to consider.

- You can express the premium as a percentage of the share price. The premium of the Fleming warrants is 11p/148p = 7 per cent. Expressing the premium as a percentage tells you roughly how much the shares have to rise before investors will earn a return on their money. It is important to decide whether such a rise is realistic in the time available, because the premium will disappear as the warrants reach expiry. Investors could find the warrants have lost their premium without any improvement in the intrinsic value.
- Warrant investors with patience or a good calculator can also work out a break-even point for the warrants – the annual percentage rise in value needed on the shares for investors to break even on the warrant. The capital fulcrum point, based on a more complicated equation, moves one step further from the break-even point. It tells you how much the share must rise a year to achieve the same capital return on the shares and the warrants. A good stockbroker should be able to tell you warrants' capital fulcrum points along with other warrant statistics. If you expect the rate of capital growth to be higher than the fulcrum point, the warrants should be good value.
- Gearing is one of the factors making warrants attractive – a small investment in warrants can mean disproportionately large returns. But it also implies more risk than an ungeared investment. You can work out the gearing on warrants by dividing the share price by the warrant price. The BTR 1995–6 warrants had gearing of 321/63 or 5 times. The Fleming warrants had gearing of 148/59 or 2.5 times. This means £100 invested in BTR warrants means rights over £500 worth of shares.

MAKING THE MOST OF WARRANTS

- Be careful. Warrants, like options, futures and other forms of derivative, offer large returns on a small outlay – i.e., they are highly geared. And like other forms of derivative, warrants can become worthless if the underlying share moves in the wrong direction. Investors make money on warrants in rising markets, they stand to lose money when markets fall. It is worth finding a good stockbroker when you start investing in warrants and subscribing to a warrants newsletter (see *Further reading*, below). Even warrants enthusiasts warn that it is easy to lose money.

- Remember, warrants bring the right to buy shares, but the warrants themselves pay no income.
- The price of warrants should move in the same direction as the share price of the underlying security, but the warrants will not be good value just because the share price is good value. Consider the two prices separately.
- Warrants priced at just a few pence are not necessarily cheap – there will normally be a reason for their low price. For example, it could be that the warrants are about to expire without the share price rising above the exercise price. Warrants can and do expire worthless if the share price fails to rise above the fixed exercise price.
- Remember, there is no obligation to exercise your warrants, and you should only do so if the warrant exercise price is lower than the share price. There will usually be some element of premium in the price that makes it better to sell in the market.
- Warrants can sometimes become worthless if a takeover bid succeeds – their premium or time value disappears. This has become particularly important as the number of investment trust takeovers has increased. Check whether the warrants have any built-in compensation for loss of time value.

Further reading

The Investor's Guide to Warrants, second edition, Andrew McHattie (Pitman)

Warrants Alert, The Sion, Nailsea, Bristol BS19 2EP (*telephone:* 0117 925 8882). This publication also offers a list of stockbrokers specialising in warrants.

Investment Trusts magazine – available quarterly in large newsagents.

Investors Chronicle also publishes regular updates on the warrants market.

Equity Warrants, Julian Redmayne (Euromoney Books)

EXCHANGE RATES

***Definition:* Exchange rates are the prices at which one currency can be exchanged for another.**

Exchange rates matter in investment for two main reasons. First, even small investors can have international shareholdings and suffer or gain from the effect of currency movements. Secondly, the behaviour of currencies will affect economic policy and company profits. Just because something is important, does not mean investors are any good at forecasting its behaviour. Exchange rates confound governments, and are a happy playground for the serious foreign exchange players such as George Soros and the other hedge fund operators. But even the likes of George Soros make big losses.

In practice, foreign currency investment attracts more than the wheeler-dealers. The main foreign exchange traders are the banks. The UK devaluation of October 1992 earned gains of 25 per cent for investors who had jumped the right way. It is risky – currencies move fast. But some investors find it easier to judge currency and interest movements than share movements. Their judgement may still be wrong, but currencies are where they feel at home. Private investors in the UK have easy access to two main types of currency fund – managed funds and single currency funds.

A typical UK investor uses sterling as his main currency, so sterling should also be the base currency for his managed currency fund.

For example, in early 1996, the highest-yielding single-currency fund in the Fidelity list was the Spanish peseta fund. Its yield, reflecting high interest rates in Spain, was 7.3 per cent. The yield on a sterling fund was 5 per cent. A higher yield looks attractive, but will Spanish interest rates stay at that level, and more importantly, will the peseta fall against the pound? The idea of choosing a managed fund is that a full-time currency fund manager can judge future currency and interest movements better than a private investor. A fund manager should also be able to make more out of currency movements, and lose less, than a private investor.

MANAGED CURRENCY FUNDS

The best-known firms running managed currency funds include Rothschild and Guinness Flight, and their funds are a starting place for finding a good currency fund manager. You may not choose one of their funds, but they can be a benchmark for judging other funds. Use your own currency as a benchmark too – you are taking a risk, so you want a better return than sterling can give. The main steps in choosing a fund are:

> ***'Private investors in the UK have easy access to two main types of currency fund – managed funds and single currency funds.'***

- Check how much risk the fund accepts. Lower risk funds tend to put most of their money into sterling, earning a higher yield by investing the rest in currencies with high interest rates. Some higher-risk funds also buy currency futures.
- Choose your tax treatment. Offshore funds, and currency funds are based offshore, can let interest build up as long as an investor likes. That is likely to be when the investor's tax rate falls. The growth and the interest will be taxed at the income tax rate applying when the investor cashes in the fund.
- Look at the fund performance tables to find whether any funds have a consistently better performance than the rest. They appear under 'Sterling converted offshore funds' in *Money Management*, a sister magazine of *Investors Chronicle*.
- Decide how long you will keep your money invested. In theory, it should be at least six months, but you need to watch what currencies are doing and to be able to move your money fast. If sterling is consistently stronger than all other currencies, a managed fund will find it difficult to deliver any growth.

- Do not be tempted into a fund based in a currency other than sterling, if sterling is your base currency. It means greater risk, and going into a single currency fund may be a better route if you want to take that risk.

STAYING SINGLE

Single currency funds give you the freedom to build your own currency portfolio and work very well for people who need to hold cash in a foreign currency – international travellers rather than DIY speculators. Fidelity (its funds are listed in Figure X1) and Rothschild are the main names in single currency funds and these too are based offshore, in Bermuda and Guernsey respectively.

Australian dollars
D-marks
ECUs
French francs
Dutch guilders
Hong Kong dollars
Italian lira
Japanese yen
Canadian dollars
New Zealand dollars
Norwegian kroner
Austrian schillings
Swedish kroner
Swiss francs
Singapore dollars
Spanish pesetas
Sterling
US dollars

Fig X1 Single currency funds – the choice
Source: Fidelity Investments

MAKING THE MOST OF CURRENCY FUNDS

- Currency investment is for people whose financial affairs are in tip-top shape. Shun currency investment unless you have already sorted out your pension, house and have a well-spread portfolio.
- Currency dealing carries far less regulation than private investors might expect. Beware investment firms cold-calling to offer foreign exchange dealing – this is the wrong way to embark on currency speculation. If in doubt about the firm's credentials, you can check whether it is authorised by the investment watchdogs (see KICKBACKS, page 134). For example, in 1996, the financial regulators clamped down on a number of firms offering 'rolling spot forex' dealing services. The firms had taken advantage of a loophole in the law that waived regulation for foreign exchange deals closed within seven days. Firms conducting such business are normally travel agents arranging holiday currency, and they do not need investment authorisation. However, some currency dealing specialists decided they could slip through the rules by simply rolling over the seven-day deals. They cold-called investors, offering what was in fact a highly speculative form of investment.

Box X1

The yen and the dollar

The Japanese yen was 80 yen to the US dollar in April 1995, and by early 1996, it was 107 yen to the dollar. Figure X2 shows the yen's progress over five years. Japan's struggle to keep its strong currency under control in the early 1990s illustrates two points about exchange rates. First, currencies tend not to behave in the way governments want them to and, secondly, exchange rates matter even to small investors. The Japanese central bank kept its short-term interest rates low in order to encourage money to flow out of the yen and into other currencies. It used its foreign currency reserves to intervene in foreign exchange market and it kept bond yields lower than they would normally be in an economic recovery. Most importantly, the country's current account surplus - the result of years of strong exports and a particular nuisance to the US authorities - started to shrink.

Economists' view was that Japan's economic recovery would have died on its feet if the yen had maintained its strength against the dollar.

As it happens, the strong yen has been good for UK investors in Japan. But private investors interested in putting money overseas, even through a pooled fund such as a unit trust, need to accept a degree of currency risk on top of their investment risk. Funds can use futures (see FUTURES, page 78) or other forms of derivatives to hedge against exchange rate movements, but hedging costs money in itself and fund managers are normally lucky if they manage to cover all their exchange rate options. It is worth pressing your fund management group to find out whether or not it does hedge its currency risk.

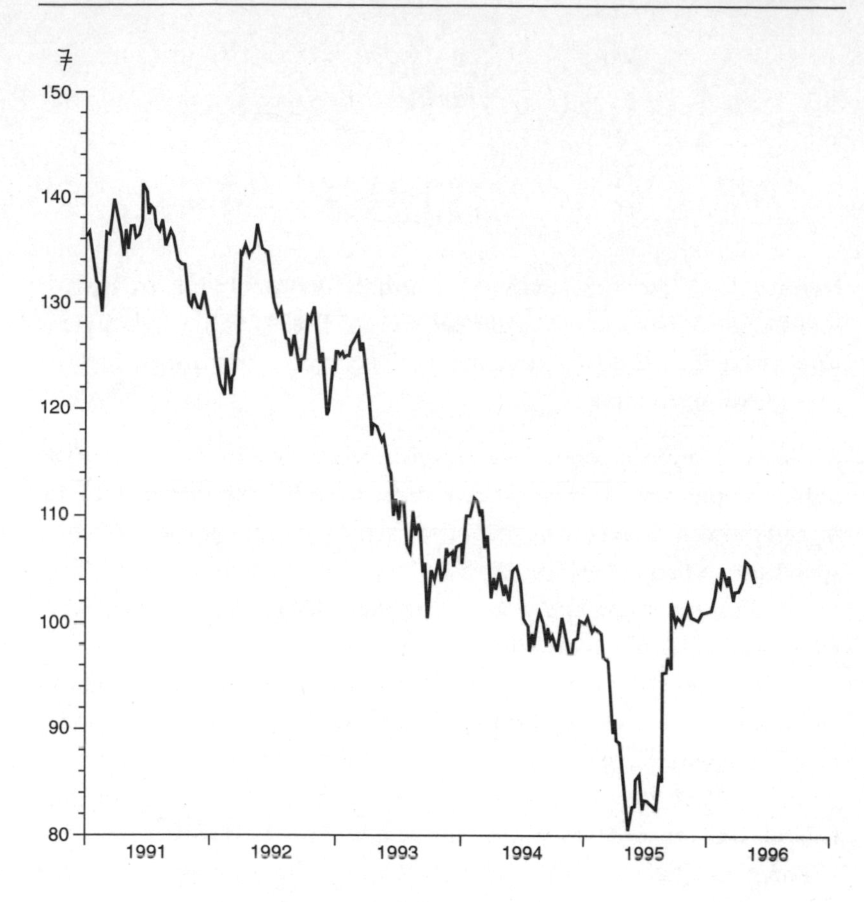

Fig X2 'The yen's little local difficulty' Japanese yen to US dollar exchange rate

Source: Datastream

YIELD

***Definition:* Yield measures the annual income from an investment against its current market price. Yields fall when prices rise, reflecting the fact that investors have to pay more for the same level of income.**

It is easy to snipe at people who, relying on interest income to pay the bills, complain about interest rate cuts. In 1992 the rest of the UK thought lower interest rates meant more jobs, a recovery in consumer spending and an expansion of manufacturing. Pensioners and others living on interest income were doing their sums, and realising they could no longer pay their bills.

In 1990 the mortgage rate was 15 per cent. Even the meanest banks and building societies could pay interest of 10 per cent gross and a pensioner with savings of £15,000 could receive £125 a month in interest before tax. Within two years the base rate had more than halved to 6 per cent and savers' interest income halved with it.

The result has been to drive investors needing income out of the safety of the bank or building society and into relatively risky investments. Money in your bank account does not rise and fall in value according to market pressures. But yield is an even more important measure in looking at most other income options where the underlying value can swing sharply – gilts (see GILTS, page 85), corporate bonds (see PEPS, page 181), permanent interest bearing shares (Pibs), unit and investment trusts (see UNIT TRUSTS and INVESTMENT TRUSTS on pages 222 and 109).

Beware of any investment that offers a particularly competitive yield. It means two things. First, as in the case of some corporate bond Peps, the income may well come at the expense of capital growth, or may even be eroding your original capital, once you add on the annual charges levied by the fund. This can be fine as long as you know it is happening. Secondly, a high yield means whoever is behind the investment is paying you a risk premium. You can earn a better income than from another type of investment, because the risk that you will lose all your money is higher. The Barings Perpetual bonds, issued by Barings Bank, yielded about a percentage point more than other types of bonds. That was because bondholders had far fewer rights to repayment compared to shareholders if the bank ended up in trouble.

A TAXING MATTER

Tax status is critical in assessing sources of income, and yields can make it easier to weigh up the effect of differing tax treatments.

Example:

A higher-rate taxpayer has to choose between investing in a building society Tessa (see TESSAS, page 219) and a savings account where he will have to pay tax on his interest. The tax-free yield on the Tessa and the gross yield on the savings account are both 10 per cent. However, the Tessa rate is equivalent to a gross rate of 16.7 per cent for a higher rate taxpayer (10 per cent divided by 0.6).

By contrast, a non-taxpayer is considering a high-income Pep and a standard high-income unit trust both paying 8 per cent. The yields are the same to the non-taxpayer because he will be able to reclaim the tax on the income from the standard unit trust. The only benefit of investing through a Pep will be the convenience of not having to reclaim his tax. Is that worth the Pep charges?

PERMANENT INTEREST-BEARING SHARES (PIBS)

Pibs are issued by building societies. They pay a relatively generous income, but are never repaid so investors depend entirely on the market to recover their investment. Rising demand for high interest investments has pushed up the prices of Pibs and, as a result, pushed down their yields. The coupons, or nominal interest rates, of Pibs run

'Tax status is critical in assessing sources of income, and yields can make it easier to weigh up the effect of differing tax treatments,'

to over 13 per cent, so when the Pibs were issued at 100p they yielded 13 per cent or more. However, Pibs prices have risen so sharply that in early 1996 their yields were under 10 per cent for the most part. For example, Bradford & Bingley 13 per cent Pibs were issued at £100. In March 1996 they stood at £133 and yielded 9.8 per cent gross.

The risk for investors pursuing income when yields have sunk so low is that they will lose capital when interest rates rise.

GUARANTEED INCOME BONDS (GIBS)

Guaranteed income bonds (Gibs) are issued by life insurance companies and are not strictly bonds at all, but life insurance policies. They pay a fixed income over a given number of years in return for a lump sum. Their rates will fall as gilts yields fall, but they can be a good way to lock into income if you believe interest rates are about to tumble. You will receive your lump sum in full at the end of the savings term. Remember that Gibs always pay income with tax already deducted and with no way to reclaim it, so non-taxpayers should avoid them.

Box Y1

Yield in action

Yield is a simple tool once you realise that yield falls when prices rise and go up when prices fall. For example, two investors buy shares in the same company, but at different prices. Each will receive the same cash dividend income, but one will have paid more for it. Yield is an easy way to judge how much you get for your money.

The first investor, Mr Smith, buys 1,000 shares in Company A at 100p. The company pays annual dividends of 5p a share before tax. The yield on Mr Smith's shares is 5 per cent and he receives £50 a year in dividends, again before tax. Mrs Jones also buys 1,000 shares in company A and receives dividend income of £50 a year. But she bought her shares at 90p a share and the yield is 5.6 per cent. She got a better deal than Mr Smith. (See also **Analysing accounts**).

MAKING THE MOST OF YIELD

- Compare the yield on potential investments with the yield on bank and building society deposits. The bigger the difference, the greater the risk of the higher yielding option.
- Define your attitude to risk by deciding how much of your capital you could afford to lose and still be able to maintain your standard of living. If you feel you can afford to lose money, some of the higher-yielding options may be worthwhile.

Z

ZERO DIVIDEND BONDS

Definition: **Zero dividend bonds, also known as zero coupon bonds, pay no income, but offer a predetermined capital sum when the bonds mature.**

Zero dividend bonds are particularly attractive to investors planning for a specific capital commitment, such as school fees. The capital payment when the bonds mature should more than compensate for the lack of income throughout the life of the bond. Shares issued by split capital investment trusts (see INVESTMENT TRUSTS, page 115) are the most popular form of zero dividend bond, or zero, among private investors, although they crop up in other areas too.

The risk with zeros is that investors will not receive the predetermined capital sum, or will receive less than expected. But in general the bonds are a highly attractive, low-risk investment. Investors need to be sure that the fund or institution issuing the bonds has the asset backing to meet its final commitment. With investment trusts this means looking at the trust's commitments to other investors, the nature of its investments and, as the life of the trust progresses, how well the trust's assets are growing. Statistics supplied by the Association of Investment Trusts are particularly useful in assessing this (see INVESTMENT TRUSTS, page 127).

Figure Z1 shows how the zero dividend preference shares of Invesco Blue Chip, due to mature in spring 1998, have fared since they were issued in 1991. The shares, issued at 100p, have risen in value as the maturity date of the trust has approached. If the trust has enough money, it will repay at 217p each zero bought to 100p.

The terms of the shares, called preferred growth shares in this case, say: 'Holders are not entitled to any distribution of revenue but are entitled to a preferential repayment on winding up by the increasing of each £1 shares at a compound rate of 11.7 per cent per annum since the date of issue. In the event that the company's assets on winding up are insufficient to meet this obligation, preferred growth shareholders would receive less than the projected 217p per share.'

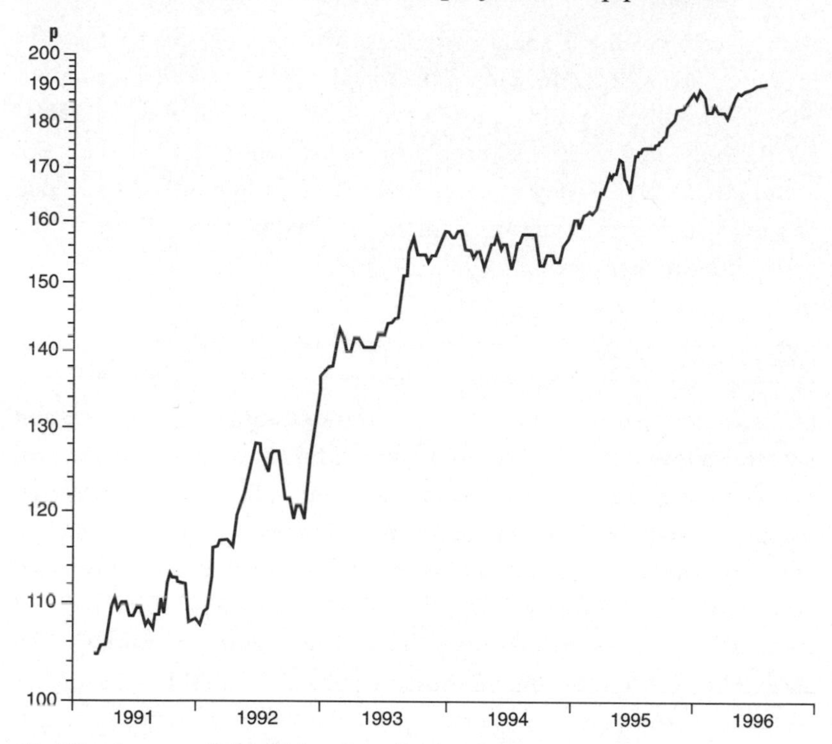

Fig Z1 Invesco Blue Chip zero dividend preference share price performance 1991–96

Source: Datastream

MAKING THE MOST OF ZERO DIVIDEND BONDS

- Check the date when the trust matures – does the trust have enough time to meet its targets?
- Look for the hurdle rate. It tells you how much the trust's assets must grow each year if it is going to be able to repay investors at the rate originally promised.
- Look too for the trust's 'asset cover' – this ratio tells you how far the existing assets of the trust currently cover the promised payout on redemption.

Z

CONCLUSION

Success in investing is about knowledge and experience. That is why investors are told again and again to take professional investment advice. This book should equip investors with the knowledge to deal intelligently with their stockbroker or investment adviser and to spot a dud adviser when they meet one. However, often only experience can teach investors some investment lessons. Here are some of the main rules to bear in mind.

SHOP AROUND

Shop around, particularly when you are looking for an adviser, and switch advisers if you find that your adviser seems unwilling or unable to keep up to date on investment issues. It is more than knowing the reasons behind significant price movements in your shares. Advisers should at least make an effort to win interested investors access to a wide range of new issues – not just the spivvy ones – and even if they are weak on areas such as warrants or options, they should be able to draw on specialist expertise in order to advise you.

ONLY INVEST WHAT YOU CAN AFFORD TO LOSE!

Invest money that you can afford to lose. Given that some highly successful investors have used bank loans to buy their first shares, this rule may seem over-cautious. However, it is a useful measure of risk. If losing your investment will be a personal disaster, do not invest in the first place.

DON'T PUT ALL YOUR EGGS IN ONE BASKET

Do not invest all your savings in one place. This rule applies as much to banks and building societies as it does to traded investments such as bonds and shares. Reduce your risk by spreading your investments across a number of vehicles. However, this only works if you have large-ish sums to invest. Trying to spread £500 across a number of investments will just mean losing too much money in charges.

SET AND STICK TO STOP-LOSS LEVELS

Set your stop-loss levels and keep to them. It is horribly easy to lose money by hanging on for better days that never arrive. Remember that your stop-loss level for a highly volatile technology stock will be more generous than the stop-loss for a share that you expect to deliver steady, if slow, upward progress.

KEEP UP TO DATE

Keep up with financial news and investment fashions, if only to avoid the latest fad. The financial services industry has a powerful marketing machine and the most widely touted products and investments are rarely the best option. *Investors Chronicle* is my recommended purchase for cutting through the marketing babble, but the weekend *Financial Times* and the *Financial Times* surveys of personal finance also give reliable value for money.